THE SURVIVAL

OF

WESTERN CULTURE

*An Inquiry into the Problem
of Its Decline and Resurgence*

BY

RALPH TYLER FLEWELLING

*Professor of Philosophy and
Director of the School of Philosophy
University of Southern California*

KENNIKAT PRESS, INC./PORT WASHINGTON, N. Y.

To My Students
in Many Climes

THE SURVIVAL OF WESTERN CULTURE

Copyright 1943 by Harper and Row, Publishers, Inc.
Reissued in 1968 by Kennikat Press by arrangement
Library of Congress Catalog Card No: 68-15825

Manufactured in the United States of America

ESSAY AND GENERAL LITERATURE INDEX REPRINT SERIES

THE SURVIVAL OF WESTERN CULTURE

INTRODUCTION

T HE ART OF prophecy is essentially practical in intent: it aims
at extricating men from some predicament into which they
have fallen. It divides itself, however, into two branches, which
may be called the *oracular* and the *rational*. Of these the former
does not argue or give reasons, but lays claims to absolute authority and prediction and flourishes upon superstitious fears. It used
to function as an excellent instrument of government, and it is
a great pity that it has been allowed to fall into disuse. For if we
now had a first-class oracle, like that of Delphic Apollo, which
was universally revered and to which appeal could be made
before our peoples or our politicians plunged into some disastrous folly, it might avert many calamities and even save the
life of modern democracy.

Rational prophecy on the other hand arises out of intelligent
reflection upon the probable consequences of extant conditions
and tendencies. It does not demand literal fulfillment nor profess
complete accuracy and certainty of prediction: it tries rather to
convey a warning. Nor is it dogmatic and fatalistic; for it per-
mits intelligence to avoid the dangers it foresees. It is the form
of prophecy in which there has been a great and greatly needed
boom in recent years, and to which Professor Flewelling's book
also is a contribution. It should be ranked with the works of such
luminaries as Mr. H. G. Wells, our most successful prophet,
Mr. Bernard Shaw, Lord Russell, Professor J. B. S. Haldane, and
Mr. Lothrop Stoddard; and I suppose that Professor Flewelling
has asked me to write this Introduction to his book, not merely
out of friendship, but also because I, too, have had the audacity
to play the Cassandra to the future of the British Empire.

Besides guiding anticipation, rational prophecy has the further
function of abating the pride of *false* prophets. These are essentially those whose prophecies are based on pseudo-science, and not
on intelligent prediction. Their name is legion and their fame is
coextensive with human folly; hence not infrequently they
achieve a reputation which needs urgently to be punctured.
Professor Flewelling's false prophet, from whom he has more or
less borrowed his title, is Oswald Spengler, who tried to extract

a universal law of cosmic history from eight or nine (more or less controversial) cases of the rise and decline of human societies. His "law" was fatalistic and he did not really extract it from the facts of history; nor did he consider alternative interpretations. He gave no reasons for the course of events except his alleged "law" itself. Yet it might well have occurred to him that if, and so far as, cyclic changes can be traced in human history, the reasons are most probably psychological. More plausibly than to an abstract formula they can be ascribed to human folly and conceit, swollen by undeserved success into what the Greeks aptly described as *hybris* or overweening indolence, *ate* or infatuation, and *phthonos,* the rancorous envy of competitors and rivals.

Actually, when the causes of the decline and fall of human societies are examined closely and dispassionately, one finds that there is always a chance of failure, even in times of the greatest prosperity, and likewise always a chance of escaping, even on the very brink of destruction. Thus progress and deterioration are permanent possibilities of social history. Moreover all the facts may always be viewed with the eye of an optimist or a pessimist, and neither of them is able to prove his case against the other. Thus the verdict of history remains ambiguous. Certainly our worst apprehensions have never yet been realized so far, and this fact is sufficiently curious. Perhaps it yields the best empirical argument for the belief in a providential guidance of the affairs of men.

F. C. S. SCHILLER

FOREWORD

· ·

THIS IS NOT a comfortable book. Speaking frankly, it was stirred up by what the writer considers the false and misleading analogies of Spengler's *Decline of the West*. Yet Spengler cannot be answered with anything like the thoroughness with which he has written. Even granted a learning as capacious as Spengler's, to which there is no claim, such an attempt would involve the impossible length of the *Decline* and would necessarily contain much that would be aside from the real point of discussion.

We must then in covering so much ground, such extent of history, such variety of intellectual interest be guilty of what to specialists in these various lines will appear oversimplification, and therefore, unconvincing. Why then write such a book? Chiefly because, in the age of specialization we are apt to lose sight of the landmarks. Many men, and these our brainiest, know so much about so little that they do not realize the wider implications of their own discoveries. They cannot see the woods for the trees. To point the way out must lay one open to the charge of knowing less and less about more and more. Even philosophy, making haste to be scientific, has fallen into a like mood losing itself in unsystematic embranglements in which completeness of view is thought a scandal. Yet the revolutionary discoveries of science, typified in the doctrine of relativity, call for a comprehensive philosophy.

Lack of attention to the deeper implications of science, and of capacity for critical thinking has made possible the perversion of Hegel's concept of history, into the contradictions of Nietzsche, Marx, and Spengler. These are reversions to the authoritarian philosophies of the Orient, as such are opposed to democracy, and have become the basic philosophy of modern totalitarianism. Absorbed in scientific research there has been too much tendency to laugh off these philosophies as negligible. We now witness in the horrors of the world's worst war the outcome of a philosophy holding to irresponsible authority, whether economic, social, or military, without the restraint of moral or religious concepts. We shall not be able to meet the challenge with physical strength alone. We must now call in the help of philosophy and of a philosophy which has not sold out to false gods. To do this we should inquire closely into the ideals which have made our Western culture what it is, and which can enable it to survive.

The undertaking of such a task might well seem hopeless. Nor within the space allotted to a modern book is it permitted to do more than to suggest broad outlines of thought, to raise questions, to disturb old complacencies. If at times we seem to be dealing with "things too great for us," let the reader be assured that the convictions spring from much reflection and the perusal of many books. No point is taken that the author does not feel he could sustain. However dogmatic he may appear, he does not profess ultimate solutions, but he does have decided convictions concerning, righteousness, justice, and the democratic way of life as the basis of permanence and peace. At any rate response to dogma must take the form of positive convictions which are often mistaken for dogma, if one is not to lose himself in an endless quoting of authorities, like that of the scribes, which dulls the point of understanding.

To recall the many and exacting steps by which Western culture has reached certain desirable characteristics, and the principles which must be relied upon to win both the war and the peace, such is the hope of the author.

The survival of any civilization is not something standing apart from its underlying philosophy. Of none is it more true than of the culture of the West. Its principle of individualism presents a unique phenomenon in the field of history and contains factors of survival little reckoned with. The elements of stability latent in individualism have to do with the spirit of freedom and creativity, of inquiry and achievement. They reside deep in the human consciousness, are psychological, and have power to overcome barriers of artifice and form because they represent the forces of life itself. They present thus a persistent power which does not end with the changing political and social forms under which they have sought expression, but rather survives all forms to accept new methods and make new discoveries. If too much stress seems to be put upon the relation between the different phases of Western culture, such as, for instance, that between the appearance of the arithmetical concept and the rise of democratic individualism, it is not meant that one is the cause of the other but that both issue from common underlying tendencies. There cannot be the slightest doubt of the attempt of the early scientists to escape by the scientific view of nature from the superstitions which had bound the pagan world to authoritarianism. Can there be doubt of the place of honor taken by their work as a contribution to the development of democracy?

The democratic order may seem weak and even ephemeral to some, but the spirit which seeks expression through it is vital and cannot perish. To the very extent that the present world situation is disillusioning according to the measure of its failure to satisfy, to that extent is the demand for a better order destined to be realized. The age of material achievements, great as they are, cannot provide the permanent satisfactions of the living spirit of man. These must be transcended with spiritual achievements as yet embryonic and almost untried, and which may be distinguished from individualism under the higher term personalism. This too provides community of feeling with what is highest in Oriental culture and offers a mediating basis for understanding and co-operation. Hereto one must look for the survival of Western culture.

Acknowledgments are especially due to my colleagues in the School of Philosophy, the late Professor F. C. S. Schiller, Professors Wilbur Long and Paul R. Helsel, and also to the late Professor Bergson, Professors E. S. Brightman, Frank Collier, John Laird, and A. C. Knudson, who have given much time to reading the manuscript and who have made valuable suggestions but must not be held accountable for the views presented. Faithful and interested students who listened to and discussed these chapters, both in America and in China, have rendered assistance by their questions. Not the least in acknowledgment should be the authorities of the University of Southern California and its gracious head, President Rufus B. von KleinSmid, and the forbearance of my own family, all of whom by patience and encouragement have made the work possible. With such reinforcement it should have been better done. Acknowledgments are also due *The Personalist,* in which has appeared some of the material here used.   RALPH TYLER FLEWELLING

November 11th, 1942

CONTENTS

....

PROLOGUE

SECTION I
INDIVIDUALISM IN WESTERN CULTURE

xi

Contents

Prologue

"CIVILIZATION," according to Lord Justice Russell, "is not dominion, wealth, material luxury; nay, not even a great literature and education widespread, good though these may be. Civilization is not a veneer; it must penetrate to the very heart and core the societies of men. Its true signs are thoughts for the poor and suffering, chivalrous regard and respect for women, the frank recognition of human brotherhood irrespective of race or color or nation or religion, the narrowing of the domain of mere force as a governing factor in the world, abhorrence of what is mean and cruel and vile, ceaseless devotion to the claims of justice."

WHAT IS WESTERN CULTURE?

THE FIRST DUTY of anyone presuming to discuss in any way the philosophy of civilization is undoubtedly to inform his readers of the definition of civilization which he intends to employ. Popular and even professional and scientific opinions upon the meaning to be ascribed are numerous, varied, and vague. Both West and East describe it in terms of their own culture and that is likely to seem barbarous which is not indigenous.

The Westerner often loves to think of the East as taking on the ways of the West. To him it foolishly seems that there would be progress in civilization in the exchange of the medley of hawkers' cries, drums, bamboos, rattles, and gongs, which characterize the Orient, for the still more raucous bedlam of whistles, horns, and bells that make night hideous in our Western cities. Some, in the name of civilization, would fill the East with unsightly factory buildings, grain elevators, and warehouses, would crown the Western hills of Peking with ten thousand times ten thousand oil derricks, and would set the children of the Orient groping in the darkness of the bowels of the earth for coal and iron and gold. Under the same dream of civilization, her narrow streets would be crowded with the traffic of automobiles, and her citizens divided sharply into two classes, "the quick and the dead." The measure of culture could then be easily taken in the wealth of five per cent of her citizens, in the ghastly toll of her mines, in the death rate of her sweatshops, and in the daily number of fatalities from her automobiles. Is this what is meant by conferring the blessings of civilization?

Ten years ago there would scarcely have been a question raised among us as to the validity of such a program of civilization. But the Western world now finds herself at pause, in a confluence of conflicting tides that raises questions in the best of minds regarding the future, and also respecting much that we have considered necessary to the progress of society. Forces have been unloosed that fill the Western mind with grave concern,

3

and we are not so certain as once we were respecting the outcome, or even what direction it is desirable to take. We are in
such a mood as has not possessed us before in the memory of
living men to inquire into the values we supposed were ours, to
take inventory of that which has for long passed as unquestioned
good. In fact we now wage a war to determine whether what we
have termed "good" shall be called evil. Or whether from hence-
forth, violence, fraud, betrayal and falsehood shall be held as
good, the essential features of a "New Order."

Contacts with the East remind us that our own civilization is
a plant of recent growth, and these contacts increasingly modify
any feeling of superiority which might arise from the cleverness
of our inventions or the forward state of our science. We find
ourselves pitched out of the old easy complacency of accepting
our civilization as the only one, and forced to define the meaning
of culture.

Before we actually do this, however, we shall have to clear the
ground of certain misconceptions that have obtained wide popularity.

I. The Fallacy of Automatic Progress

Before we can settle upon a definition of civilization we shall
have to consider something other than we have been discussing,
the concept of the man in the street, that of the uncritical multitudes who know not their right hands from their left. Let us inquire after the interpretation of the scientists, the anthropologists,
the ethnologists, and the sociologists.

Here we find that society is thought of as ranging all the way
from the primitive to the sophisticated, and that much of our
concept has been spun on the thread of the theory of evolution.
It is to be doubted whether in the last fifty years any book of
any considerable importance has been written on human culture
which did not assume the development of society from the simple
to the complex, by an automatic progress. Any proposal to question this venerated dogma of Western society would in the common opinion have marked a man as insane or a fool.

There have, however, been some curious effects of this scientific dogmatism in leading us to overestimate the cleverness of
our own minds, and the superiority of our own culture, often
to the disparagement of others, present or past. It is very certain

that the assumption has been misleading in the interpretations it has induced in anthropology, and often even in historical criticism. The most disastrous effect has been in the field of the understanding of contemporary cultures which we have considered inferior to our own by reason of certain adventitious or superficial differences. We have also been gravely misunderstood by the peoples represented by those cultures and very properly disliked.

When we reflect upon the term "primitive" we shall find that our common use of it carries a fallacy. First, we assume somewhat gratuitously, that we are the climax of the evolutionary process without admitting that the question is debatable. Next, we assume that our particular line of descent has been in continuous progress while others have not. Their very lack of our own standards constitutes them in our minds backward or primitive peoples. Further, since evolution is assumed as automatic, it is of the very essence of time. Because ours is the superior culture it must have had a longer development than these "primitives." Thus we make a complete round of special pleading which proves nothing quite so much as our credulity.

So long as the theory is unexposed to the facts it remains a most flattering and comfortable conception. But reflection on history shows that all other races have, so far as we may determine, been developing as long as has ours. The Chinese could make the supreme claim of age, continuous development, and on this basis have a right to claim superiority. If there is anything in our dream of automatic evolution for society, it must hold for all others as well as for us. Furthermore, a study of history shows that the movement of culture is not necessarily in one direction—upward. Civilizations fall as well as rise. The sting of this fact now looming on the general intellectual horizon gives poignancy to the disillusionment of our times.

Such researches as those of Aleš Hrdlička[1] in the culture of the Kodiaks of Alaska show how a race at first possessing a degree of culture and the use of well-wrought pottery can descend by reason of isolation, difficult physical condition, to an art concerned principally with making spearheads and fishhooks out of the materials available in their situation. Art, as well as

[1] Aleš Hrdlička, Curator, Division of Physical Anthropology. United States National Museum, in the *American Scholar*, October, 1935.

civilization and philosophy, is the child of leisure and plenty. None of these higher forms of culture can be achieved by a people whose universal necessity is the struggle for food. This need not be interpreted as a lack of intelligence. In fact, any society of today cast on desert shores, lacking the implements of civilization, would quickly drop to the measure of physical necessity, though it would not necessarily drop in brain capacity.

There is no primitive culture now in existence. If there ever has been, in the sense in which we use that term, we have no record save in a few rude artifacts of men who lived beyond the dawn of history. That they were the possessors of inferior mentality cannot be sufficiently established by a few scraps of skull indicating a low brow and their presence in the stratum of stone implements. All historical demonstration is against such an assumption rather than for it. Perhaps we should revise our anthropological dogmas. We have guessed at the primitiveness of early races by the crudeness of their implements, by their ignorance of metallurgy. We have little justification for the conclusions we have commonly drawn concerning a dawning mentality or lack of it. The judgment that the mentality of the men who used these crude artifacts was in close proximity to that of the apes, anthropoid or otherwise, is wholly fortuitous and not sustained by any real knowledge of which we are at present possessors.

It would be pleasant to think that our mentality is proved superior by the development of our implements, but there is not evidence of a scientific nature that man has more brain power now that we have the steam engine, the automobile, the radio, the airplane, and the high-powered telescope, than he had before. Apparently Socrates, Plato, Lucretius, Boëthius, and Isaac Newton were our intellectual peers though they knew nothing of unit heat, electrical refrigeration, bedtime stories, or the antics of Mickey Mouse. The youngster that races down our streets in America at sixty miles per hour in a high-powered automobile is not necessarily the mental superior of Archimedes, though he doubtless would, if Archimedes were to cross his path, command "the old 'hick'" to "get out of the way." Such reflections as these concerning modern mentality may be galling to our pride, but they show how boastfully we have built about the pyramidal apex of unproved hypotheses a considerable structure upon which our interpretation of civilization has depended. Under the light of fact and of criticism, some opinions that have seemed to us indubitable may disappear as completely as the baseless and unsubstantial fabric of a dream.

This weakness in much of what has dignified itself without protest as science would not have required this unpleasant exposure were it not that the false notion of automatic progress in human culture has become the unconscious background of our thought, and unless we exorcise it at the beginning we cannot clear the way to any but the old conclusions. That we should think clearly is important, since the older concepts have exerted a pernicious influence on interracial understandings in days when only sun-clearness can make for the peace of the world.

II. How Then Shall We Define Civilization?

By this time it is fully apparent that we cannot get anywhere in our discussion of civilization without first attempting a definition of the term.

It is established that the common idea of civilization is the presence of bathtubs and furnaces, motorcars and radio, airplanes and television. Very often the possession of brains is left out of the picture in the interest of cleverness, shocking manners, pornographic weeklies, and movies in bad taste. One may be quite the child of his own age, however, and still confess a misgiving here and there. The view is too simple. From the dawn of time alien peoples have looked askance at each other across the barriers of ocean or mountain or artificial boundary, and each has found one descriptive word for those on the other side, "barbarian." This term is not so deep in meaning as it is in prejudice. In meaning it might be, though without much etymological justification, only "the bewhiskered one," which term obviously applies more fittingly to the white race than to any other. In prejudice it has been annihilating, the source of misunderstanding, suspicion, hatred and war. But if we cannot define civilization in the terms of the multitude, and if we must reject the former concept of the primitiveness of people unlike ourselves, let us see if we could define culture in terms of education.

Probably all would unhesitatingly agree that the degree of education among any people might well form the measure of their civilization. Here we would seem to come to rest on a bottom fact. But what do we mean by education?

Education is of two varieties at least, the training of the mind and the training of the hand. Of what consists the training of the mind? To an earlier generation it meant, ultimately, at least, a knowledge of Greek and Latin and of the ancient classics which they represented: it meant a knowledge of mathematics and of music as a branch of mathematics. It meant also logic and rhetoric as a sort of mathematics of thought and language. With the Chinese, for hundreds of years it implied a knowledge of the Chinese classics so intricate that the scholar could repeat both the text and commentary. Added to this was required a facility in the use of language evidenced by agility in composing verses. In our Western world education has become more and more a training in science, with a tendency to omit subjects of merely disciplinary or cultural character.

In the strictly professional sense, education has become the study of pedagogy based on an already obsolete and discredited psychology. The further we inquire the more difficult we find it to agree on just what should be meant by an education. In recent times it has swerved sharply away from mental discipline, intellectual independence, and tends to become an ability to use mechanical devices for computation and otherwise, of whose origin and principles the user may be ignorant.

A similar situation faces us with regard to education considered as a training of the hands. If in the former case civilization seems to be in retreat, what can we say of the latter. Here the complicated inventions of modern mechanics threaten to leave the fine old arts high and dry, since there are apparently no operations of the hand which may not be more accurately executed by the machine. At this point it seems almost as if civilization, as we conceive it, were about to destroy civilization considered as a capacity for fine handiwork.

If further we judge civilization by the quality of its arts, its appreciation of beauty, a little digging below the surface will disclose a like confusion. The forms created by the ancient basket weavers of the Mesa Indians of America or the pottery of the jungle tribes of Africa show an eye educated to the appreciation of beauty, and an accomplishment of artistic expression which

Prologue 9

rival the classic age of Greece and excel some of the productions of either civilized individuals or modern machines.

Since we seem to find adequate definition of civilization neither in mechanical invention nor yet in education of mind or hand, let us submit the question whether it might not mean the art of living together. In the history of the West this seems the theory most likely to receive the next trial, if indeed we are not altogether destroyed in this war. Already civilizations have arisen that have shown conspicuous mastery of the art of living together. It may have been true of Egypt, it was quite surely true of the Aztecs, but the longest surviving example is that of China herself. More than any other people those of China have mastered the art of living together. It would be easy from this basis to prove this the highest civilization yet developed. Certain enthusiasts of the West would welcome this conclusion, but I doubt if it would gain the approval of the Chinese themselves. Most of the civilizations that have so far mastered the art of living together have done so at a great price. They have possessed great powers of resistance until new factors have come into the field, as in the case of the Aztecs, whose civilization fell overnight because they knew nothing of firearms. Their social success and their international failure both sprang from the same sources, and were due to the stern repression of individuality in large portions of the community, repressions that hindered both initiative and discovery.

The danger of such a tragedy to modern civilization is at the present hour most menacing. The world is full of the doctrine of regimentation for the sake of national, or even of provincial advantage in a non-provincial world. This is the underlying meaning of Nazism on the one hand and of Communism on the other. Their principles, based in class, or racial, conflict, are, for practical results, identical and equally dangerous to civilization; the one, a tyranny by the privileged, the other a tyranny by the hitherto unprivileged. Both are essentially enemies of freedom.

Perhaps from this discussion we can now draw some tentative conclusions respecting the nature of civilization. All these concepts seem to have come short at one point. Mechanical devices, while the result of the greatest modern genius, now threaten to standardize our workmen, destroy initiative, artistic response, and even mentality. Education is falling short in that it does not sufficiently provide a discipline of the mind but drops more and more into the vacuity of mere professionalism which is deadening to personal development. The destruction of art seems threatened by the invasion of mechanics into the field of education, turning emphasis away from the creative genius and expression of the individual. Social amenity or the art of living together, as now attempted, achieves only by the suppression of the individual and leads to the deterioration of the finest values. In so far as any or all of these expedients have failed, it has been at the common point of the welfare and highest self-expression of the individual.

Whatever else it may or may not signify, a real civilization apparently must be one in which is possible the highest disciplinary self-expression of the person. It must foster the intellect by putting a premium on mental discipline. It must cultivate and inspire the sense of the beautiful, and provide the means to the highest artistic self-realization. It must achieve the art of living together but that without the suppression of the nobler powers of any citizen. We can then safely say that the degree of any civilization is to be measured by its success in the cultivation of the achieving person, among all its members.

A civilized society would then be a society so well-ordered as to encourage to the highest degree the free development of the individual in intellectual, moral and spiritual accomplishment, in invention and education, in social and economic order.

A true civilization is one that provides the proper environment and inspiration for the highest type of personal achievement and happiness, and at the same time conserves the highest good of all.

It seems true then that only that organization of society has a right to the title "civilized" which holds persons to be the supreme value. Such a civilization must be so ordered that it will provide for the development of each individual up to the highest range of his possibilities, physical, mental, and moral. It will supply opportunity for free self-unfoldment, freedom of opinion, speech and action within the limits of the common good. It will take on a higher range than merely that of universal suffrage, free education, or freedom of religion. It must cherish and perpetuate the principle that the person is of surpassing worth. It will be alert to the perils imposed by injustice to any class or neglect of any individual however defenseless or weak. Such a civilization will realize a community of individuals who are educated to live together harmoniously not only within the national boundaries, but with all the world.

Such a civilization would in the truest sense be a democracy but it would be a misnomer to think of it as represented in any particular type of organization. Humanity has caught glimpses of the ideal and has in some degree realized it from various types of political organization. In Greece, in Rome, in Judea, the dream arose. Democracy does not, however, mean an unrestrained freedom to do as one wishes. The basic platform of democracy is self-restraint. Men have the choice in any ordered society of governing themselves from within, or of being governed from without. Behind democracy is freedom, but behind freedom is the self-control of persons. While we hold the dream of the true civilization, we must continue in deference to common usage to apply the term to those imperfect efforts after a social order already achieved.

Of course it is apparent that in this sense no section of society has yet been altogether civilized. Civilization has yet to be achieved. We are now living in a world in which the old watchwords and expedients no longer help us, because within the memory of living men it has shrunk in length and breadth to the narrowness of a village street. Let us here attempt to discover something of the history and development of Western culture, to point out its weaknesses and failures, and to ask some questions concerning the possible future of civilization in this already narrowed world. No longer is it a question merely of what one-half of the world proposes to do. We are now so close together that what any smallest state does is of moment to all the rest of us, for we shall fall or rise together. Contrasting concepts lie at the base of the civilizations of East and West and the time has come when we must come together and amicably work out that which shall be for the good of all.

Some years ago, Spengler, in his work entitled *The Decline of the West,* indicated what he calls "sense of destiny" as the motivating spirit of the West. If that interpretation is true, it will be interesting to discover how his sense of destiny arose and to trace its historical development. We might easily picture to ourselves the parting of the Orient from the Occident on the central Asian plateau. One branch of the human family would be visualized as separating to the East and destined to be stopped by an impassable ocean, and to settle down, forming the intensive cultures of China. The other branch faced westward with horse and cart and had no insuperable barriers to stop it until it reached the Atlantic. Once there, and before there was time fully to conquer the wilderness, and begin intensive development, the mariner's compass, enlarged ships, and the China trade set it on a new trek westward before the old land lust had died away. The early nomads had flung out wide advance guards of horsemen, who became the terror successively of the unsettled peoples of western Asia and Europe. The carts, carrying wives, children, stock, and impedimenta, brought up the rear. Wherever these latter delayed was home and the rallying point of the tribe in seasons of peace. One of the strangest parallels of history was the similarity of these first migrations to the last: the Mongol carts to the prairie schooners that crossed the American desert and mountains. To men whose faces were set in the one direction, the desired conditions of life were just one more trek across the ranges or the plains. Happiness, wealth, freedom were just a little farther west, and men began to look upon themselves and their race as having a destiny to conquer the remaining wildernesses of the earth.

More than "sense of destiny," the whole movement tended to cultivate individual initiative. What one acquired of that promised fortune in the new land of pilgrimage was largely dependent upon one's own exertion. The Occidental, in addition to becoming a predestinarian, became also an individualist. This outlook began to express itself in his philosophy with the dawn of written language. As his philosophy developed into science, his individualism dictated that the method of science should be the individualistic one, that is, the method of analysis of arithmetical progression and democracy. Since his tribal and national existence had been conceived as made up of individuals, so he conceived of reality as made up of ever and ever more separable particles, until he came at last to the indivisible atom. His has been a long experiment in analysis, in individuation, in extension. He sought the ultimate unit of reality; his Oriental brother demanded the ultimate and all-embracing organism.

A contrasting development took place in the Orient. Here the migrations soon came to the end of the trail. Successive influxes could only settle down upon, overlap the previous ones. The land was soon cultivated to the limits of arability to provide the common living. It was seemingly the most fertile spot on earth, and few were willing to take the backward track to plateau and desert. People were forced to live in close proximity. Both farming and living had to become intensive. The individual could subsist only as he fitted himself into the close-knit fabric of society. The very segregation intensified family relationships. To assert individuality in any drastic way was to put one's self on the outside, to cut himself off from means of support, to make himself an outcast. Nowhere except in the Orient has such a premium been placed upon conformity. It had certain advantages as well as disadvantages. While it built up imperviousness to new ideas, it was useful in the preservation of the established social order, not only against revolutionary notions, but, by a strange paradox, against foreign amalgamation. The invaders have ever, by force of circumstance, been compelled to sink into the common picture or perish. Thus there arose in the Orient the most intensive and the most enduring of world civilizations.

But did development cease in the Eastern world while the Western world was forging ahead? To many, such will seem a foregone conclusion, but, in the light of the facts we have cited, it is not so apparent. May there not be an intensive development that is progressive quite as well as an extensive one? Is an extensive analytical civilization more civilized than an intensive organismic one? I do not believe that the opinion so fondly entertained by the West can be maintained.

The Westerner has been more than an individualist. He has also been a lifelong spendthrift. He began by destroying the forests with ax and fire. What matter? Were there not untold forests still unburned? This was done in the frenzied attempt to clear the land for a few crops of wheat that flourished for a limited time, until the virgin soil was exhausted. We have been such spendthrifts of soil that the United States government recently suggested the turning of extensive tracts of former tillage back to the desert, as insufficient to support even a sparse population. We have ripped open the bowels of the earth like pillagers to appropriate the last treasure there, in sublime indifference to the coming generations or the future of society. We are now wastefully depleting our resources of oil with scant respect for the common good, the national defense, or anything but private gain.

Unfortunately, for a race so constituted, with such an economy as ours, the days of exploitation are ended. The world is now so narrowed that our wild nomad feet must halt. We are now obliged to learn the lesson in which China has been tutored for four thousand years. The early backwash of her migrations turned her whole effort inward toward the internal relations. It focused the attention of the individual upon the simplest associations in which he found himself, those that were necessary for his own maintenance. These simplest relations were of the family and the village, and so intense was the struggle for life that the common man had no opportunity to look beyond it. But it taught him social economy; it taught him the indissoluble nature of human relationships. It taught him thrift, the conservation of food, the conservation of soil, how to get the most from little. These are qualities of the utmost importance in the present overcrowded world.

East and West must come together in mutual understanding and helpfulness if civilization is not to perish. Each has lessons of value to teach the other. If it is true that the world has grown too small for the West, it is by contrast true that the world has grown too large for the East. We must move together for the building of the new and better world which is yet to be. In the finished dream of civilization there are many factors to be contributed from the race experience of both East and West. This harmonization cannot be brought about by violence nor by propaganda, however well-intentioned, but only by mutual respect and understanding. Such is the collaboration immediately demanded by the narrowing boundaries of our present world.

SECTION I
INDIVIDUALISM IN WESTERN CULTURE

CHAPTER I

THE CREATIVE IDEA
OF WESTERN CIVILIZATION

· ·

THE ATTEMPT TO discover the single creative or dominant
idea in Western culture will seem to many not only foolish
but impossible. If such should be hit upon, it might fall victim
to the ordinary fallacy of the universal. The dictum, "All generalizations are false, including this one," still holds true. While,
then, it may prove of profit to diagnose a culture and discover its
fundamental motif, the principle discovered must be used with
caution, and great restraint must be exercised in drawing conclusions.

Spengler in *The Decline of the West* has pointed in a remarkable way to a single dominating idea which seems to him to lie
at the seat of Western development. This distinctive idea he discovers in "sense of destiny." He declares that the Oriental world,
as indeed other races and ages, has been lacking in sense of
destiny. It has not been conscious of playing an historical role.
Indifferent to time, there has been wanting the idea of progress,
of tasks to perform, of coming civilizations to achieve. This
peculiarity of Western culture he believes to be accountable for
former progress, and since that role has now been played, since
there are few uninhabited and unexploited parts of the earth,
he considers the Western cycle about to close, and our civilization doomed to definite decline.

There are, no doubt, many events which favor Spengler's contention; but when one approaches phenomena of any kind with
a conscious or unconscious hypothesis the tendency is to exalt
and emphasize sustaining facts and to overlook those that are
contradictory. Thus it is possible to build what upon casual
examination appears unanswerable argument. We feel that this
is the weakness in the Spenglerian pessimism, though we believe
in facing the darkest facts in the situation and in allowing fullest
expression of judgment.

17

One of the oversights in the "sense of destiny" theory seems to be the assumption that its flowering is the particular characteristic of the *Aryan* stock. The historic reasons for the acceptance of this dictum are almost innumerable, since the main propagation of the principle in historic time has been on the part of the West. But as a swallow does not necessarily make a summer, so it is scarcely ascertainable that all other peoples in all other times have been without this sense. In fact, a great portion of the Oriental world which is named as devoid of it—the Indian—is itself of the Aryan race. Added to this is the admission that there was no time sense and thus no sense of history among the early Greeks. These exceptions make the generalization exceedingly weak, and indicate that other factors than racial must be sought in explanation. If the principle of racial peculiarity were to be established, it would be necessary to show that there are in the make-up of Aryan personality certain factors impossible of development in any other family stock. Until we have the benefit of older historic records we must admit that the first evidence of a linear philosophy of history which affected Western thought was the gift of the Semites. The Hebraic philosophy of history was charged with "sense of destiny." Zion was conceived as the lawgiver to whom the whole world should eventually turn for judgment. There is scarcely any portion of the Jewish Scriptures devoid of this underlying concept. It provides the deep under-tone and background of Jewish political thought which found resurgence and expression in the darkest hours of Hebrew history. It appears in the works attributed to Ezekiel and Daniel and was repeated in the Christian Book of Revelation. The influence of this concept of historical destiny was so formative in Western life as to outshine all other forces and to confute the Spenglerian proposition that "sense of destiny" was a strictly Aryan idea. The brilliant author of *The Decline of the West* seems to fall prey to that principle of necessitarianism which he himself so ably criticizes, namely, the presumption of mechanism. In the development of society he overlooks the possibility of human choice and its effects upon large portions of society. Society is not a mechanism except for purposes of statistical and scientific description. Society can undertake new social motives under the spur of outstanding leadership, or by an act of will. Not only so, but these considerations can leap the boundaries of nationality and of race, setting at naught the whole theory of race peculiarity. Essential blindness to this fact is the foundation on which *The Decline of the West* is built, and it is likewise one of the greatest menaces to the survival of Western culture. This result is always repeated whenever human interests are viewed from the mechanistic, the statistical, or the impersonal standpoint. It is ever possible to hypostatize the early extinction of society in some Malthusian manner and to give the elucidation the form and convincing force of mathematical exactitude. The only difficulty lies in this, that it may be scientific but it is not true. For, as Spengler has himself shown, science is unfitted to deal with life and personality. The best it can do is a guess, and a guess based on statistics from which personal or concrete meaning has been largely removed.

It is necessary then, to ask some deeper question than the racial one respecting "sense of destiny" as a Western characteristic. We must inquire what are the creative elements in this "sense." These again have already been indicated by Spengler. Sense of destiny arises out of space-time consciousness. When analyzed, we discover that some degree of space-time consciousness is necessary to any experience of personality whatever. While it may be true that in the West this experience has been emphasized to a marked degree, it is likewise true that it is neither national nor racial but the common experience of all persons. The importance of this fact lies here, that if space-time sense is common to all experiencing individuals, a magnified space-time concept can under favorable conditions leap all racial and national boundaries. The lack of space-time consciousness in certain races is not due to fundamental differences in persons but to differences of outlook, education, religion, and social, political, or physical environment. If this be true we are not dealing at all with a mechanical process, which rolls its ruthless cycles of flowering and decay, but with one that may involve permanent achievement for all races and all humanity. In other words, some phase of "sense of destiny" may become a world-gripping factor of the future, and the dominating idea of Western culture need not entail a decline.

I. HISTORICAL SOURCES OF THE SPACE-TIME IDEA

If we seek the sources of the space-time idea as characteristic of Western thought, we shall have to take into account, first of all, a physical one. Our ancestors, since they parted from their Oriental brothers on the central plateau of Asia, if some much disputed conjectures be true, have been continuously on the march. Always the face has been turned westward to greener pastures and richer inheritances. Always the dream has been of better personal opportunities, easier living conditions, more assured freedom. The famished hordes have looked continuously to the West as a fabled Garden of the Lord, promising new abundance and new opportunity. Any man with his face set in that direction, away from the old, away from the established, soon acquires a sense of destiny for himself and for his descendants. He becomes simultaneously a believer in novelty, change, and in freedom. Forevermore the more comfortable condition is just ahead of him. The perfect freedom is to come. The utopian civilization is on the horizon. Society is in process of evolution and the culmination is ahead. Thus out of sheer physical change a sense of movement and direction has become the main hypothesis upon which the Western world has built its culture. Whenever the discerning Westerner sees a Peking cart he is thrilled as no Chinese could possibly be, as he is reminded of the place its forerunner has filled in the history of the West, and the uses to which his ancestors have put it. Such, it seems to me, is the physical source from which began the peculiar space-time consciousness of the West, and its sense of destiny.

It might very well be that in this one concept is to be discovered the dividing characteristic between Occidental and Oriental civilization. The striking contrast of this spun-out, infinitely-divisible-line notion of space-time to the circular cyclic concept of the Orient might well be taken as a fundamental difference between East and West. By a strange coincidence Spengler bases his prophecy of *The Decline of the West* upon the Oriental concept and thereby incurs the charge of special pleading. In final analysis any cyclic concept of history ends in staticism. Only that which has previously happened can be expected to happen again. The historic cycle revolves only to repeat the old situation. History becomes self-repetition. Change is an illusion. Such a

concept would seem to explain the agelong political indifference
of peoples accepting it. If the cyclic theory of history be true,
there could be no real decline of the West but only a momentary
descent foretokening a future rise. The lowest point of the cycle
is the necessary step in the coming resurgence. In such a scheme,
decline and disaster can be only apparent, a part of an ongoing
process in which real advance is impossible. Under such conditions, "the decline of the West" is a contradiction in terms, a
bit of special pleading. Using Spengler's own theory, the decline
can be but the beginning of its rise, and his contention becomes
meaningless. Nor does resort to the Hegelian dialectic of a spiral
cycle of nationalisms help much unless we admit pan-Germanism
as the goal of universal history.

If we would seek the intellectual sources of the space-time
idea in Western thought, we shall need to go back to the beginnings of philosophic thinking. To Heraclitus, perhaps more than
to any other, is due the breakup of former world concepts. He
opposed the monism of the Eleatic Xenophanes with his doctrine
of a world in perpetual process. The only permanence was a
law of change. Though this idea did not gain immediate response, nor universal acceptance in Western thought, it was
peculiarly provocative and creative. It was one of those ideas
which, officially repudiated, lives on under the main current of
thought until the time for its recognition is ripe. The philosophy
of change was aided by its opponents as no other system in the
history of opinion. The arguments of the Eleatics, particularly
those of Zeno and of the Sophist-Eleatic Gorgias, to disprove
change and movement were so contrary to common experience
that they left grave questionings in the minds of their own ad-
herents; the arguments proved too much. All men long for certitude. They wish a dependable universe. The natural and lethargic
inclination is to keep the *status quo,* whether in religion, in
society, or in science, in the face of desperate situations. Men
look askance at theological, social, or scientific change which
involves the readjustment of positions with which the individual
is familiar. One does not wish to give extravagant praise, but it
may very well be that the challenge flung down to Eleaticism by
Heraclitus in the morning of philosophic and scientific thinking
had more than a little to do with saving the West from the
domination of a static absolutism into which it is easy for the

human mind to fall, for two reasons—the first, the apparent grandeur and finality of an all-embracing idea like that of the Absolute; and the second, the sheer inertia of the human mind in the face of any system which calls for continual readjustment.

The paradoxes by which Zeno attempted to stem the disconcerting tides of a changing world were just too much. The mathematical contention that, given a start, a tortoise could forever outdistance Achilles, while mathematically demonstrable, was too much for triumphant common sense. "If you want to prove the impossibility of motion, stop wagging your tongue," cried one of Zeno's audience it is said, as he walked out of the lecture. The denial of movement to the arrow because any mathematical placement of it demanded it be in a certain spot did not arrest its deadly course. It needed only that Gorgias should complete the folly by making nihilism still more ridiculous to consign Eleaticism to the junk heap of discarded ideas. The mastering grandeur of sweeping conclusions, the inertia of human thinking, and the demand for unshakable certainty, an *ataraxia* of the human mind, continued to haunt the chambers of thought, and remains to this hour a potent factor in the realm of ideas.

A striking phenomenon in the history of philosophy is the way in which contradictory and initially conflicting theories absorb and sustain each other. It may have been the effort of Leucippus to solve the antimony between being and becoming, between permanence and change, that led him to conceive the cosmos as made up of quantitatively equal atoms, whose movement gave the qualitative differences of which common sense is so conscious. Democritus advanced the concept, and finally Lucretius gave it to the Roman, and hence to the modern, world in sublime literary form. The attraction of atomism for the ancient world and ours lies in its promise to give us both concepts, staticism and change, and to make them lie down in peace together. The unchanging mathematical and physical laws under which atomic relations are conceived give us our Absolute, and movement gives us change. And furthermore, we seem relieved of all theological implications, under the cover of mathematical concepts. Critical thought is only beginning to reveal the contradictions of this ancient and modern self-delusion.

Notwithstanding, the challenge of Heraclitus had broken the spell of absolutism and had launched the notion that the world is a process. The foundations had been laid for pluralism, for mathematical science, for individualism, for democracy. Nevermore could Western civilization fall completely under the concept of the static.

II. SPACE-TIME AND THE INDIVIDUAL

So far we have dealt with but one portion of the formative influences that entered into the rising sense of destiny. Another concept had to do with the place of the person in his world, the contribution of mind to cosmic process. Among the Greeks Anaxagoras seems the first to have arrived at the fundamental principle of selfhood or personality. For him, mind is that which can be in all things, can direct them, and yet differentiate itself, from the things it controls and creates.[1] Though this statement would be disputed by many philosophical writers, the final asser-

[1] *Frag. 12*: "All other things contain a portion of everything, but mind is infinite and self-ruled and is mixed with nothing. For if it did not exist by itself, but were mixed with anything else, it would contain a portion of all things. . . . For in everything there is a portion of everything, as I have said above. And in that case the things mixed with it would prevent it from having power over anything else such as it now has, being alone and by itself. For it is the thinnest of all things and the purest, and it possesses all knowledge and the greatest power. And whatsoever things are alive, the largest as well as the smallest, over all is mind, the ruler. And over the whole revolving universe mind held sway, so that it caused it to revolve in the beginning. The revolution first began in a small area; now it extends over a larger space, and it will extend still farther. And mind knows all things, whether mixed together, or differentiated and separate. Mind also regulated all things—what they were to be, what they were (but are not now), and what they are; and mind regulated the revolution in which revolve the stars, the sun and the moon, and the air and the ether that are differentiated (from the primal mixture). And it is this revolution that caused the differentiation. The dense is differentiated from the rare, the warm from the cold, the light from the dark, the dry from the moist; and there are many portions of many things. Nothing, however, is altogether and distinct from anything else, excepting only mind. And all mind, whether greater or smaller, is alike. Nothing else, however, is like anything else. But whatever portions are predominant in each individual thing, these it has always been taken to be, because they were the most conspicuous things."

The principal reason why these fragments have been interpreted in a materialistic sense seems to have been due to the bias of materialistic philosophers who set a pace with which later commentators dared not or felt it not worth while to disagree. There have been notable exceptions, however, as cf. Max Heinze: *Uber den Nous des Anaxagoras*; Mary Mills Patrick: *The Idea of Spirit in Greek Thought*; F. M. Cornford: *Anaxagoras' Theory of Matter*; E. Rohde: *Psyche*; cf. discussion by Paul R. Helsel in a doctoral dissertation, University of Southern California, 1935: *The Concept of Nous in Early Greek Philosophy*.

tion that "nothing is altogether differentiated and distinct from anything else excepting only mind" would seem to present overwhelming evidence against the materialistic interpretation, and not to be overridden by the theory that such ideas do not comport with the contemporaneous state of human progress. At any rate, the simplest and most necessary fact concerning intelligence, mind, self-consciousness, individuality, or personality, was hit upon by Anaxagoras. For the most elemental characteristic of personal or even mental experience lies in the power of differentiating one's self from the surrounding world. If personality enters into higher ranges, it is due to capacity for greater differentiation in unity. We are able to distinguish between the self and its ideas, and also between ideas. As these distinctions through memory take on the form of succession, the time factor becomes a reality. Thus we see the entrance of the space-time idea as necessary to all self-consciousness. It is futile, then, to argue as does Spengler that the space-time experience is foreign to certain races or nationalities; its domination is a matter of degree, and whatever is so essential to all personal experience may be cultivated into a national, race or world consciousness.[2]

It was Socrates who in Greek thought raised this principle to the dignity of moral idealism and freedom. To him, as to Plato and Aristotle, Anaxagoras was the first of the Greek philosophers "to have been awake." We may take this to be the Socratic-Platonic emphasis upon the truth that in the interpretation of individual experience the real problems of philosophy first swam into view. Thus in the Western world arose the space-time idea, carrying with it the notions of freedom, moral responsibility, and sense of racial destiny. In the history of the Roman Empire it became dominant in part through the influence of Stoicism, in greater part through Epicureanism and Cynicism, all the schools having claimed Socrates as their fountain and inspiration.

The advent of Christianity into the Graeco-Roman world brought a new stream of destiny consciousness, and this from Semitic sources. Here it seems to have arisen out of the clan warfare which characterized the welding of the Jews into national entity. Their disorganized tribes, like those of the Greeks across the Mediterranean, were in the position of a buffer state between

---

[2] The Oriental world has a space-time consciousness but it differs from that of the West by being circular rather than linear.

opposing and overwhelming states. With this difference—the opponents who fought across the borderland of Judea were more highly organized and more cultured, and exerted the pressure more continuously and through long centuries. This condition would drive any people to internal amalgamation or dissolution. That Judea was not dissolved was due to her national religious convictions which differentiated her from her oppressors and from the surrounding clans. In this she was aided by her high-land isolation just off the main routes of commerce and war. Yet her position made her a menace to the line of communication between Egypt and Asia. Out of the long struggle came the sense of national destiny. As Judea had been the barrier between states, the battleground on which they came together, she might also play the role of arbiter, and some day the law should go forth from Zion unto the ends of the earth.[3]

No account of the rise of the sense of destiny, or the linear concept of history can be complete without recognition of the fact that Judaism played a principal role. National abhorrence of idolatry, purged and intensified by the Babylonian captivity, led Israel to consider her national mission as centering about bring-ing the Gentiles to the observance of the Law, the worship of the one true God, the Lord of the whole earth. Ezekiel, who wrote perhaps the first great philosophy of history, under the effects of that captivity, attempted to turn Hebraic thought from an intense nationalism to a more cosmopolitan personalism. Righteousness was something more than national or racial loyalty, it was an individual achievement, open to and demanded of all men alike. The judgments of God are both national and indi-vidual. He denied the totalitarian claim that sins were only national when men sought to escape personal responsibility by

[3] Though implicating the "sense of destiny" the Jewish idea was essentially Oriental in form and shows the dangers that lurk in such generalizations as Spengler's. Zion's destiny was to become the center to which the Gentiles should come for the Law. The Chinese in the same conceptual way thought of their emperor as the Son of Heaven and thus the ruler of the whole earth. All space diverged from the Emperor's seat, which was the fifth direction: e.g. East, West, South, North, and the Emperor's Seat. This Oriental "sense of destiny" seems now to urge the Japanese mind to bring the world under the scepter of one divine ruler—the Mikado. The main difference between Oriental and Occidental "sense of destiny" would be that the one is centri-petal whereas the other is centrifugal.

declaring: "The fathers have eaten sour grapes, and the children's teeth are set on edge" (*Ezek.* 18:2).

A still further intensification of feeling followed the persecution of the Greek conquerors in the compulsory worship of the Emperor in the days of the Maccabean revolt. Therefrom grew the Book of Daniel with its more detailed philosophy. History was held to gather its meaning from the unfolding purposes of a Divine Spirit to whom kings, men, and nations were but the actors in the supreme drama of creation. When under similar persecutions in Rome the Christians sought to unravel the meaning of events, they built on the earlier concept of the Book of Daniel a more modern and contemporaneous theory known as the Revelation. This was in a real sense an echo and development of the Book of Daniel, revised for the times and it had a formative influence in fastening on Europe the linear concept of history, the sense of destiny yet to be fulfilled. The concept was at least as early in Judaism as the author of Genesis to whom Abraham moves out to the Land of Promise to inaugurate a national role in world history.

Not until the Exile did this national dream begin to break into the Messianic and more spiritual, as well as more individualistic, concept. All great idealisms are flowers that spring from the soil of early and more materialistic defeat. It was the full force of this finer sense of destiny carried over into Christianity which was added to the Stoic impulse to become a dominating factor of Western civilization.

For the third time, if we suspect that Zeno, the founder of Stoicism, was Semitic, Semitism provided a further impulse toward individualism and the space-time idea. This occasion came with the Moslem invasions, carrying Jewish scholars on the flood of the tide of conquest, with their knowledge of and devotion to Aristotle. The Moslem world also under the double spell of Judaism and Greek philosophy felt called upon to play the historic role of destiny in the West. This also provided a thrilling moment in the history of Western culture bringing in its train a new triumph of democracy.

III. SPACE-TIME AND PERSONALITY

It can be said that no civilization rises higher than its religion and its art. This is not only true because religion and art are the highest elements of self-expression. It is true because only something akin to, or substituting for, religion can lift a fertile idea into a mass consciousness and so make it hold for wide populations and for considerable periods. Judaism, Stoicism, Mohammedanism, and Christianity were such religions. National or racial sense of destiny is a plant of slow growth. It is the result of a thousand accretions. The principles upon which it is founded permeate their way but slowly into the popular mind to become a national or race-consciousness. They require the force of long habit, of particular outlooks upon the world, of political and geographical exigency; they require the building up of permanent institutions and settled conditions. The most potent factor in inculcating the masses and bringing about a mass consciousness must be religion or some parallel substitute for it, if nothing more than a so-called "religion of humanity." For religion is the great melting pot in which men of diverse interests, tribes, races, blend their differences into political and institutional amalgam. The totalitarian states afford the current example of the fact. Sovietism attempts to displace the old religion with an emotional appeal all its own. Its problem is whether it can permanently hold its own against the older faith by mere violent negation and without the construction of a more positive worship than Marxism now affords. Nazism makes direct appeal to the ancient heathen religion for its emotional force while with Fascism it would revive the ancient concepts of the Roman Empire, with the worship of Caesar not so far in the background. In Japan there is already at hand the worship of the Emperor and the effort thereby to displace all other forms of worship. He would delude himself who would try not to think that these facts bear an internal connection. They are steps toward raising, or should we say lowering the national consciousness to blind obedience, and mass action. It is due to the particular spur which religion gives to the emotional and creative elements of imagination. Under the impetus of a masterful religious idea the revolution may be sudden and far-reaching—as the conquest by Christianity of the Roman Empire, the rise of the Moslem states, or the efflorescence of Gothic architecture. All such movements are infilled with the space-time idea, and sense of destiny is itself one of the most religious and creative of impulses. It is the soul of all missionary enterprises whatsoever.

But so far in Western civilization these creative factors have scarcely got beyond the nationalistic stage, for religion bears a double function in history. It may be only racial or national, and it may be cosmic.

Christianity, by reason of the diverse elements that have already entered into it—Jewish, Greek, Roman, Gothic—and by reason of its universal characteristics, stands best fitted perhaps for a cosmic role. For it is, in its highest teachings and spirit, plainly cosmic. But Christianity in this larger sense has never been tried. It has fallen prey to racialisms and nationalisms that have exploited it for their selfish interests and have never yielded themselves to its cosmic demands. This is today the principal block in the way of its progress. It but needs overnight that Christians become really Christian to give to Christianity a cosmic significance and to bring to it world-wide acceptance. For the objection of men of other races and religions is not to the principles of Christianity itself but rather to the unchristian practices of its avowed devotees, added to their parochial interpretations of its spirit. The confusion in the mind of the world arises from the disparity between professed faith and practice and the perniciously narrow channels set for what might be a cosmic faith; the meditating principle of all religions. This is not the basic fault of Christianity itself, but of its race-proud and narrow-minded Western interpreters. The mind of the Founder of Christianity was cosmic in its outlook. It was steeped in the lore of Judaism, and was touched by the culture of Greece in a way which has never been properly evaluated.[4] The first Christians were familiar

---

[4] If this statement seems extreme it is well to remember the graciousness with which the inquiring Greeks were received, and Jesus' appeal to the concepts of their own Orphic mysteries (John 12:10); his position with respect to the Samaritan woman, who was astonished that he, a Jew, would speak to her; his treatment of the Syrophoenician woman (Mark 7:26). The Greek culture of the cities of Phoenicia and the Decapolis might quite naturally have affected the outlook of Jesus and the Disciples. The Stoic philosopher Antiochus, teacher of Cicero, and the Grammarian Ptolemeus were natives of Ascalon. Gadara, where the demoniac was healed, was the birthplace of Philodemus, the Epicurean poet and philosopher father-in-law of Julius Caesar; of Meleager the poet-philosopher, anthologist, and epigrammatist; of Theodorus, the rhetorician, tutor to the Emperor Tiberius. At Sidon was the seat of the Epicurean school presided over by Zeno of Sidon. In the face of these facts and the oral and disputatious nature of the teaching of the time, one must possess a certain hardihood to deem it impossible that one who also deigned to teach should be thought quite uninfluenced by the intellectual tides amid which he lived. The general atmosphere tended toward a cosmic universalism foreign

with a tradesman's Greek and around the Nazarene sea gleamed the templed hills of the outstanding Greek culture of his day. The mind of Jesus was able to see past the narrowness of nationalistic, racial, or ecclesiastical pretensions to include all men of good will. He laid down as the requisites of religion no standards of belief, except in the saving grace of righteousness, love for and devotion to God as the Father of all men, implicit obedience to and love for the Higher Will. This devotion was to be proved by an equal passion for the supreme good of men. The appearance of such service was to be recognized as inspired of Deity whether it sprang from Jew, Samaritan, or Gentile. He sought to welcome to his discipleship without further tests all men of good will and righteousness without respect to theological opinions. The day will come when the soundness of this position will be recognized and will become the platform of all true lovers of religion. Until that day Christianity cannot be truly said to have been tried.

All this has particular bearing on the destiny consciousness of Western civilization; for sense of destiny is a menace to the world until it becomes cosmic in its sweep. While it remains on the plane of the nation or the race it can lead only to diversion, war, and destruction. It was the *Mittel-Europa* idea that lured Germany to welcome war, as indeed some similar role has been conceived at times by every European nation and threatens again to engulf us. It is rampant heresy against humanity which lies concealed in all imperialistic ambitions on the part of any nation. Our sense of destiny must include the welfare of all mankind without distinction of class, race, religion, or condition. We must rise to this cosmic consciousness now or civilization must perish. In a world as now constituted we cannot maintain the old national and racial outlook and survive. This is what gives force to the Spenglerian indictment. Only something with the cosmic, creative, and emotional appeal of religion is powerful enough to meet the situation. The individual as self, state, or nation considers its own interests at the expense of all others; the person

---

to the narrowness of Phariseeism which Jesus continually opposed. This cosmic consciousness also pervaded the message of Jewish prophetism. Note Jesus' introduction to his ministry (Luke 4:16) which was based on Isa. 42 —a ministry to the Gentile. For further discussion of Hellenistic influences see Fairweather: *Jesus and the Greeks,* Charles Scribner's Sons, New York, 1924.

finds himself and his highest good only in the well-being of all. This latter is the heart of personalism and the soul of Christianity, and unless it becomes part and parcel of Western sense of destiny the decline of the West becomes an assured fact.

IV. SPACE-TIME AND THE DEVELOPMENT OF THE WEST

What has served to exalt the space-time consciousness to such exaggerated proportions in this modern age? It is undoubtedly due to the mathematical character of modern science which has been able to color all the thinking of the West—its philosophy, its religion, its business and social practice. In a sense, the space-time idea as extension is the crowning achievement of Western culture. It has never been brought to such completeness in any other era, nor has any concept been so widespread or so potent. We think of everything in terms of mathematics. We are worshipers of statistics. We apply them to political and social forms. We attempt by them to evaluate educational systems and look to them for the confirmation of religious success. And the success of the principle lies in its wide orientation. Great numbers of men are thinking in terms of mathematical relation. Out of this have sprung the multitudes of mechanical inventions dependent upon the laws of physio-dynamics. Once an idea becomes so imbedded in popular conceit, in subconscious thought, it becomes the fructifier of countless creative imaginings. Our own age is history's best example of a mechanical complex seizing upon the imagination of the world. The result has been to give us new patterns of space-time itself. The application of steam and steel to mechanical problems, telegraph, telephone, electrical invention, airplane, radio, television—these practical children of our mathematico-time-space ideas have transformed the very minds that have created them. But this is no reason why the world should grow drunken on the wine of a single idea. For two generations the whole world, and for five generations a part of it, has held the captivating hypothesis to be the only possible one. Whatever could be made amenable to the space-time model of mathematics was declared knowable and real. Whatever stood outside the statistics has, sometimes very blatantly, been called unreal. Counting has passed for wisdom, and mechanics has been the only god. We have been strangely moved to dream that what was in some senses only a mathematical progression was the high star of our destiny, that gospel for which our civilization was born into the world.

Nor can we be blind to the part which the sense of destiny and the linear concept of history has played in the Western dream of liberty. Men moving out to found new civilizations were sure to make the occasion one for the seeking of new opportunities and new freedoms. For the most part they were men escaping from the thralldom of tradition, or social necessity, of political autocracy, or ecclesiastical tyranny. They were moving out from old conditions that had hampered and bound them. They must form a society which would improve upon the old, which would make impossible for themselves and their children the old repressions and slaveries. Such an achievement of freedom would have been impossible in a more settled state of society, particularly of one in which the cyclic concept of history controlled the popular mind, and a social passivism held it in thrall.

Now on every side we hear the troubling voice of the prophets of disenchantment and doom. We know not which way to turn. We begin to doubt our destiny, and that when it seemed about to be fulfilled. For the first time, perhaps, since those tramping hordes beyond the dawn of historic time faced westward we are riven with doubt. Is there any way out of our dilemma?

Only now that we have plunged into the social, educational, and religious morass are we discovering the one-sidedness of our beliefs, and the existence of values that can in no way be revealed in the logarithmic tables or actuarial statistics. So long have we been accustomed to treating our problems in the one way it is difficult to conceive any other. So with the large gains and the heaped up riches that should prove of great benefit to our future progress, this richest of the ages mourns in single-mindedness the "decline of the West."

What has been true of a great constructive idea, even so poor a one as that of numbers, once it gets into the subconscious mind of masses of men, may be true of ideas even greater, and having moral, social, and ameliorative values. Instead of deploring the incapacity of mathematics to answer all questions and achieve all values, it may be that the time has arrived to follow some other concept to its fulfillment. The human mind shows no exhaustion of resources, and when it can concentrate on ideals great enough and commanding enough, we shall achieve a new world.

Perhaps the day has come when we are summoned to something vaster, to something far more difficult than the long road that meant a pioneer subduing of the earth, and a development of physical resources. The greatest conquest of all awaits us, namely, the subduing of our own hearts, the conquest of our own spirits. The long road taken under a sense of destiny will have been in vain and our own will take its place with the buried civilizations of the past unless we can now lift it to the higher level of moral and spiritual achievement.

CHAPTER II

THE RISE OF INDIVIDUALISTIC MORALS

. . . .

W
HEN HERACLITUS BROKE from the old forms of a static world to set forth the concept of a world in constant process of change, he introduced the whole time-space problem into a society that, at least so far as the Eleatics were concerned, had agreed to ignore or deny it. His doctrine, given to the world through the atomism of Epicurus and later of the Roman Lucretius, laid broad and deep the metaphysical concepts from which modern science has never been able to clear itself. The whole mental habit of Heraclitanism is away from the static to the moving, away from death to life, away from the One to the Many. When Heraclitanism absorbed the further emphasis by Anaxagoras on mind as the metaphysical fact behind all differentiation and movement, and Protagoras had added the humanistic doctrine of "man the measure of all things," the philosophic way had been prepared before Socrates with his doctrine of individual certainty, not, this time, of sense perception, as with Protagoras, but of moral intuition. The moral discovery of Socrates was the most brilliant and significant that up to his time had been made in the history of Greek culture.

That the primal impulse of modern civilization should have arisen from the search for moral self-realization is no detached or insignificant fact of social progress. It may seem incongruous to ascribe the role of revivalist to the quaint, silenus-like figure that made himself so obnoxious to his fellow citizens just after that burst of Periclean glory that preceded the twilight of Greek civilization. But with all his quaintness, his comic appearance, the sharp practice of his dialectic which sought to convict every man of ignorance, there was also the assurance, the unequivocation of spiritual passion, that went directly to the mark and accepted no subterfuge in the search for moral truth. Some have discerned in this strange figure only the mock-heroic who could drink all night (without getting under the table) and walk

33

steadily home at dawn while his companions slept where they fell; but the clear moral vision of this man who refused to flee from death by poison for the sake of a principle he had nailed high to the Athenian masthead was not the moral vision of the self-indulgent, the gluttonous, and the alcoholic.

The undying truth which Socrates discovered and proclaimed in the midst of a caviling and degenerate world was no less than that of individual moral responsibility. Man could know what was wrong, and had the power to do the right. We cannot assume that until Socrates' time there had been no truth, honor, nor righteousness in the world, but he did discover that righteousness was confirmed by the light of reason: It had a philosophical basis: it was a certainty of the cosmic order. The Athenian tyrants might strut their day, and the tricky and uncertain Demos might rise in sudden wrath and put to death its saviors and benefactors, but his was the appeal to history, to time, to destiny, if you will, against which all unrighteousness would rage in vain. The cosmos was righteous, and only righteousness could permanently endure. The cosmic order behind the individual made his triumph sure.

If that social firebrand who moved across the Arabian desert clad in the skins of beasts and feeding on locusts and wild honey could be called the forerunner of Jesus, there was yet a vaster and a stricter sense in which Socrates could be called the forerunner—he who prepared the way before the feet of the Lord. For Socratic sense of righteousness wrought into Stoic integrity prepared the Roman world for that concept of truth upon which, if man should fall, he would be broken to pieces, but if upon him it should fall, it would grind him to powder.

If there has been anything about Western culture that is praiseworthy or has lifted it above the ruck of time, it is not political nor legal achievement, art, nor even science, but this consciousness of the eternal nature of truth and righteousness founded in freedom which for the West was the primary philosophical message of Socrates. And it was because of the emotional element, the religious appeal with which it became involved, that it touched the springs of creative imagination in the Western world to give us our highest achievements in law and democracy, in education and art and science.

Reference has already been made to the fact that righteousness did not arise with Socrates, nor was the idea of righteousness peculiar to western Europe. Its chief distinction there is that it is an individual thing. The individual cannot lose himself in the body corporate. His nation goes to war but he himself is driven by the sense of individual sin, which is never quite absolved. This very fact makes him the eternal critic of his own unrighteous and often unholy institutions—which capacity for self-criticism has become almost the special characteristic of Western culture.

I. HISTORICAL ASPECTS

It would be impossible to unweave all the intricate fabric which went to determine the direction of Western morals. But Western moral feeling has been characterized, as have other elements of Western life, by individualism. The rise of morals in any society is dependent upon a certain sense of isolation in the individual in the midst of social relations. Call it egotism or what one will, the first sense of moral responsibility marks the birth of the moral person, as surely as the consciousness of the experience of the "me" as over against the "not-me" marks the beginning of the individual. The first moral consciousness is the response of the unit to certain recognized social relationships. For this reason, individual ethical conviction exists everywhere, is primal and elemental. Where the individual sinks himself into the group, it is a condition brought about by willed orientation. Individualism in Western morals is an emphasis rather than a peculiarity due to race. Its appearance has been characterized by a sense of sin, of deep individual responsibility for one's acts, now against some ideal perfection, as of God, and now against one's fellow men.

Among the Jews, it began to take on a more individual aspect in the prophet Ezekiel, as the welfare of the commonwealth threatened to become merely the responsibility and welfare of individuals. Men who had largely identified themselves with the tribes were driven to question their own relationship to and responsibility for the beloved society which now found itself decimated and exiled. Religion ceased to be a corporate act and began to take on more individualistic forms. It is impossible not to feel that the great growth of priestly ritual and sacrifice for the atonement of specific and individual sins sprang up after the exilic period.

Possibly the prime mover of all was Egypt, for here earliest

of all we find a definite teaching of immortality with a future
rigidly assigned by the moral acts of this earthly life. In all
probability Egypt exerted powerful influence upon Judea, as
indeed it undoubtedly did upon Greek culture, through the
spread of the Orphic mysteries. Into the factors that made up
the general result must be brought also the religion of Zoroaster
and later of Mohammed. In all of these systems, for which
Alexandria and the regions around became the melting pot, the
great trend was toward personal responsibility, until it finally
emerged in clear and institutionalized form.

II. THE SOCRATIC PRINCIPLE

In Greece individualistic morals found their great protagonist
in Socrates. In him, divorced from the extreme mysticism of
Orphism, the principle of personal morals was clearly set forth
upon a scientific and philosophic basis. It is difficult from fragmentary information to appraise the character of Socrates. What
were the factors which led him to his unique philosophical principle? There was the calm and persistent search for truth. There
was the Protagorean background of man's significance in the
scheme of things, as the measure of them all. There was the
unutterable confusion of Sophistic, which had broken down into
a sheer moral relativism, combining the worst features of Pro-
tagoreanism and Eleaticism. There were the festering sores of
Greek demagoguery in political life. Into the midst of a moral
darkness that promised no relief came Socrates, one of the most
amazing figures of history. For this unexcitable man, who could
calmly arrange his dress and rub his sciatica in the presence of
the official poisoner, arrived at his conviction by an act of
mysticism, a religious conversion at the bivouac of the Hoplites.

Distressed about the access of the individual man to a knowledge of moral good, there came to him as an inspirational revelation the fact of the eternal validity of the moral self-consciousness.
If any man would look within his own soul he would find there
condemnation of every evil act. This was "the true light that
lighteth every man that cometh into the world." He called it his
daemonium, which would not, indeed, lead him unerringly into
the right, but which would at least unerringly warn him of moral
evil. It is significant that the two greatest religious teachers of
Western civilization should have hit upon this principle as the
starting point of their moral teaching: Socrates in the negative

way, an inner spirit that would warn him from evil; Jesus in a positive way, a spirit of truth that should guide into all truth.[1] The significance lies in this, that whatever is good and distinctive in Western culture is owing more than anything else to these double influences.

This, then, was the Socratic principle, and upon it Socrates based his whole philosophy. In fact, the power of the principle lay in its philosophic background. The fact of the common *daemonium* was, to Socrates, cosmic. It was a method of ascertaining truth, but it was more than that. Its sanctions arose out of the metaphysical facts of existence. This was to him a moral universe, man was by nature a moral being. There is no doubt that Socrates' enthusiasm for this principle led him to overlook some of the darker phases of human experience. In its negative character it led too much to an attitude of *laissez faire*. To his mind, verdant and hopeful even to death, it but needed the work of an intellectual midwife to release the mind and soul of any man from its moral misconceptions. A few deft questions after the dialectical method, a confession of ignorance, and lo! out of the assembled fogs of passion and self-interest would stand clearly revealed the moral truth. It might have been sufficient, if all men had been blessed with the intellectual honesty of a Socrates. The fact seems to have been that he had never altogether lost his way amid the fogs of passion and self-interest. Nevertheless there was the drawing power of a sublime faith in men which enabled him to bring others to his own high level of faith and to transform life by the contact of a spiritual inspiration.

III. The Stoic Contribution

It is impossible to understand Stoicism apart from its place in the field of history. It arose as a defense against the breakdown of civilization. It was the bridge over which Greek culture passed from an ancient to a new world. Absorbed again into the body of Christian thought, it bridged the Dark Ages and helped in the Renaissance. Stoicism sought that *ataraxia* or apathy of spirit which it shared in common with Epicureanism, Cynicism, and Skepticism, but it was born from a world of political tumult and mental confusion, of religious defection, and of moral anarchy.

[1] John 16:13.

We get some faint notion of the rottenness to which Greek moral fiber was reduced by one of the Greek plays[2] recently revived in America, for no reason at all except in the hope that the rottenness of a past age would appeal to the rottenness of this and bring shekels to the box office. We ought to understand, however, that it was no compliment either to our morals or our classicism. Into a world of moral degradation, of ethical relativism, in which men were saying it is impossible to know what is right, good, or true, and adding to this the cry of political partisanship for the prevention of justice: a world somewhat boastfully claiming its emancipation from ignorance and the trammeling customs of the past: a world which with glee had announced the death of the gods and the lapse of higher sanctions than the lust of the flesh and the pride of life; a world rotten-ripe for the dictatorship which was so soon to crush even the lingering relics of democracy; this was the world into which Stoicism was born. But more than all this, it sought some respite from fear in a day when human life and liberty were held ever at the pleasure of demagogue and tyrant. How was the true man to rise above any circumstance that might befall him? How could he dig down to the deep rock of what Carlyle called "the center of indifference"? It was essentially a reform movement, a fore-running spirit of Puritanism arising out of a morally decadent and politically tyrannical national life—for the rise of Puritanism was in a very real sense a revival of Stoicism with some Christian features added.

The Epicureans had sought *ataraxia* in physical satisfactions. It is true that not until late did Epicureanism develop into the licentiousness which gave it a bad name. It is true, also, that Epicurus was more than Stoic in his simplicity of life and his dependence upon nature. The difference must be found, I believe, in the contrasting character of their metaphysics. For Epicurus this background was material only, while for Stoicism it was spiritual.[3] The later development of Epicureanism is not to be laid up against Epicurus but against the principle of materialism whose historic development has always been the disparagement of man in his world. It was just the insignificance of

[2] *Lysistrata.*

[3] It might be charged that Stoicism was also materialistic and fatalistic but its materialism was largely abrogated by its doctrine of the supremacy of mind.

man in the universe that yielded the apathy which Epicurus sought. Matter was supreme and would inevitably win. Why, then, trouble about life? Bring desires down to the compass of the hour and the opportunity, for we are "a long time dead" and the clods of the valley will soon rest sweetly on the best and the worst of us.

The Cynics' apathy attained a measure of indifference to the world, its conventions, its honors, its rewards, its hardships. It had some things in common with Stoicism, but its real *raison d'être* lay in its disregard of the refinements of life. The Skeptics were less practical and more rational, and held that apathy could be attained only by complete suspension of judgment. Conviction was held to be the spark which disturbs our clod, and only he could be happy who was utterly without it. Opposed to all these "ways of life" was Stoicism, which believed not only in the supremacy of reason but in the conquering power of the individual.

The founder of Stoicism was Zeno, a Cyprian Phoenician, perhaps a Jew, of Citium, and there is within the system not only that confidence in individual judgment and capacity for moral action which characterized Socrates, there was added to this the unifying principle and sense of cosmic order which was the peculiar gift of the Jewish prophets. It is only by some such assumption that we can account for certain elements in the Stoic scheme. Stoicism, even as Epicureanism, Cynicism, and Skepticism, laid claim to a Socratic beginning, but Zeno seems to us to outrun even Socrates in the capacity for reverence. It was this capacity which ennobled the more naturalistic Greek thought. So Stoicism is perhaps to be understood first by a Jewish setting of reverence, and next by the Socratic background of individualism; and finally, because a man or a movement is frequently made quite as much by enemies as by friends, Stoicism must be understood by its opposition to the Epicurean materialism. One must be aware of the difficulties that lie in the way of such distinctions, because systems, attitudes, philosophies never present a clear case of either/or. We judge by general principles and historic trends quite as much as by any specific doctrine, for many a philosophy must eventually be known not by its profession but by its results.

The moral system of the Stoics was bound up with their metaphysics, for they had the wisdom to see that no pragmatism, no philosophy of action, could be intellectually self-sustaining unless it were conceived as an expression of the universal order. They rightly felt that a theory of knowledge, a system of ethics, the forms and norms of beauty, could not be isolated from the whole. This demand for wholeness is much decried in days of specialization in the interest of detached and partial thinking, when it is more or less of a scandal to adhere to a "system." But the Stoics were right: the final test of any way of knowledge is not its brilliant spots, nor even its eclecticism, but its consistency.

The Stoic task was this, to show that a system of morals was grounded both in the nature of man and in the nature of the cosmos. If they did not altogether succeed in this, yet they made the farthest religious advance of any purely philosophical movement, and they founded a culture under the protection of whose institutions we yet live. They knew that morals as duty could not be maintained unless the world itself, and its natural processes, were basically moral. Nature must have a care for the good and a hatred of the evil. If reason was disclosed in man, it must be because there was reason in the world of nature. Understanding of the world was based upon an intelligibility which resides in the world and in that which has produced it. This metaphysical and epistemological argument has never been excelled nor logically refuted.

Cicero in the *De Natura Deorum* quotes Zeno as declaring:

> Nothing destitute of consciousness and reason can produce out of itself beings endowed with consciousness and reason: therefore the Universe is itself not destitute of consciousness and reason.[4]

As the Epicureans had depended on Heraclitus with his eternal change for their conception of nature, so the Stoics based their physics, but with this difference: the present world was not the product of chance but of reason, purpose, and intelligence. The primal principle was fire, or fiery breath, but it contained also the meaning of *logos*. The mind or the life was to them something ethereal, but it was none the less conscious, intelligent, and purposive. The world, the whole cosmic order, was infilled with intelligence. This Creative Intelligence was God. Thus they

[4] *M. Tvlli Ciceronis*, Edidit Otto Plasberg, Fascicvlvx II, Lipsiae in Aedibvs B. G. Tevbneri MCMXI, p. 271.

based their doctrine of knowledge on that trinity of principles, the intelligent nature of man, the intelligible nature of the world, and both springing from and accounted for by a divine Creative Intelligence, or Reason.

This, then, was the basis of Stoic morality: to live in accord with nature was to live in unison with reason. Man was not to live by Epicurean bread alone. Any attempt to look on nature as something apart from man and his highest moral and spiritual requirements was a distortion, a failure to comprehend the full meaning of nature. This argument against a popular naturalism and in favor of a higher naturalism is as forceful as it was then. If we start out to account for the world, we must account for the most important element in it, namely, the mind and spirit of man himself. And as Dante taught that in God's will is our peace, so Epictetus taught that in our acquiescence with nature lay our true freedom.[5]

It is impossible to sum up in a brief paragraph, as is here attempted, the contribution of Stoicism to civilization. Indeed, it could not be exhausted in many books. All one can do is to enumerate rather casually, without essaying explanation, a few of its leading gifts to humanity. The most direct gift was, of course, through the Roman Empire and institutions themselves. It is a far cry from Nero to Marcus Aurelius, but the moral dis-

[5] "Lift up your head at last, as free from slavery. Dare to look up to God and say, 'Make use of me for the future as thou wilt. I am of the same mind; I am equal with thee. I refuse nothing which seems good to thee. Lead me whither thou wilt. Clothe me in whatever dress thou wilt. Is it thy will that I should be in a public or a private condition, dwell here or be banished, be poor or rich? Under all these circumstances I will make thy defense to men.' . . . If Hercules had sat loitering at home, what would he have been? Eurystheus, and not Hercules. Besides, by travelling through the world, how many acquaintances and how many friends had he? But none more his friend than God, for which reason he was believed to be the son of God, and was so. In obedience to him, he went about extirpating injustice and lawless force. But you are not Hercules, nor able to extirpate the evils of others; nor even Theseus to extirpate the evils of Attica. Extirpate your own, then. Expel, instead of Procrustes and Sciron, grief, fear, desire, envy, malevolence, avarice, effeminacy intemperance, from your mind. But these can be no otherwise expelled than by looking up to God alone as your pattern; by attaching yourself to him alone, and being consecrated to his commands. If you wish for anything else, you will, with sighs and groans, follow what is stronger than you, always seeking prosperity without, and never able to find it. For you seek it where it is not, and, neglect to seek it where it is." *Moral Discourses,* E. P. Dutton & Company, Inc., New York, chap. 16, sec. 4.

tance of the one from the other is very largely due to the impact of Stoicism in its conquest of Roman society. The contribution of Stoicism to the glory which was Rome is seen no less in those Roman institutions that passed away with the fall of Rome than in those which did not thus pass away. The dream of the life of culture in an ordered society, under a legal code insuring the equal protection of all men without distinction of class, race, or condition—in fact, the main undergirding of present civilization—is itself the precious gift of Stoicism to the world.

Stoicism has been mentioned as the highest religious achievement of pure philosophy, but beyond estimate is the preparation which it gave the Roman world for the reception of Christianity. It is difficult to see how Christianity could have gained a foothold without it. Furthermore, its literature and its ideas flowed into and helped to form the Christian concept of the religious life. The modern contrasts between Jesus and Paul, just now so popular, rest upon the intellectual background of Stoic Tarsus which everywhere influences the Pauline concepts.

And not the least contribution of Stoicism was the inspiration to modern democracy. It conceived of slave and freeman, poor and rich, low and high, all men as being equal before God. The legal formulation of this theory created the Roman code, the basis of Western law. The force of this principle has proved too great for any but temporary tyranny, and must eventually become the ruling tenet of all organized society. It formed the moving impetus of the revival of letters, the Gothic architecture, the Protestant Reformation, and modern democracy.

For a movement that has contributed such colossal and undying gifts to humanity there would seem to be no ground of criticism which would not react with force upon the critic. But Stoicism professed to a complete rationalism, and as such it failed. The consciousness of that failure made a place for the moral philosophy of Christianity.

In the first place, the Stoic rationalism was too complete. It was rather too good to be true. It reckoned without the time sense. An utterly rational universe is a completed universe. The Stoic fell into complacent agreement with a static world. Since this world was founded on pure reason, whatever is must be right. It is the best possible of worlds. There is nothing to do but accept it. There has to be something pedantic or inconsistent about such a declaration in the face of the glaring inequities of society and the sufferings of the innocent. Their world order had no future; it was without perspective. It could be no better than a recurrent cycle of imperfect worlds. For all that is here, the good and the evil, the righteousness and the sin, the justice and the injustice, all are a part of the necessary world order. There can never be a consummating triumph of the good. The divine is ever hampered by the "given" in his own nature.

This led to an impasse in the problem of evil. There was fate, *Moira,* ruling forever in the background, over which God himself could have no power. In the last analysis, there was no hope in the world. For life, defeated and broken, the sum of whose joys was outbalanced by its miseries, there was Epictetus' "Open Door" of suicide. The inadequacy of this philosophy, the failure of its rationality, seems disclosed if legends are true, in Zeno's suicide, because in a fall he had broken a finger, or in that of Cleanthes, who found a toothache more unbearable than death. Under such circumstances there would seem to be a failure of Stoic principles or an eagerness on the part of God to indicate the "Open Door."

But the reason for these failures all lay in the Stoic neglect of the emotions. Such is the weakness of any thorough-going rationalism. Normal man is never all mind any more than he is ever all emotion. The Stoic criticism of Epicureanism was that it failed to include in its universe mental and spiritual man himself as a part of nature. The Stoic also failed because, doing this, he neglected to include the whole nature of man. Though later Stoicism modified the position, the early Stoic exercised neither compassion nor forgiveness. Even to the intimates of one's household any display of affection was a descent from the Stoic ideal. They would have sympathized deeply with the Puritan law that jailed a Boston sea captain returning from a three years' voyage who kissed his wife at the doorstep, thus outraging public decorum.

The road to reformation lies not through rationalization, however perfect, but through capture of the emotions. This is the main historic reason why Stoicism failed and why education of itself alone can never insure the progress of society. The springs of emotion control the creative imagination, where reason can only assist and direct. No lesson is more needed in the world,

and particularly in America, today. No civilization can long survive without religion, and a religion which captures the emotions.

What in particular is the message of Stoicism for our day? The
message seems rather simple, but very fundamental. The greatness of Stoicism sprang from its doctrine of the supremacy of the
individual over all circumstances. We need to read anew the
legend that the sources of happiness are internal. We have too
long considered that happiness could be purchased with the
baubles of social standing, fame, and wealth. The Stoic looked
ever to those inner sources of comfort which we have too often
affected to despise.

Along with his deep sense of the innate worth and dignity
of the individual went also a profound sense of moral responsibility, of which our materialistic and behavioristic enthusiasms
have well-nigh relieved us. The working of that virus is disclosed in the "scrap-of-paper" incident of the late war, and the
succeeding easy repudiation of debts, promises, and honor.

The Stoics emphasized the possible divinity of man, as Christianity had the supreme right to do but has seldom had the
courage to do.

IV. THE JUDAEO-CHRISTIAN IMPETUS

The system of Stoicism was incomplete without the spiritual
élan of Judaism and Christianity. Judaism had provided the
setting of uncontaminated monotheism, the concept of a holy
and righteous God to whom both nations and individuals are
responsible. Their prophets had issued the call for social righteousness which demanded the amelioration of the lot of the
oppressed. Wedged into the small no man's land between violent
and assertive nations, Egypt on the one hand, as opposed to the
Babylonian and Assyrian cultures on the other, they had come
to abhor national sins as much as individual shortcomings. They
had evolved a philosophy of history deep with the sense of
destiny and looking toward a time when the knowledge and
service of a holy and righteous God should fill the earth as the
waters cover the sea. They advanced the idea of a good time
coming through the leadership of a just and righteous ruler
commanding all men by the power of justice. They had evolved a
literature of right conduct, the greatest literature of all time, of
such high order as to provide a Holy Scripture for the rising

movement of Christianity, to furnish its ritual, and to become a mighty factor in its success. Thus was the way prepared for the triumph of Christianity which took on a vital note by proclaiming that the looked-for leader had already come, and Christianity now became the main rival of Stoicism. The very similarities of virtue in the two systems which led to immediate hostility between them could only bring a later conciliation. The harshness of Stoicism was unnatural and inhuman. It cast too much of strain upon the regular amenities of life. There was needed the softer note brought in by the teaching of Christian love. Nor in the long struggle that preceded the acceptance of Christianity in the Roman Empire did the Christians show themselves any whit inferior to the Stoic in fortitude. In this they rather outdid the Stoic, for in them was no dull, uncomplaining bearing of ills; under the spur of the new faith the early Christians ran to meet these ills and faced martyrdom in holy ecstasy of triumph. This was what astonished their persecutors and finally persuaded them.

Here again the secret of their power lay in an intense personalism, in which they outplayed the Stoic at his own game. The peace they sought was no peace of Nirvana, a unity with the cosmos let down from above. It was a unity which arose first of all within their own experiences, and because it was an inner unity based on moral integrity, a divinely personal order, it became thereby eternal and cosmic. Viewed from this standpoint, perpetuation of the individual through immortality became a universal necessity, the broken fragments of life through self-realization being a part of the divine life and "the communion of the saints."

The role of such a faith is in the very necessities of the case revolutionary. The greatest foe of Christianity has always been institutionalism. The early defeat it suffered in Rome was not in the fiery persecutions it was called upon to undergo. The hours of deepest triumph were those recorded in the catacombs. The heaviest blow received was the conversion of Constantine, and with it the official conversion of the Empire. One need not enter into the prejudiced claim of Gibbon that Christianity was the cause of the downfall of the Roman Empire, nor the feeling of many good Stoics in the matter, to express the opinion that they may have been partly correct—and to add this proviso, that the institutionalized Christianity which came into power did not deserve the name of Christian. As to the disintegrating power of Christianity in undemocratic types of social organization, they are correct. Christianity is plainly revolutionary except for that ultimate condition when the kingdoms of this world have in principle and in fact become the Kingdom of Love. The Kingdom of Christ means rule by conviction in the individual conscience, in good will, and Christianity has never been tried in world politics. It is in the world as a revolutionary power until the seemingly impossible has been achieved. Therein lies its glory and its inevitableness. There is no settled and institutional condition with which it can rest, because it is of the very essence of life not to stop. This is no evidence of failure, but rather the evidence of life.

When we begin to take account of the rise of sense of destiny in the moral idealism of the West, we shall plainly have to take into account the special impetus of Christianity. It added to the Judaic concept of righteousness a missionary passion hitherto unknown. For the narrower racial outlook of Judaism it substituted cosmopolitanism. In its very essence the demand of Christianity is not for the prevalence of a given theological *credo* but a missionary passion for the prevalence of certain moral ideals in human life. Wherever it goes, its immediate attack has been on social wrongs, and it has never permanently yielded to evil social custom. This has been and ever will be the source of its compelling power. To say this is not to overlook the plague spots that fester under the surface of our Western life, nor the many shortcomings of institutionalized Christianity. We need to remember that according to Christian teachings no nation nor civilization has yet earned the right to be called Christian, and that in the very nature of Christianity (as an *individual* experience of God) no earthly institution, including the church itself, has yet a full right to call itself Christian. In the light of these facts, the oft-heard demand that Christianity begin by Christianizing the West, or even begin by Christianizing itself, has little force. Christianity is an appeal to the moral idealism of individual men of all races and nations, and her justification is in the righteousness of the idealism she presents, and does not rest upon its acceptance by any man or group of men. This is the cogent fact behind the missionary endeavors of Western ideals, and one which more than any other, perhaps, has endowed Western culture with the sense of destiny.

V. THE MORAL CONSCIOUSNESS OF THE WEST

Having traced the genesis of the individualistic morals of the West, it becomes necessary to mark out the features which differentiate Western moral feeling from that of other races and periods. In this no claim is made for the superiority of Western morals. We are only attempting to arrive at certain distinguishing features. We have seen the closeness of relationship of Occidental moral ideals with Judaism, Stoicism, and Christianity, the great religions of the West.

Religion is ever presented with two temptations which Christianity has never fully escaped but to which it has again and again risen superior. This supremacy has made it effective in the development of Western moral idealism. The temptations are, on the one hand, the temptation to institutionalism, and, on the other, to the quietism of the mystic. Both these elements have been strong, and at times institutionalism has threatened to prevail. At such times, however, the revolutionary principles of Christianity have asserted themselves, thus assuring progress and changing opinion. While mysticism has taken a leading part in Christianity, it has never flourished, except sporadically, as a distinct outlook. Thus Christianity has developed in morals the emotional element which Stoicism rejected, and has made it the spur and incentive to the Stoic ideal of righteousness. Herein lay its superiority for the diffusion of moral ideals, the progress of education, the existence of great art. It civilized emotion without becoming its slave. Its successes imply the strong aid of the very element which the Stoic spurned, emotion.

The spiritual passion which lay behind the idealism of Christianity entered into the moralism of Western culture and made it a growing thing and hence powerful in propagation. However ideal any system of ethical precepts may be, it can never get anywhere, can never become dominating, can never move masses of people, without embodying the emotional element.

This is the reason why Western culture has felt that it had a mission on earth, a manifest destiny, though it has again and again surrendered to and been a prey to the mercenary spirit and freebooting both of individuals and of nations who have misled their naive and conscientious followers. Had Western civilization been true to Christian principles, these would now dominate a happy and united world. Instead, it is now called upon to enter a plea for its misdeeds, to fight for its very existence at the moment it stands convicted in the light of its professed principles.

CHAPTER III

LAW FOR THE INDIVIDUAL

. . . .

N O STORY COULD be more fascinating than that of the rise of the concept of law in Western society. Its roots lay deep in the contrasting cultures of Greece and Judaism, and its fundamental principle was respect for the individual. There is no claim to be made that European law is the only code that looks toward individual right, but it was unique in its long and philosophical development and in its abstract nature. Because of this inherent principle, though often called to meet the challenge of autocracy, it has always overcome, and all sorts of despotism have been but passing phases of its progress.

Law as a philosophy of conduct might be said in Grecian thought to have begun with Anaxagoras, who was the first of the Greeks to call attention to the ruling or controlling character and self-sufficiency of mind. This idea became the center of the Socratic system, where it was given the added note of sufficient moral judgment. Then came the great practical schools of Greece, all claiming Socrates as their inspiration and setting forth philosophy as a way of life. Whether "the way" was that of suspended judgment, as with the Sceptics, or limitation of desire, as with Cynic and early Epicurean, or of self-control, as with the Stoic —in all, man was seen as the arbiter of his own destiny, and was conceived as subject to abstract principles.

The influence of none of the other schools, however, was comparable with that of the Stoics. Stoicism was fitted by its special emphasis on moral responsibility to exercise the determining influence in Western legal theory. This circumstance arose from assent to the Socratic principle of the universal validity of the moral self-consciousness which made it possible for every man without outward instruction or mandate of authority to know what was wrong. To this the Stoic added a strong insistence on the supremacy of the self over all circumstances, so that in the individual there never could be real excuse for failure to realize right conduct. It was in the province of every man to know and to do the right. These emphases became the controlling axioms of Western legal procedure, and are the basis for such a maxim as "Ignorance of the law excuses no man."

It is almost superfluous to mention the contribution of Judaism to this general result, for, although Hellenism and Judaism were presumed to be in bitter conflict, that conflict was more racial than rational. One can be quite aware of the difficulties at this point, and the long controversies presumably settled in favor of incompatibility. Nevertheless, at least two facts remain, and they are unanswerable.

First, if we are to consider the great prophetic leaders, rather than the priestly and ritualistic, as representative of Judaism, the incompatibility dissolves. For it will be seen immediately that the message of Socrates on the moral responsibility and obligation of the individual is in strictest line with the Hebrew prophets from Ezekiel down.

Second, it is well to remember that in a sense Stoicism could be thought representative of the Jewish liberal spirit as well as of the Greeks, for there is some reason to believe that the founder of Stoicism, Zeno of Citium, may have been a Jew,[1] or at least, was a Phoenician Semite, peculiarly open to Jewish influences. Whether founder of the sect or not, it is likely that he had much to do with the moral direction of Stoicism, and there was nothing in it which was incompatible with the highest principles of Judaism.

If someone arises to object that prophetism was not the whole of Judaism, nor Socraticism the whole of Hellenism, it will be apropos to remind the objector that neither was hierarchism nor Olympianism the whole of Jewish or of Grecian culture. In fact, the balance is on our side if we consider the argument from the standpoint of what the principles were that survived and made strongest contributions to civilization in each of these cultures.

---

[1] There is no external evidence for a Semitic origin for Zeno. We follow here the suggestion of Windelband: *History of Ancient Philosophy*, Charles Scribner's Sons, New York, 1924, p. 303, and find it in accord with the internal evidence of Stoic doctrine itself. There is not of course sufficient ground for an unqualified statement that Zeno was Jewish. We cannot but be impressed with the fact that his father, Mnaseas, was a merchant and that he himself was first drawn to Athens as a merchant, where he was captured for the philosophical interest by a manuscript of Xenophon's *Memorabilia* discovered in the market place.

In which case there is but one answer. For Judaism the high-watermark of achievement was prophetism, and for Greece, correspondingly, Socraticism. It was exactly the supranational, supraracial elements in both that enabled them to coalesce for the benefit of Western civilization.

1. Law as the Expression of Universal Conviction

Any consideration of the Socratic principle will reveal, behind the claim that every man[2] has direct approach to the knowledge of right through his own conscience or what Socrates called his *daemonium,* the assumption of a friendly ground of the universe. This easily develops into the concept of a cosmic consciousness which is the source of universal conviction.

If there is a *daemonium* that enlightens every man with respect to correct social conduct, then there must be an eternal rightness about law which should command respect from the evil as well as from the good. Socrates is often classed with the Sophists, with their doctrine of the complete relativity of moral good, but the adoption of this principle was his real advance beyond Sophistic and puts him forever outside the Sophist category. It is this belief in a universal conviction or universal consent to law which is the first distinguishing feature of Western culture. Here the emphasis is not placed upon institutional authority, as of the mandate of a prince or of a despot, but an authority which wins recognition by reason of the universality of its claim upon every rational mind. It is an internal authority bearing conviction to every man. Herein lies, of course, an inherent democracy. The power of the law is presumed to lie in this universal conviction which will be recognized by every normal or right-minded individual. In this connection, it is significant that in the rendering of difficult judicial decisions, where there is neither law nor precedent, it is good practice to decide according to the principles of common sense and understanding.

And it must be remembered, also, that this recognition is the gift of every man without regard to his social condition of poverty or wealth, of freedom or slavery, of education or ignorance.

---

[2] The objection may be raised that Socrates considered the *daemonium* peculiar to himself; but this claim seems contradicted by the fact that he expected every man to see as clearly as himself, once the obstruction of false notions had been cleared away by the employment of the Socratic method.

Furthermore, this universal recognition of right was presumed to be in accord with universal fact. Society, the conditions of life, labor, happiness, all that could conduce to individual well-being, were in strictest conformity with individual conviction, so that the universe was found to be in harmony with the law-keeper, and the everlasting enemy of the lawbreaker. This conviction has perhaps been the source of that respect for law which in general has characterized the West, and this respect has been sufficient to carry through periods of the worst reaction both on the part of demagogues and tyrants and the revolutionary impulses of the masses. If Western culture is ever successfully assailed, it will be at this point—the suspicion that law has nothing about it cosmic or compelling but that it is only the whim, caprice, or greedy demand of a ruling class, a despot, a privileged few, or the emotional reaction of the mob spirit.

II. Law as the Expression of Universal Capacity

Not only is Western legal theory based upon the concept of universal conviction but likewise upon that of universal capacity. Capacity to keep the law is assumed in the same degree as intelligence, so that only those are excused who are incompetent by reason of insanity or of idiocy to the extent of being unable to discern right from wrong. This theory is quite distinguishable from the notion that law is merely conventional. Such a belief could never have built the long-surviving respect which has characterized Western society.

The essential part of this principle lies in the belief in the moral capacity of all normal men irrespective of birth or education. It is established on the assumption of the freedom of the human will, its power to choose between courses of action in spite of evil influences. The presumption is that nothing can excuse a person from moral obligation and responsibility. Obviously, any theory of conduct which tends to break down the belief in the freedom of the individual or to remove the sense of moral obligation strikes directly at the foundation of Western civilization as at present organized; for individuals cannot be held amenable to laws which for any reason they cannot understand and cannot obey.

III. LAW AS THE EXPRESSION OF UNIVERSAL RIGHTS

The whole fabric of Western political organization is interwoven with the belief in universal rights. When the Stoics taught the essential worth of every human spirit without regard to conditions, they were scattering the seeds of countless revolutions which are not ended nor can be ended until those rights are achieved. It so happened that to the Stoic sanctions were added those of the Jewish prophets, which rose to their highest expression in Jesus of Nazareth. Thereby was introduced, through the Christian religion, a new emotional background which gave unconquerable impetus to the movement. To the prophets as well as to the Stoics the right of the individual lay basically in the Divine Fatherhood. The best reverence that could be paid the Supreme Mind or the Supreme Father was, then, through respect for the least and feeblest of his children. Official and priestly Judaism was quite incapable of confining this benefit to the children of Abraham; prophetism broke down the racial barrier; and finally Christianity, most revolutionary of all, and more than Stoicism, erected it into a religion and blended the love of God with the love of one's fellows.

It is puzzling to account for the slow growth of this principle through Western society until one reflects upon the stubbornness with which favored classes defend sanctions which appear to favor their interests, and it is further discovered how complete is the real surrender involved. This means nothing less than that the individual can find his highest self-realization only in the common order. This obduracy in the so-called upper classes is matched in the lower by a selfishness that resents moral responsibility. It demands a high degree of moral intelligence, and can be achieved only with the assistance of the emotional gifts of religion.

The basis of Western law, as of Western democracy, then, is the right of every individual to life, liberty, and the pursuit of happiness so long as the pursuit does not involve an invasion of the rights of others. Thus it was early seen that law was necessary as between man and man, and that essential freedom for the individual lay in that measure of self-restraint which guaranteed the rights of all others. Hence the law became the expression of this supreme warrant.

IV. THE BASIS OF LAW—THE COMMON GOOD

The outcome of such a system of legal theory, then, will be seen as the recognition of the individual, with this important proviso—the individual can be the possessor of no rights which run contrary to the common good. The political history of the Western world has been one continuing story of the struggle of vested interests to resist the surrender of special privilege. There was the struggle of noble against king to share special privilege, and then of middle class against noble, and finally of serf and slave, for a division of responsibility in government and with it equality of opportunity. In every such contest the struggle has been against vested power, entrenched might, the mandates established by arms, force, wealth, or custom—and, with varying fortune, yet, one by one, those one-time "rights" that have proved inimical to the common good have had to be surrendered. The so-called revolutions which have often threatened the complete dissolution of Western civilization have been revolutions in the interest of the common welfare. With many discouraging setbacks it has on the whole been a story of essential progress. It can be predicted with assurance that whatever may be in store for Western society, it has a choice between only two ways. One is the complete collapse of civilization and relapse to anarchy; the other is the completion of the program on which so much of blood and treasure has thus far been spent—the full realization of the common good—through political and social organization, education, and freedom.

The revolutions of the Western world have so far been the meeting of successive crises, and have ended special privileges for the few and have given them to the many. There is no logical stopping point in the movement until the basis of our legal theory is reached—the prevalence of the common welfare. Even the right of private property has been legally maintained only with reference to the common well-being of society. That this has long been the theory is indicated by the existence of our laws of eminent domain.

CHAPTER IV

INDIVIDUALISM IN THE STATE—GOVERNMENT
AS SOCIAL CONTRACT

. . . .

OUT OF THE welter of influences that provided the inspiration and determined the form of Western democracy, it is difficult to choose the most important. Any survey of these influences is certain to seem incomplete to the student of the period. One can only hope to strike at the more salient influences.

We have more or less revised our opinion of Greek democracy since the sympathy aroused by the struggle of the Hellenes for independence filled our histories with romantic idealizations. We realize better now how cramped was the feeling for democracy in a political setting wherein one set of tyrants or bandits succeeded another in mastery. Particularly in Athens, the lot of woman and slave received no consideration at all. It was at its widest but limited, a suffrage accorded to men who bore arms. To the Greeks there was no annoying incompatibility between freedom for some and slavery for the rest. It was a long time before the teachings of their philosophers worked down into the consciousness of their privileged class, if indeed they ever did. For the stormy experiment of Greek independence and freedom, the reign of the city-state—did not provide sufficient coherence to survive the inner conflicts of parties and factions in the face of jealousy and strife between cities. Nevertheless, that experience, brief and stormy as it proved to be, did present an ideal of democracy in such contrast with Oriental despotism that the dream could not altogether be lost. Moreover, the dream did not pass until it had found expression in the immortal *Republic* of Plato, which became the standard and pattern for all utopias for twenty-five centuries.

Whatever may be said of the socialistic quality of *The Republic* —and Plato was an aristocrat, if there ever was one—the ruling thought was of the value of each individual to the state, and the surrender of individual liberty to the common good. This was in a way the culmination of that individualism that had begun with Anaxagoras, had been emphasized by Protagoras, and had reached practical grounding in Socrates. Plato seems to have been strangely driven to his dream of a new social order by his very disgust at the failure of a democracy which was only the fertile field of demagoguery and political chicanery, and particularly as it had been evidenced in the condemnation of Socrates. Plato was followed by the Stoics, with their insistence upon individual sovereignty and equal rights, whose late disciples managed to gather up the fragments that remained of the early Roman dream of popular sovereignty and to get them written into the Roman code as the legal basis for Western government. Their dominating idea was the dignity of the human spirit and its superiority to circumstance, and the application of it to slave as well as to freemen. Christianity came, erecting the doctrine of care for the weaker members of society into a religion. The Gothic invasions, while they threatened to destroy completely the fabric of the social order, brought an added interpretation to individual right and intensified the love for freedom. All of these elements entered into the training for democracy.

1. Rise of the Free Cities

After the establishment of the Roman legal code, the next great impulse toward democracy in Europe probably arose out of the growth of the Free Cities which came at the end of the tenth century. Already Christianity was in the ascendant, and where it was most active and compelling there had grown up the belief that the year 1000 would mark the close of the Christian epoch and the end of the world. This belief led to the widespread manumission of slaves. Since the world was about to end, when slaves could be of no further benefit, and since both Stoicism and Christianity had taught the religious equality of slave with master, much embarrassment would be saved in the next world by recognizing that equality in the world that was present. Thus were turned loose from their masters the most efficient members of European society—skilled workers, tradesmen, and craftsmen. These, gathering together for self-protection and furtherance of trade, began the guild system which became of such importance in European arts and government. In the guild each accepted craftsman had a voice, and the various guilds united in government. Thus arose a wider and more successful effort at democracy. The great wealth and power that came to the Free Cities soon enabled them to treat with other powers as independent nations, and fired the European mind, as nothing else could have done, with the dream of popular sovereignty. In spite of the breakdown of government that came in these cities, as it had in the Greek city-states, through the rise of organized parties, gangs, and tyrannies, the dream of a wider freedom remained.

II. FEUDALISM AND THE INDIVIDUAL

The vision of individual rights survived the breakup of the Carolingian Empire into its feudal fragments. It was true that the common man had to pay a heavy price for protection, but there was about his subjection the nature of a contract. He traded days of service in the army for individual protection. Within the more or less benevolent slavery there was a strict recognition of individual prerogatives, frequently overridden by the lord, it is true, but generally observed and never forgotten by the ruled classes. This spirit of freedom was like the theme of a fugue running through the music of Western life, rising now and then to ominous expression in hours of oppression and attendant revolution.

The artisan brought his business to the vicinity of the castle, where he could easily flee in times of siege, and where he could be of service in meeting the needs of retainers and lord. The agriculturist likewise found it expedient from such a vantage point to manage the cultivation of the noble's land. But throughout this arrangement there was the recognition of free contract. Only sporadically and among the very lowliest was there an unquestioned serfdom—the slave belonging with the land. Where this did appear it was bitterly contested.

On the whole, therefore, while feudalism was a temporary state in the reorganization of society after the Teutonic invasions, it did not prove fatal to the concept of common rights and a government resting on the consent of the governed. This idea has been dominant in the West, and it has been one of the threads running through its history that gave the peculiar impression of progress which Spengler has symbolized in the term, "sense of destiny."

III. THE GROWTH OF NATIONALISM

There could scarcely be a better example of the revolutionary changes brought on by war than the growth of nationalism under the disturbing pressure of the Crusades. Here it seemed as if there had been a permanent setback to the spirit of individualism and freedom. The absence of feudal lords and their armies on Crusade gave the opportunity for the stay-at-homes to carve out for themselves kingdoms by war and intermarriage, and the lapsing of rights through the death of noble Crusaders. Nor did the movement toward nationalization reach its culmination at once. Not until the sixteenth and seventeenth centuries did it threaten Europe with widespread autocracy.

Paradoxical as it seems, the growth of nationalism and the rising autocracy were not unattended by popular gains. The movement offered the common people, at least the middle classes, exemption from feudal exactions that had become oppressive by raising a higher and an interfering power. In the beginning and for a long time in this development the king was looked to as a source of higher justice, the protector of the people from the rapacity of baron and lord. The earlier part of the struggle was attended by the securing of constitutional guarantees and parliamentary representation.

This period saw likewise the extension of several great popular causes. Even the Crusades did not originate among the nobles themselves. They began within the church and involved many ranks of society. Eventually they touched all classes, as was evidenced in the Children's Crusade. It was the period of such popular activities as the rise of chivalry, with its insistence upon the rights of the defenseless and its deference to the cause of womanhood. Even greater in popular participation was the growth of monasticism, Mary worship, Gothic architecture, and the universities. Monasticism placed men on the common level of religious vows. The worship of Mary voiced the demand for an approach to divine protection which should be open to the last and feeblest. The erection of the cathedrals was not only the building of this dream into stony form and symbol, but became itself the expression of an extreme individualism, as it embodied the labor of the masses. The university, begun for the training of the clergy, became the hotbed and breeder of democracy, as it recognized the intellectual possibilities of all and closed its doors to none.

Here was pent-up individualism enough to save the day when in later centuries consolidation of power led king and potentate to think more highly of themselves than the case justified, and to lay claims to aristocracy by divine right. Such had succeeded in buttering the political side of their bread, but while they had been doing it, they had overlooked the growing institutions of freedom whose influence was destined to sweep away every claim of absolutism.

IV. The Church as Exponent of Democracy

It is significant that the liberalizing tendencies of which we have been reminding ourselves grew up under the patronage of the church, and arose, likewise, during the very period in which the church was consolidating its authority. Sometimes measures of freedom were proposed in order to give the church advantage in the struggle between sacred and secular power. Sometimes the popular movement was granted approval by the secular arm for an exactly opposite reason; but in almost every instance it represented an eventual gain for the common man.

The early contacts of the church had, on the side of philosophy, been altogether with Hellenism, which represented an extreme Platonism. The Greek fathers, many of them, were converted only after considerable training in Platonism. This Platonism had already felt the transforming touch of Judaism, so that the early Christian community had ready at hand a philosophy and a theology from the trinitarianism of Philo Judaeus, up or down. There could not have been a more appropriate vehicle for theological expression, nor one so well uniting their established views and the new ones into which they had come.

Thus it happened that the early church was built on a Platonic —not to say a Neoplatonic—foundation. Such a foundation could but exalt the doctrine of authority. All things visible were for it but the emanation of things invisible—the supreme Idea which represents the uttermost reality. All lesser things found themselves gathered up in this most real Idea and, apart from this, were but shadows and ephemera. Thence grew the notion that the church, proceeding from God, represents the fundamental reality and is the recipient and ground of all authority. It was this theology that gave substance to Augustine's dream of the *City of God,* and superimposed upon the falling ruins of imperial Rome the dream of an eternal ecclesiastical empire. This concept was a relic of Oriental geometrizing, a totalitarian distrust of democracy.

But there were inherent in Christianity certain principles that render such an interpretation of it ultimately impossible. The heart of Christ's evangel had been a protest against superimposed and hierarchical authority, and an appeal to the direct access of the soul to God—the authority of life as it speaks within the individual conscience. This element in the Christian view was bound to get itself uttered just as soon as Platonism had so run its course as to seem finally triumphant.

The Moslem invasions were the plow that turned the hard soil of contented Platonism. Not only did the church find its outward authority 'challenged—it saw its theological claims threatened, and then its intellectual pretensions, and that by an individualism that gained ready ally within Christianity itself— the concept of individual religious consciousness that had already, under hard repression, been chafing for expression. Mohammed-anism, which, through Jewish scholars, had introduced the full text of Aristotle, had only culminated a movement already well under way. Aristotle stood for the full reality of the individual. The early universities were organized to study the *Organon.* The first glow and springtime of Renaissance was in the air, with great peril to autocracies of every kind. It was a flood of power which the church herself could not dam nor repress. She had to adapt it and transform it or be overcome by it. Not long after she had declared Aristotle heterodox, Albertus and Thomas Aquinas had done their work of adaptation, and Aristotle was installed as the philosopher of the church. So complete in the Western world had been the triumph of individualism.

v. The Enlightenment and Revolution

There could be nothing more inevitable than that society could not rest in a compromise, largely verbal and legalistic, be-tween Platonism and Aristotelianism, between authority and untempered individualism. It must go on, if only from curi-osity, to see the outcome of so fascinating a movement. Once the change had been made, it was easy to presume that a philosophy emanating from a Supreme Idea being out of the way, one emanating from the individual, spun from itself as the spider spins its web, would prove not only more to the heart's desire but more potent for change. However halfheartedly—or should one say, lightheartedly—he may have undertaken the task, it was Descartes with his "I think, therefore I am" concept of indubitable self-existence that became the spokesman of the movement.

With the utterance of those fateful words the carefully builded structure of external authority fell down—though for nearly three hundred years ecclesiasticisms of every sort, Catholic and Protestant, have, by skillful patching of here a roof and there a wall, been pretending that their ramparts remained unbreached. When the movement that began with Descartes had worked itself out into expression, it was but a step to the initial skepticism of Hume and the "nature" philosophy of Rousseau. But the movement was like dynamite in its effect upon accepted ideas. Nor have these ideas yet run their revolutionary course. They are the sources of much of the confusion of the present. They cannot be further discussed here, but will be deferred to a later chapter for consideration. Suffice it now to say that not only did the Enlightenment philosophy open the floodgates of the French Revolution; it has been the source of a more silent, because more prolonged, and a more complete revolution which is not yet ended.

This is the incomplete and halting story of the rise of individualism in the Western society and state.

CHAPTER V

THE DREAM OF UNIVERSAL EDUCATION

....

THE CONFLICT BETWEEN Platonism and the church, which
exalted the hierarchy as the supreme authority and source
of all truth, and Aristotelianism with its individualism extolling
the worth of private judgment, took place for the most part over
the question of the reality of universals as against that of particulars—or what is known in the history of philosophy as the
Realist-Nominalist controversy. The problem had never been absent from the minds of the theologians of the church, as we have
it set forth in the *Isagoge* of Porphyry, a commentary on the
Predicamenta of Aristotle. The question was further saved for
debate by Boëthius, whose notes on the *Isagoge* bridged the centuries and kept it alive.

The conflict of ideas between universalism and individualism,
or between external and internal authority, autocracy and democracy, is perfectly mirrored in the life and writings of Augustine.
It was as agonizing in the body of society as was his personal
conflict with "the world, the flesh, and the Devil." His early
writings, *The Confessions*, like his early career, were marked by
an overpowering individualism. *The City of God* was in the
nature of a retreat. Before the overwhelming force of the barbaric
invasions the old man lost the vigorous faith of youth in convictions which arose out of the personal contact of the individual
soul with God. In his *Confessions* he had written: "Thou hast
made us for Thyself, and our hearts are restless till they rest in
Thee." But he began to doubt the general efficacy of the inner
call. Against the rising tide of heathenism the appeal to the individual seemed insufficient. It must be met by an institutional and
visible authority. It was not the last time that proponents of
democracy were to withdraw in distrust from the results of their
own system. But democracy was a great creative idea. It made
the widest possible appeal to the imagination, and, once begun,
had a way of rolling on like a flood fed by uncounted streams

on the way. In the face of violence, democracy will always appear weak. It will seem especially so to dictators and advocates of violence. All the impressiveness of autocracy can be marshalled for inspection, is always in evidence. The strength of democracy is hidden and internal, but being grounded in the nature of life, and of the universal order it cannot ultimately be defeated without the complete destruction of the social milieu. Autocracies may flourish for as long as they can keep the upper hand. Their weakness is that they are against the nature of things. They violate the nature of persons, and their end is sure.

The first universities grew out of the demand to gather the wisdom of the newly recovered individualist, Aristotle. The mental air was like the bracing springtime, dynamic with promise and beauty. One's college course of four years was spent in the study of Aristotle's *Organon,* Cassiodorus' *Seven Liberal Arts,* the *Encyclopedia* of Martianus Capella, and Boëthius. For a time it looked as if Europe, victorious in battle over the Moslems, was to fall conquered by Mohammedan and Jewish learning. That the surrender was not utter and final was largely due to the genius of Albertus Magnus and the diligence of Thomas Aquinas, in making Aristotle orthodox. They did so at the cost of the Protestant Reformation. Aristotle was stronger than institutionalism, and could not be omitted and ignored. Like the fateful genii of Pandora's box, once out, the forces of individualism could never be reconfined. Learning became universal in the sense that it was open to all who sought it. The *studium-generale,* or the college of students and scholars, was the earliest organized democracy. Great numbers of scholars roamed the highways from university to university, bearing the dream if not the benefits of education.

This tide could not come to logical rest until it had brought forth the American doctrine of popular education, and the Rousseauan maxims had found modern expression through Froebel, Pestalozzi, Montessori, and John Dewey. The final outcome in America has been enthusiasm for free education for everybody, in every conceivable subject, mingled with a dread of Communism.

Certain master individualists began a literature in the popular speech, and destroyed the monopoly of Latin learning. Raymond Lull, Petrarca, Boccaccio, Dante, were the forerunners of individualism in literature, the beginners of a movement which would not stay until it had run its course through Montaigne, Rousseau, and Nietzsche.

I. THE BEGINNINGS OF UNIVERSITY EDUCATION

Western Europe had before it the model of university educa-tion in the great philosophical schools of Athens. Hope of the preservation of classical learning added sentiment to the impulse toward those models. It was not, however, until the church had overcome her distrust of pagan learning and had become awake to the need for education that real organization of schools began to take place. The centers of education were of two kinds, those that gathered about the palace and those of the monastery.

Charlemagne called in Alcuin of York to organize and teach in connection with the court, so that the Emperor might have at ready hand clerics for the copying of state documents, and like-wise to form a general center of education in the palace school. Later, Charles the Bold, successor to Charlemagne, gave a similar position as minister of education to John of Salisbury. The most significant development, however, took place within monasticism itself. From the past there were many historical incentives. Haarhoff[1] points out that in Marseilles, previous to the fifth cen-tury, the people were trilinguists, using the Greek (because of their origin as a Greek colony), Latin, and Gallic. At Arles, as late as the sixth century, we are told that Caesarius could cause his Christian congregation to sing in Greek. From these centers was but. a step in space and time to the monastic establishments of Treves, Autun, Marmoutier, and Tours. Thus there was at hand a tradition which united learning with a knowledge of Greek, and made precious the translation of Platonic and Aristotelian fragments.

As the monastic establishments grew more prosperous and not so much attention was needed for work in the fields, men began to be trained and set aside for the copying of precious documents, the Scriptures, the works of the fathers, and of such Greek and Latin manuscripts as had come by this time into the possession of the church.

The existence of medical baths at Salerno, noted from of old

[1] *Schools of Gaul.* See also Glover: *Life and Letters in the Fourth Century*; Gilbert Murray: *Ancient Greek Literature.*

for healing virtue, gathered at that place not only the diseased
from many lands, but skillful physicians, likewise, who began
to teach their arts to others. Out of this grew the first medical
school, and the beginnings of a university at Salerno. Governmental organization demanded, likewise, a knowledge of the
law, and from this demand grew Bologna and Padua. Paris
became famous for theology, and thus began that university.
The first organized and most effective liberal arts course, offering
training in classical language, was at the Cathedral School of
Chartres. Education became a matter of national emulation. No
nation cared to be behind in presenting advantages to her own
citizens. Soon Oxford was vying with Paris for distinction as
the leading university. It was deemed advantageous to keep the
young men at home for study, and to preserve their patriotism
from foreign corruption.

It is to be noted that the term university did not mean an
institution consisting of both liberal arts and professional
schools. It was a general term applied to students and faculty
without regard to the curriculum offered.

II. Aristotelianism and the Revival of Letters

One of the profoundest influences in the development of the
universities must, however, be reckoned in the revival of Aristotle which resulted from the contacts set up by the Moslem
invasions. Just enough of Aristotle had been saved to western
Europe to keep some knowledge of his work alive, principally
the *Organon,* or *Logic.* For long years it was to flow very much as
a surreptitious or underground stream, until it broke into the
open in the nominalist controversy.

But the Moslem-Jewish scholars were in possession of the
full body of Aristotelian writing, and this began to be eagerly
sought after. Papal ban and restriction could not eventually keep
back the tide. Soon these scholars were invited to the leading universities, first of Italy and finally of Paris. Aristotelianism was
itself, as we have seen, a great bid for democracy. In Islam it had
been chiefly sought for its scientific contribution. Knowledge
of the stars and of botanical lore made it the special care of the
Moslem physician. Hence when reintroduced to a Europe which
had been aware of the *Logic* alone, it had an electrifying effect.
Not only was enthusiasm for classical learning advanced, but a

new interest was introduced—the scientific interest. Logical deduction had long been the sole method of the learned. There
now began to grow up a respect for the inductive method of
experiment.

It is true that Moslem learning had put the taint of astrology
and magic on all this interest. The earliest period of scientific
investigation was that of the alchemists, who hoped by experiment and the discovery of hidden lore in the writing of the
ancients to transmute baser metals into gold, or to discover the
elixir of immortal youth. The latest proposition to transmute
lead through the change of electronic balance is the echo of an
older hope. Nevertheless, out of such superstitious and despised
beginnings arose the triumphs of modern science. Nor should
the ancient alchemists be despised, for they frequently paid with
social ostracism and sometimes with their lives for the hardihood
of their experimental interest. The bridge at the foot of St. Al-
date's at Oxford is still known as "Folly Bridge" because in the
little guardhouse over the original bridge, Roger Bacon had in-
stituted a chemical laboratory. Here we have one of the most
conspicuous examples of how the folly of one age becomes the
science of the next.

The impact of Aristotelianism, moreover, went out past the
revival of classicism and the initiation of scientific method. The
repercussion was felt in the world of letters. If all was not to
be settled by an authority emanating from above, but by the
multitude of concrete examples, then the individual experience
was of worth and there was set forth in the world all the evidence
for individualism and novelty. All this argued the opening up
of information to the long-despised common man. There began
to be at last such a thing as common letters. Dante's *Divine
Comedy* was such an experiment and an appeal to a wider
clientele than that of the learned. The dependence of Dante upon
the Koran for his concept of Hell[2] is startling even to modern
students, and shows how deep and how vital were the influences
of Aristotelianism and Mohammedanism. Thus was swept into
Christian concepts a demonology and superstition that represented the worst of Mohammedanism, introduced through the

[2] See Miguel Asin: *Islam and the Divine Comedy*, tr. by Harold Sunderland,
E. P. Dutton & Company, Inc., New York, 1926.

vehicle of the vulgar or common tongue, which immediately gave it wide and even universal acceptance.

The literary movement was confined neither to time nor place. Raymond Lull, Jean de Meung's, *Romaunt de la Rose*, the yet earlier *Chanson de Roland,* Petrarca, Boccaccio, established the common literature and gave letters to the people.

If there was ever an illustration in history of the results flowing out of philosophy, surely it was nowhere more evident nor pronounced than in the effects of the Aristotelian revival in Western Europe.

III. CONTRIBUTION OF THE UNIVERSITY TO DEMOCRACY

The sense of educational need and the far-reaching vision of Charlemagne gave a popular set to education at the very start. Any aspiring youth who had a passion for learning was encouraged to attach himself to such influences, noble or monastic, as would provide him with the desired privileges. Especially was this true of the monastic schools, which offered special encouragement to any youth who showed ability. He could, by becoming a novitiate, have access to learning, and that without mortgaging his future to the full demands of the priesthood. Thus there grew up about the traditions of the early schools a great liberality, which was continued when monastic, cathedral, or palace school passed on into the full development of the university. The university was not alone for the rich. The poor boy whose mother could spare but a goose for the rector, as in the cases of John Huss at Prague and Pierre Ramus at Paris—seems to have provided enough to insure some sort of livelihood while the education was going on. The democracy of scholarship, too, brought to such, if they proved worthy, the highest honors, despite their lowly origin.

Thus there arose in Europe, in addition to the church, another institution of democracy. Where there were open doors of rapid advancement from the lowest to the highest position of society, an atmosphere inimical to special privilege and divine right was the inevitable consequence. Those open doors of ecclesiastical advancement and university learning were the inlets which increased the dream of popular right and popular sovereignty when the times were ripe.

IV. THE CLASSIC IDEA OF EDUCATION AND THE MODERN

A civilization which had begun by receiving the strong trend of Platonism, which viewed all things as emanations from the Supreme Idea, could of course hold but one theory of education. All authority lay behind, and it behooved the individual to put himself in the attitude to receive the oracle from above. Deduction in such a system is the supreme method. The classical learning was based on this method, and the general effect is to minimize individual research and opinion and to exalt the discoveries of the past. Ancient writings thus came to be looked upon with awe, since the older they were the nearer were they presumed to be to the supreme sources of authority. This feeling of the Middle Ages was quite different from the antiquarian interest with which the modern man venerates and preserves ancient manuscripts. Our interest is strictly historical, to glimpse if we may the development of thought and to picture another day in living terms. The medieval scholar hoped to run upon some lost formula, some buried secret, that would disclose knowledge of the ancients now unknown. The nearest approach to this feeling that we have in modern times is in the recent flurry to discover dark secrets in the supposed cipher of Roger Bacon. The best comment is that Roger himself had entertained the same hopes concerning the cabalistic signs of those who had long preceded him.

The change from Platonism to Aristotelianism, from universals to particulars, from deduction to induction, was a revolution in the idea of education which has been going on even to our own time. The tendency is now to neglect utterly the lore of the past and to proceed on individual investigation. Frequently this takes an extreme form of disregard and ignorance of the past that sends men on many wild and vain searches from which a little more learning would deter them. The tendency is again to exalt a single method. And though it is in contrast with the medieval one, it, too, will prove inadequate and misleading.

V. THE NATURE THEORY OF EDUCATION

The culmination of these movements in educational theory found expression in Rousseau's *Émile*, which is substantially what has been followed for fifty years in America, as the latest educational discovery. It is based upon an extreme individualism which not only rejects the past but also exalts the value of individual discovery to the *n*th power. The anomalous thing is that it has exalted even the idiosyncrasies of the individual into a place of importance—and has done this in the name of science, at the very moment that the scientist was dismissing the individual as a negligible and unimportant element in the vast machinery of nature. Thus we have had the paradoxical situation in which our intellectual tycoons have been insisting on a scientific knowledge free from all personal bias, and a theory of education which expects the unassisted infant to arrive at all wisdom by consultation with his own personal desires.

The Rousseauan doctrine fell in line with the social and political revolution of which Rousseau was a part, and, at least so far as America is concerned, he was undoubtedly the most influential man in education of the last three hundred years.

Today we witness the culmination of the movement—the dream of universal education which began with the ideal that every man was worth educating, that educational privileges should be extended to all, but which could not limit itself. The very principles contained in it led it finally to exalt the *contribution* which every man should make to education. Thus we have come upon a period when we study the lispings of babes in order that we may discover therein matters that are hidden from the wise and prudent. The search takes a different turn—the superstition is the same.

CHAPTER VI

THE GOTHIC SPEAR

. . . .

IN ONE PASSAGE Spengler [1] calls attention to the way the rising individualism found expression in language. The Latin "*sum*" and Gothic "*im*" became in English "I am," in German "*Ich bin*" and French "*Je Suis.*" He adds that "I" and "thou" are the key to the Gothic architecture; the spires of Chartres are but two colossal digits representing the first personal pronoun, thrusting themselves into the sky. The statues that line the porticoes are but further "I's" and "thou's." Whether or not his contention is defensible, there is no doubt that individualism distinguishes the Gothic. It depends no longer upon conglomerate masses for its strength. Everywhere we witness a new manhood standing upright in pillar and porch and flying buttress, as well as in steeple and in arch. It marks the increasing tide of individualism and democracy, like a volcanic upthrust from the midst of a plain. Even its details are individualistic, each man working out what is more or less of his own idea in line and ornament, each feeling a profound responsibility, each leaving the carved symbol that indicated the individuality of the worker.

Whether we accept the more fanciful theory of Spengler, or turn to the more apparent one of Henry Adams, [2] the result is not materially different. To the latter the Gothic grew naturally out of the Norman and has for its principle the grouped spears of the Northern invaders. At any rate, it was something new in the world. It represented a new authority which did much more than worship a dead past. It had all the philosophy of self-assertion and individualism.

I. THE STRUGGLE OF BYZANTINE WITH GOTHIC

Before Western culture could emerge into unquestioned individualism it had two forces to face and overcome. Both of

[1] *Decline of the West*, tr. by C. F. Atkinson, George Allen and Unwin, Ltd., London, Vol. I, pp. 262-263.
[2] *Mont St. Michel and Chartres*, Houghton Mifflin Company, Boston, chap. IV.

these were from the Orient. The first was the Oriental influence exerted by the Byzantine. How deeply this entered into European life and how nearly it came to domination is written in the architecture of Italy, most notably in Venice. "St. Mark's Rest," as Ruskin poetically calls the Cathedral at Venice, is the high-water mark of this influence. Its opulent magnificence, with such vast attention to detail, its grottoed splendors, none of which seeks the open air or the light of the sky, are quite foreign to the Western spirit. The richness of St. Mark's is the richness of shadows, but shadows lighted up with jewel and mosaic. One is tempted to say it was the work of men whose deeds were darkness, but to do so would be utterly to mistake and falsely to condemn. It is all a part of that Oriental mysticism which seeks for the hidden, which feeds upon mystery, to which magic and occultism are the more sought expressions of religion. It is the religion of quiet and contemplation which detests being disturbed by the noise and clamor of a practical world. All this comes upon the visitor to St. Mark's the moment he steps within the portals. Already has he been prepared for it in the deep and ornate porches, but once inside the door he feels he has left the world behind. No contrast could be more obvious. The gay and sunny square, thronged with merchantmen and traffickers, bright with gay awning and the flight of birds; then suddenly one finds oneself faced by the depth, the darkness, the unearthly quiet of an internal world into which no noise or intimation from that outer world can creep. Here is nothing suggestive of that forest-roaming Goth whose wilds were dark but whose lancelike pines pointed ever to the light and to the stars to bear to his soul the message of an untrammeled freedom. For a time it looked as if the East would win, but its mysticism was too powerless before the Gothic youth of a future yet untried. Youth won the day.

The victory was not final nor complete, for soon the battle with Orientalism was to be met upon the Western front and in a vastly different way. Here Western culture faced a virile foe, strong in the strength of a new religious enthusiasm and an urge for expression which has scarcely been equaled in history. It represented a civilization in many respects superior to that which was at last to overcome it. It was marked by the wealth, the finesse, and the learning of the East. It had the historic background of the oldest cultures. It had taken to itself the richness of the Greek culture of which the West had been deprived. More than all else, it armed its sword with religious emotion, and it is difficult to say why, with all these advantages, it did not win. The only answer that comes immediately to mind is that it was impossible to impose foreign tyranny upon a people who had already tasted the fruits of individualism and liberty. Nor is this conclusion to be disturbed by the fact that for a long time Islam may have presented a higher, a freer, and a more enlightened government than was achieved in the Western world. The Moslem appeal to the sword turned the sword against her and helped to make triumphant the spear of Norman and of Goth.

ii. The Moslem Menace

What Western culture might have become without the Moslem menace is difficult to understand, for it formed the strongest impetus to the next great developments in Western life.

First of all, it was the uniting force which brought together the warring factions of Christendom within the church. It swept into the tides of overmastering religious emotion well-nigh the whole populace. It gave drive to the development of chivalry, since it gave to the unemployed knight a *raison d'être* and a career. The great knightly orders were organized to keep open the highroads for pilgrims to Rome and the Holy Land. Beaune, the beautiful little walled city in the Côte d'Or of Burgundy, became the center from which the Templars rode forth, while their rivals, the Hospitallers, established headquarters but four miles away. How much the feminist movement of modern times may owe to the rise of chivalry is impossible to say, but to believe that the different status of womanhood in Christianity from that in Islam owes something to this influence is not difficult.

The Crusades were the more direct effect of the Moslem threat. Their influence on the customs and habits of the Western world is beyond computation. The West acquired a taste for the luxury and refinement of the East—silks and satins replaced homespun—and the rough and ready manners of the Gothic man-at-arms were replaced by a growing demand for elegance. Courtliness of manner became the mark of a gentleman. Warriors who set out with racial contempt within their hearts soon discovered both superior culture and superior education in those they had despised. Out of the Moslem menace came a new desire for learning which eventuated in the universities. But before all, perhaps, was the fact that Mohammedanism had taught the European hand to war.

III. THE INDIVIDUALISTIC CHARACTER OF THE GOTHIC

The individualistic character of the Gothic has already been touched upon. Henry Adams [3] has called attention to its belligerence. Belligerence is the price which must always be paid for individualism, so it may well be said that the two are inseparable.

The Gothic spear had been sharpened first against the Roman, whose dying empire was to conquer in his laws, customs, literature, and religion, but who could not, because of internal weakness, oppose himself successfully to the rising prowess of a new people. The feeling that success lay in the spear, in the virile individualism of battle, had no little part in determining the direction of Western culture. Michael became the patron saint of the West. On this theme Henry Adams traces the development of Gothic architecture out of the Norman beginning with the abbey church and castle of St. Michel, and culminating with the west portal of the Cathedral of Chartres. Everywhere it appears, the Gothic architecture bears the impress of individualism, belligerence, and self-confidence. Spear or ego, its towers threaten to pierce the heavens; and good St. Michael, with sword which has been "bathed in heaven," stands ready as the special emissary of the Almighty to maintain whatever ground has been already won. Beneath the crypt, individual men laid foundations, each portion marked with the seal or symbol of the builder, to bear eternal testimony to the honesty of the individual who laid it, and eternal testimony, as well, to the fact that upon the individual rests the fate of the church itself and of all Christian society. In out-of-the-way places, as well as in the full glare of the sun, individuals did their most beautiful work, working with an individual freedom of detail and a devotion uncramped by the fact that the rising structure would hide their carving in utter darkness. Most often the craftsman must have worked with little conception of the completed whole, but almost always with the purpose that, so far as it was in his power, the result should be utterly glorious.

[3] *Op. cit.*

The result all now can read. As one faces the Cathedral of St. Gatien's of Tours the impression is that these towers which gave name to the city are exactly alike. The moment the details are studied, they are found to be nowhere alike. They are not even of equal height. The marvelous and well-nigh miraculous fact is that all this individualism sinks into so vast and complete a harmony, repeating nothing save some new example of the common principle that binds all into the whole.

The general result may be an other-worldliness that rivals St. Mark's Rest, but it is an other-worldliness that belongs to this world, is set firmly upon world bases, the saints and Christ in judgment, and even God himself reposes upon the foundation of apostles and martyrs that throng the porticoes, reaching down at last to that dark and silent place within the crypt where an honest mason laid the stone and the mortar that should last till time should be no more. And all this pile is instinct with this-worldliness—with life and movement from vaunting spire and fragile arch to flying buttress; it is as being in the world and yet projecting beyond it.

This is the rich lesson of the Gothic—a reading in stone of the ancient text:

The Kingdom of God standeth sure, having this seal; the Lord knoweth them that are his, and let him that nameth the name of Christ depart from iniquity.

IV. THE GOTHIC AS A POPULAR MOVEMENT

As the significance of the Gothic lay in its individualism, so its power lay in the fact that it was a great popular or mass movement. A mass movement so far-reaching in results could have come about only through the prevalence of religious emotion. Those who so ruthlessly destroyed the Cathedral of Rheims were destroying something from the earth, something which neither they nor any other living people can restore. The individualism upon which we have been reflecting could have found the restraint and self-control of all true art only through the aid of religion. More than mere co-operation was necessary. Such a result is never attained through collaboration alone. The seat of such mutual enterprise could rest only in a common impulse, an overmastering emotion, and such inspiration it was within the power of religion to furnish. The turn toward Mary

worship was a revolt from the theologians, and, in deeper phase
—though it dared not own it—from the theologians' God. It was
a protest against a God that was unapproachable because he was
lost in the Absolute, and a conception of Christ that denied the
very essence of Christianity, as a "word made flesh that dwelt
among us." The only outlet for that protest was a stark paganism
or a more effective approach to God for the common man. This
approach appeared possible through Mary the mother. The common people now filled the niche which the theologians had
vacated, with a divine love which cared for the common man.
And so to the "Queen of Heaven" it was that they brought their
choicest gifts. Long lines of toiling men, women, and children
tugged at the ropes that drew the giant monoliths to Chartres,
and at each mile they stopped to sing a mass. Their gold and silver, fruitage of uncounted days and years of toil, was brought
as sacrifice to the crucibles from which flowed the cathedral bells
and the inimitable glass—for here at last was one who held it
in her heart to have compassion upon the toiling, suffering multitude. It was in religion a part of that demand for individual self-
expression which had been made otherwise evident in law, in
education, and which was working in the structure of society.

The modern man may look upon this movement with super-
cilious contempt, but it was the spiritual element involved that
lifted Europe from barbarism and society from corruption. You
will pardon me if, heretic and dissenter though I am, I slacken
pace at the sound of the Angelus and offer a silent prayer. I am
determined that neither theologian nor institution shall rob me of
that inner fellowship with these men of a far-off day. There are
values here that may be appropriated by all humanity. Let us cast
no slur until we have shown an equal devotion and a parallel
genius. Though the Protestant Reformation which was yet to
follow singled out the Gothic for special reprobation, its heart
really beat to the same tune, showing again that the most undying
hatreds lie not between opposites but between dissenting divisions of the same cult, or within a common family.

The religious struggle of our Western culture, whatever the
outward form it has taken, has been a struggle to free the individual. Buried deep under privilege, authority, papal, biblical,
or creedal, lost in institutionalism or ecclesiasticisms, it has ever

tended toward individualistic expression. It has shown the main characteristics of Western civilization.

v. Individualism in Modern Religion

The advance of individualism precipitated in the development of the Gothic and evidenced in the religious controversies of the Middle Ages could not be checked by the repressive forces cast up to dam back the tides of change. At one point the bulwark of ecclesiastical infallibility was raised against the dissipating dangers of free and diverse religious opinions. Protestantism having revolted against the papacy was restricted to the appeal to an infallible body of doctrine enshrined in that portion of the Scriptures which it chose to consider "inspired." Neither expedient was altogether successful in setting up an authority which could effectively combat the further growth of individualism. Within papal authority were discovered multitudinous avenues of personal freedom, working through the divergencies of multiplying monastic orders. In Protestantism the common allegiance to infallible Scripture yet allowed a multiplicity of interpretations which led to the founding of almost innumerable sects based on casual and unimportant distinctions of sacramental method, ecclesiastical organization, doctrinal refinement, the preference for hooks and eyes on the clothing, or the presence or absence of whiskers on the face.

Having run into such banalities, the next movement of individualism in religion must necessarily be upward, since apparently the range of religious absurdities has been exhausted and a growing enlightenment cannot be satisfied with the continued emphasis on unessential differences.

CHAPTER VII

INDIVIDUALISM IN SCIENCE—EVOLUTION

. . . .

ANY CONSIDERATION OF Western civilization would be incomplete without an account of that element which, to many, will seem most significant and most important of all, namely, the advance in scientific knowledge.

Attention has already been called to the roots of Western science in the philosophy of Heraclitus and Lucretius, and of the "master of those who know," Aristotle, that first systematic scientist. The scientific impulse really took its rise in western Europe from the Oriental interest in astrology and medicine. With the closing of the Greek schools of philosophy, Greek scholars fled to the East, bearing the priceless manuscripts of Aristotle. Since the principal interest was the cure of disease, Europe received Aristotle the second time through the medium of medical men and hence of science. The whole philosophy of Aristotle was bent upon concretes, the individuals, which could be classified but which were themselves the realities, rather than the class, which they composed. Thus was paved the way for that method of induction usually ascribed to Francis Bacon, and which became the cornerstone of modern research.

Here again truth was held to be nothing esoteric. It must commend itself to every man. Its generalizations must rest on the special occurrences of phenomena common to all. It is impossible to reckon the importance to the modern world of the new method; for it lifted science out of the realm of the abstract and mythological, out of the chaos of hearsay and make-believe, into a realm of law and order. To us it seems unaccountable that hitherto men should not more generally have thought of basing scientific generalization upon the observance of phenomena.

To hypostatize an animal origin for the best of us was only the logical sequel of this progress toward individualism. The theory of evolution was the last great leveler. It placed all upon a common ground. It was the scientific triumph of democracy.

77

Not alone did it proclaim the commonness of our humanity *inter pares*; it made man only the errant brother of the atom. Weighing and measuring had at last placed human beings among the other atoms of matter and brought to pass in scientific thought the phrase of an ancient skeptic:

> Dust thou art and to dust thou shalt return.

Darwinism was the final triumph of scientific individualism, representing as it did that "kind" arose out of the accumulation of individual differences.[1] All since then has been an unquestioning acceptance or fulfillment of his theory, or else something quite different, looking toward the present scientific revolution.

I. DEPENDENCE OF SCIENCE UPON GREEK MODELS

The peculiar success of Western science was due to its individualism. For this method the way was prepared by Heraclitus and Democritus. The first suggested change as the cosmic principle.[2] To Heraclitus the whole order of nature was a continual flux. So many centuries have passed, and only in the present has science discovered in the modern doctrine of relativity, the anthropomorphic nature of time and space which ruled Heraclitan thought.

The next step was due to Leucippus and Democritus, who conceived the cosmic substance as made up of similar and irreducible entities, or atoms. The differences which we call qualities were thus all of them grounded in quantitative change. This theory presents an awkward logical impasse to understand how things can be alike and different at the same moment; but when the time came for science to rely upon this dogma, it was accepted with unquestioning faith, and until recently few have had the temerity to call attention to the contradiction involved.

Nor can the work of the Pythagorean sects be overlooked. The modern scientist might frown upon the suggestion that here lies the beginning of the scientific method, but such is undoubtedly the case. The Pythagoreans hit upon the notion that number is the sole constitutive principle of reality. Their chief interest

[1] Vide F. C. S. Schiller: *Formal Logic*, pp. 56-57.
[2] Compare Diels: *Fragmenta*; Burtt: *The Metaphysical Foundation of Physics*; Article "Heraclitus," *Encyclopedia of Religion and Ethics*; Lossky: *The World as an Organic Whole*.

seems to have been astronomical and astrological, but they developed mathematics to a high degree, laying the basis for early geometry and perhaps of trigonometry. From these beginnings it was easy for Lucretius, Epicurean and atomist, to represent the universe as springing out of chaos through a fortuitous concourse of atoms, and we have the basic theory of modern science easily at hand. We have likewise the main reason for its outstanding hostility to everything but a mechanistic and materialistic universe devoid of purpose and of mind. Thus the modern scientist has been put to it to explain his own intelligence in a universe in which intelligence is by fundamental assumption declared to be unreal.

II. THE MOHAMMEDANS AND THE NEW SCIENCE

Modern science could never have gotten under way nor have developed the mathematical method prepared for it had it not been for the impact of Aristotle brought to it through the Moslems.

The Moslem interest in Aristotle was mainly scientific. They were in possession of his more scientific works, which they studied for purposes of health and divination. This meant that they were physicians, deeply interested as a race, even before Mahomet or Aristotle, in astrological lore. The effect of the stars upon human destiny, upon health and happiness and the vicissitudes of war, trade, and love, had already been established among them as a scientific interest. Therefore Aristotle's cosmology offered them a rich field for research. His botanical work was quickly caught up for its value in the crude materia medica of the day. Undoubtedly the Moslem knowledge of Aristotle's scientific work, yet unknown to Western Europe, had given them a great advantage over Christendom. The introduction of their scientific achievement into the Western world under the authority of Aristotle was undoubtedly one source of the rise of Western science.

Moreover, the first scientific achievements in western Europe, as they had been in Greece and in southern Italy and in Islam, were mathematical. This helped to give the mathematical set to all Western scientific investigation, and made the mathematical the basis, if not the sole method of science. The constitution of the human mind is so closely in accord with the system of nature that any method of investigation which is in keeping with common sense is bound to wrest from nature some of her secrets. There is no doubt that the mathematical method has been the source both of the great advances of modern science as well as the source of unappreciated limitations.

III. THE MATHEMATICAL TREND SINCE DESCARTES

With Descartes, whose discoveries were chiefly mathematical, and with the modern development of mathematics through the analytical geometry, the calculus, and the invention of logarithms, the modern world had at hand scientific tools entirely unknown to the ancients. Analysis became the one path to knowledge. The search began for the discovery of an ultimate unit. As one invention after another disclosed the pluralistic character of this unit, new names were invented for new unknowns until we have a long vocabulary of words that at one time represented the indivisible unit of being: molecule, particle, atom, electron, proton, neutron, *alpha*, *beta*, and *gamma* particle, photon, positron, negatron—and so down a constantly increasing list. And ever the unit is an unknown and unknowable quantity.

So deeply has science identified itself with mathematical method that it needs only the magic touch of number to erect any claim into scientific cogency for some. This is especially true in affairs having to do with social disciplines, such as sociology, psychology, political science, and economics, where the indeterminate element is far more powerful than the determinate, and in which mathematical method is frequently inept and misleading. It was this insane confidence in mathematics that has given the world its Malthuses and Adam Smiths with their unwavering confidence in numbers that have no real meaning.

At any rate, we have come to live in an Aristotelian world, where information about the whole is conceived as made up of a knowledge of the minute particles that comprise it. Our only difficulty seems to be to get our jigsaw universe together again, once it is taken down, to show scientific reason for considering it as a unit or a system, or to account for its complex adaptations and co-operations. The real wonder is not the multitudinous existence of flying particles with their all but irresistible energies, but rather in their harmonious co-operation full of purpose and intelligence to create a meaningful world.

IV. THE INDUCTIVE METHOD

Much controversial energy has been wasted to claim for the various European nationalities the credit of introducing the inductive method. Nicholas Cusanus, Roger Bacon, Regiomontanus, Leonardo da Vinci, Francis Bacon, and René Descartes have each had their enthusiastic followers who were ready to set forth extravagant claims in their interests. Among English-speaking people the all but solitary credit was long bestowed upon Francis Bacon as the father of the inductive method. Although he may be claimed to have preached it, it is quite certain that he never practiced it.

However, the inductive method seems quite adapted to the unemotional nature of the English, and it is not strange that there it should find a great development. This cannot be said, however, without recognizing the practical scientific experiments of the French, which were not a whit behind and might be claimed superior to those of the English in actual invention. In fact, any attempt to evaluate scientific progress by national lines is foolish and can be made to appear otherwise only by unforgivable oversights. It seems rather to be the gift of those times and places in which the open expression of opinion is allowed and the spirit of free inquiry encouraged. Scientific progress is the child of democracy.

V. THE THEORY OF EVOLUTION: THE ULTIMATE EXPRESSION OF INDIVIDUALISM

The inevitable outcome of the mathematical method was the theory of evolution. Here organisms are taken not as wholes but as the combination of parts. The same old method of analysis is found to be still with us, and though there is a question about its applicability to biology, we shut our eyes to the opposing facts in our enthusiasm for the theory. Thus we have pushed back of the organism to discover the secret of the cell, and back of the cell to trace its ancestry in chromosome and gene, and so the greater part of our lore is microscopic and often hypothetical. Of course, the fundamental assumption here is materialism, and we refuse to believe in anything but mechanical causes. We cannot conceive of organisms as not made up of parts, quanta which have some significance or existence within themselves before they come into existence through an organism. We think of them as in some magic way creating the organism, rather than of the organism itself as furnishing their sole purpose and cause.[3]

The present practice is quite akin to the crude fancy of Empedocles, who dreamed of the bodily organs as existing first by themselves and then drawn together by mutual attraction. Thus arms, legs, eyes, ears were assumed created and coming together by a natural affinity to form a man. Present theories are only sufficiently refined to close our eyes to the old materialistic difficulties. We think now of these members as if they were already embedded in some material way in chromosomes, and implying but the need of a better microscope to reveal them to us. This is but a refinement of the ancient thought—the pushing of individualism, or sanctified numerology, to the limit. Thus the genes are assumed to carry traits and yet not to carry them, for frequently there are jumps of several generations. How material facts, such as these are assumed to be, can both be present and absent seems not even to have occurred to the theory-bound devotee of popular science.

Whether or not individualism can profitably press its discoveries further is a grave question. For there are a multitude of inconsistencies which the evolutionary theory cannot untangle. The situation is like the boy who found it easy to dissect the clock but who could not put it together again because he had never learned the intricate purpose which was in every part as surely as the metal from which the parts were fashioned. Today we have all the parts, but not the purpose. The unfortunate circumstances under which the theory was set forth, with the bitter hostility upon the part of the church, have prevented the reappraisal of the doctrine which is long overdue. The bitterness that early met the suggestions of Darwin and Wallace; the ex cathedra statements of Spencer; the neglected testimony of the Lamarckian theory, which has found itself incapable of proof and yet which is necessary to the maintenance of any mechanical theory of evolution, at times show how far we are still from the goal of under-

[3] These must be assumed to be effectively present and absent at the same time. Atavism is a convenient fallacy of the abstract when used as an *explanation* of what is undoubtedly fact, e.g., the repetition of characteristics through different generations. Our quarrel is not with the fact but with the assumed explanation.

standing. There are certain respects in which our pronounced individualism has led us away from fact, but it was essential in the development of individualism that we should apply the theory to life itself.

CHAPTER VIII

THE DEVELOPMENT OF INDIVIDUALISM IN PHILOSOPHY—PLURALISM

IN PHILOSOPHY, INDIVIDUALISM is paradoxically both the beginning and the end of doubt. When the individual is set forth as the judge of his own perceptions, there immediately swim into ken a multitude of questions that had never occurred before. What is the relation of this perceiving mind to the world of objects? Why do these inner perceptions represent an outward world of reality? Does the contrast between inner perception and outer world present an insoluble contradiction? If not, how can both be brought into harmony? The crude realism that satisfies the common and the materialistic mind never becomes conscious of these problems involved in the simplest perception. The success of common realism rests upon refusal to recognize the questions at issue. Individualism is called upon to face the issue at once—to place the individual mind with relation to the validity of knowledge before it presumes to know. The crude realists assume knowledge without raising a question as to the possible validity of cognition claims, or without establishing a technique by which it can philosophically determine between the true and the false.

Practical issues demand that there shall be at least an end of analysis. There must be some point of rest, some ultimate position, some fundamental platform from which to work. A refined and philosophic realism takes the place of the old in varying degree, so as to include perception, intelligence, the human mind in the constitution of reality, the sum of things. The farthest advance in this direction is made by a ·personal realism which declares that the ultimate reality is personal. In the series of causes, when we get back to a causal personal will, we can analyze no farther. We have to accept something as true and not needing demonstration. If we accept matter as the indubitable reality, we have taken the way of materialistic realism and cannot account for mind. If the idea or the thought seems to us the only unconditioned reality we are headed for an absolute idealism which denies the external world. The personal realist suggests that our own existence is the only reality that does not have to be proved to us, and that here must be the beginning of all perception and thought, the alembic in which thought and thing are brought together. Whatever external influences may have entered into action, none of them is completely determining without the will of the acting person. Here, then, is a reality which is itself not determined and must be assumed as a starting point, a minimum of causal reality. Thus causal intelligence is seen as included in the very constitution of reality.

I. INDIVIDUALISM AS A REVOLT FROM SKEPTICISM

Perhaps it was Anaxagoras who first in philosophy raised the question of the reality and place of mind in the cosmic order. Protagoras made critical the issue by declaring the mind of the individual the measure of all things. It was not strange that such an assumption, unattended by an adequate theory of knowledge, and without the grounding of metaphysics, should have developed into the sheer relativity of the Sophists. For the Sophists were chiefly concerned not with finding a correct and indubitable rule for discovering truth; they were trying to show that truth did not exist. With the abstract principle they had no concern. The theory fell into the hands of those bent upon misusing it for their own ends. If truth were relative to the individual, then whatever they wished could be considered true. This was the early deadlock into which the philosophy of individualism fell. The result was a skepticism more and more complete until it was met and combated with the personal realism of Socrates.

Repeatedly in the history of Western thought this has been the answer to skepticism. Against the Sophistic denial of moral truth Socrates raised the assurance of his indwelling *daemonium*. This assurance did not come to him without mental struggle. He, too, had been enamored of the specious conclusions of an artful dialectic, but he had been equally convinced of its falsity and emptiness. He arrived at the unequivocal conviction that, in spite of all argument, he knew within himself whenever a contemplated course of action was wrong. This inner conviction he saw as stronger than all the stifling voices of self-interest backed by the smoothness of false dialectic. His doubt was ended in the sure conviction of the eternal validity of the moral self-consciousness. Nor was this self-consciousness his alone. It was metaphysically grounded in cosmic reality. For this reason he could assume it to be possessed by all men. In this manner equipped, he set forth to face the skepticism of his time. Through his pupil Plato and his followers, the Stoics, he provided the organizing center about which Western society gathered its moral and legal codes. Socrates might truthfully be called, because of his discovery, the father of Western civilization.

II. Augustine and the Supreme Certainty

Social institutions are the reflections of ideas that have gained common or dominating acceptance, and have been precipitated or formulated into social practice. There are many influences that had been at work making the world into which Augustine was born. Chief among these were Stoicism, Judaism, and Christianity. Their inherent theories had established legal practice and moral code, and had built the institutions of later Roman civilization. All of these were now collapsing under the onslaught of Gothic invasion and the internal weakness of the Empire. As always happens in such a case, the underlying philosophies of the old order were being questioned. There was a cynical doubt of theories that had been thought invulnerable to change. There was mistrust of ruling political institutions. There was suspicion of the prevailing social organization, and there was skepticism of the church and the whole moral and spiritual order. All seemed to stand or fall together. To Augustine, it threatened the collapse of law, order, learning, and morality.

Again it was a personal realism that solved the doubt. Augustine had, through a remarkable conversion, received certain indisputable personal assurances, and it was out of these assurances that he drew the lesson for his times. He asserted the certainty of personal apprehension of the truth. So sure was he of the final triumph of this truth that he foresaw the power of the institution which he visualized as possessing the truth to build a spiritual kingdom on the ruins of the ancient order. Out of his unquestioned romanticism and individualism, as voiced in the *Confessions,* he was able, ideally, to construct the new organism which is set forth in *The City of God*. Again it was personal realism finding within man's own soul not only the doubt but its solution. Augustine's dream of an eternal empire of truth held together the shattered fragments of Western civilization until the barbarians had been cultivated to appreciate the surviving legal and moral code.

III. FROM CARTESIAN FAITH TO HUMEAN SKEPTICISM

Once more in the history of Western culture personal certainty and affirmation found itself the victim of the institutions its own faith had fostered. Again it had to meet the challenge of skepticism.

But each time the skepticism took on a different hue. Augustine had invested the concept of truth with absoluteness and authority. The new skepticism was destined to take a deeper range. It could not stop with moral conviction only, as with Socrates, nor with absolute spiritual assurance, as with Augustine. This time it was a challenge thrown down regarding the validity of knowledge itself.

Descartes raised the problem in his famous dictum, "I think, therefore I am." It was the defiance of an overfed and top-heavy civilization which was asking the question whether there was anything which could escape the universal doubt. Descartes held that the one reality which could not be doubted was doubt itself. Upon this seeming frailty he proposed to build up a complete philosophical system. Of one thing he was sure, that unless one could believe in his own reality and the validity of his own mental processes, he could not believe in the reality of the world of experience. The question of reality was fought out on the field of the theory of knowledge, but it was tagged with a fatal dualism of mind as over against matter. Two contrasting worlds of thought and thing were set in eternal opposition, and the wonder grew that they could not be brought together again. The natural outcome was the relativism of all knowledge, reached by Hume.

IV. THE KANTIAN UNITY OF THE SELF

There is sure to be violent difference of opinion respecting Kant, not only concerning his place in philosophy but also concerning the interpretation of his work. Nevertheless nearly all would agree that this philosophy marks a turning point in the history of thought. The system of knowledge had in Hume been reduced to a hopeless and helpless skepticism. This time the possibility of knowledge itself was in doubt, and had reached the conclusion that we could not know that we know, or that there is to our presumed perception any corresponding reality. This was the fatal conclusion that awoke Kant from his "dogmatic slumbers."

Kant began to pick his way back to positive affirmations by searching the categories—meaning, by these, the affirmations or presuppositions without which thought itself would be impossible. These he nailed to his masthead as the a priori ideas which must be considered constitutional or functional. The method so far was little more than a mechanical supplement to Hume's associational psychology; but it led to two important discoveries. First, he uncovered the weakness of the Lockean sensationalism, which had considered the mind *a tabula rasa* on which the activities of the external world wrote meanings. He discovered that the mind itself was not the passive recipient of knowledge but must itself be active in all judgments whether of perception or reflection. A thousand meaningful scenes might flash unmeaningfully on the eye of ignorance. Rich truths fall futilely upon unappreciative ears. Truth is conveyed only as the processes of thought are set up and wilfully pursued by the receiving mind. The teacher can never do his thinking for the pupil. There must be a corresponding mental activity in the pupil's mind or there is no thought. This discovery was so clear that it seemed strange that it had not been disclosed before.

The second great discovery of Kant was closely allied to the first. It might pass under the phrase, "the synthetic unity of the apperception in all judgment." This was in no way an adequate formula for personality, and its use as such has been sharply disputed. Kant probably intended it as a mere description of the logical function exemplified in all selves. Nevertheless it pointed out the deeper lying nature of personality which could not be successfully controverted. Kant discovered space- and time-transcending capacity in perception which enabled the perceiver to witness the present experience in the light of its past. There were, then, no simple perceptions unless the first perception of childhood could be so called. The perceiving individual, instead of being passively written on by the external active world only, was himself actively contributing to the result—was himself in very large way the creator of meaning. As in the case of the activity of the mind in judgment, so here, without the unity introduced through personal experience and integrating past, present, and future, no meaning could arise from the world of experience. Apperception was merely that storehouse of the past from which the individual drew; which he brought to shed light upon the immediate perception. This present caught its meaning because it was unified or synthesized with other meanings in a personal world.

These were the significant contributions which Kant made to the thought of his time, and these are two of the *dicta* which remain secure in human experience. There is tremendous significance that, once more in the history of thought, fundamental skepticism was faced and looked out of countenance by the appeal to the realism of personal experience.

Again in our own time we face the crisis of progress in civilization. Again the slowly won liberties of generations, the securities gained for the individual are falling about us. Who can doubt that the impending changes are even more momentous than ever before in human history? It is in some respects the same old problem crying for solution but its face has changed. It is not now as with Socrates the problem of the validity of moral truth and the demand for the right of personal moral judgment; it is not as with Augustine the vindication of an eternal order of truth based on personal conviction; neither is the present problem one of intellectual skepticism, the validity of personal interpretations of an external world. The conflict has moved on to a new phase. The problem now rests on the value of the person rather than upon the validity of his judgments. Has he an intrinsic value that is worth conserving. Does this value exist in spite of his social position, his learning or lack of it? Are some persons by nature fit only to be enslaved by others? Can others without detriment to their own supreme personal interests accept the services of slaves? Or on the other hand is the only ultimate society a free society, in which men are free because of good will, a determination to realize themselves in the common good? The solutions of the past indicate the character of this one. There must be a new discovery of the person and of his value. We must see that any organization of society which smacks of a regimentation that is not self-regimentation is an offense against the person.

SECTION II
THE PRESENT DILEMMA OF CIVILIZATION....

CHAPTER IX

THE DISILLUSIONMENT OF ACHIEVED OBJECTIVES

I T IS NOT a pleasant task to discuss the present dilemma of civilization, or the "decline of the West," as Spengler has put it. Any criticism of Western culture will seem to many a sin, and the consideration of its weaknesses worse than sin.

The memory of inflated prosperity is still with us. The dreams of rejuvenated society, so bright before the world wars, brought rude awakening, dwell in the memory of the older of us. Men are not often willing to be disillusioned but rather make a virtue of blindness as a sort of patriotism, or a species of orthodoxy, hugging the old ideals as if they had become, or might very shortly become, facts. So, though it is not an agreeable exercise, it may be well for us to take account of our shortcomings. Sometimes the surgeon's knife is the path to life.

There will be those, of course, who will contend there is nothing much the matter with society. Some will affirm that our only trouble is the fall in the stock market. Others more penetrative will lay our troubles to general loss of confidence. If this latter be the case, it may indicate a disease more virulent than appears on the surface. Loss of confidence is likely to indicate loss of integrity, and something approaching moral collapse. That may be the road to general disintegration and ruin.

Very few stop to reflect upon the fact that we face what is in its physical characteristics an essentially new world from that of a half century ago. Persons of middle life are living in a different world from that in which they were born. Transportation has now put Los Angeles nearer to Shanghai than it was a short time ago to Denver. Shanghai is much nearer than San Francisco was in the days of the padres. Radio communication has aggravated the situation. In one day one may listen in to a speech from the Vatican, one each from China and Japan, and one from the King of England. The world has become a vast whispering gallery. In such circumstances, foolishness is

93

more widespread and disastrous, and silence more rare and more golden than ever. War does not wait on a diplomacy which depends on information three months old. In fact, it seems of late to run in advance of diplomacy or declaration. Leaders of men must think quickly—there is need for them to think straight and without a moral strabismus. Yet we are trying, in the face of a new cosmopolitanism to settle questions after the manner of the ancient provincialisms. We have been freed from the old world of action, but we have not emerged into a new world of thought and of spiritual achievement. The world has outgrown its mental and moral clothes at the very moment that science has given it unreckonable power. This constitutes the main dilemma of the present day. In this discussion perhaps no method can be more profitable than to take inventory of those very movements described in the previous section as the chief claims for distinction in Western culture.

I. Achievement and Life

Any culture or society which can be viewed from the standpoint of progress should be considered from the biological aspect. In the living organism change is the dominating principle. The higher we go in the scale of life, the greater are the possibilities of change and the power of readaptation to environment. It is, then, no condemnation of a civilization to point out that it is in continual process, nor is it a mark of civilization to show a settled quality which enables it to survive without change by the mere inertia of tradition. Failure to realize the living nature of human society and hence the naturalness of change is the inherent weakness of the Spenglerian system, especially since it is committed in advance to the cyclic view of history, that there can be no real progress. In other words, it is only by treason to his own principle that he can create perturbation about a decline of the West.[1] That the theory could have caused so much holding of the breath was further due to the rapidity of social change at the present

---

[1] If history is but a repetition of cycles, we should, like Chinese sages, look upon decline with complacency, since it necessarily precedes the eventual rise. One could even be optimistic over the *depth* of the decline, since that would indicate a contrastingly higher achievement at the upper side of the arc. But history viewed in this sense could scarcely be considered a progress, nor even a true decline, since decline is necessary to the corresponding rise. This view negates the very meaning of history.

time and to that social inertia on the part of the comfortable portions of society, which look with alarm upon any change. The greatest glory of Western culture has been its capacity for readjustment—its ability to create new ideals of freedom and of the common welfare. It will break and fail only when it is no longer able to create these larger ideals as an effective element of social imagination.

The social process is a genius for life, and it is not containable or discoverable in any set form. Neither that of science, nor of dogma, nor of authority can set it forth, because it is a living principle, continually breaking old forms and old boundaries, and for that reason definitely unpredictable. No actual achievement can ever, therefore, satisfy a living society. To arrive at one goal means to bring a multitude more in sight. To satisfy one need means to raise a hundred others which call for satisfaction. In such a case the social milieu frequently forgets the multitude of its satisfactions in contemplation of its ever-growing desires. The more multiplied the satisfactions already obtained, the more complicated and numerous are these new demands. The result, for a surfeited society, is a sense of disillusionment and futility. What man wants seems all out of proportion to what he can get. This is the disease that attacks not primitive society—which has to do daily battle with elements for bread—it is the affliction of the highly organized and full-fed.

From this it will be seen that, after all, the affliction is more mental and spiritual than physical, though it never could arise without the basis of physical well-being. This must be the justification lying behind the demand for the material welfare of all men. The greatest advances of society arise out of the revolutionary possibilities contained in this mental and spiritual dissatisfaction with things. We must have the things first before we can see how little and imperfectly satisfying they can be. The fault is not, as is so commonly assumed, in the mechanism of society. The difficulty lies in the growing appetite for things which the existing state cannot provide; and in the ultimate, though undiscerned, it is an appetite which can be appeased only through spiritual achievement. The existence of such conditions is not something to be deplored. It should be seen as evidence of a growing insight into life. Without it the world has no soul. It is the mark of a living society.

II. THE SUCCESSIVE OBJECTIVES OF WESTERN CULTURE

The successive objectives of Western culture should be viewed in the light of these facts. We usually accord to the Greeks the credit for the first achievements of democracy. From the standpoint of contemporary efforts toward government, the Greek city-state which sought to base order upon the consent of its influential citizens was a long advance upon the merely tribal and local, as well as upon that unquestioned despotism by which the large states had built themselves out of the small ones through conquest and the overlordship of a powerful military ruler with no respect for the consent of the governed. But the Greek democracy entirely overlooked the acquiescence of two very large classes in society. Even the ideal *Republic* of Plato assumed the slavery of the producing class. The early practice of democracy likewise did not often include women. Rule was really established on the basis of possible military service. The time was sure to come when the inconsistencies of such democracy would lead to a sense of failure and disillusionment.

Rome, likewise, built her power upon a certain ideal of democracy under the title, "republic." Like the Greeks, the Romans, dependent upon military prowess, had early trial of a military commonalty which, though destined to pass away, left a tradition that autocracy could not outlive. Rome bent herself upon the achievement of a universal law before which all should stand with equal footing—at least within a given class. So limited a conception must, in course of time, give way to the larger interpretation of "all men equal before the law." The barriers of special privilege were long in being broken down, and survive in practice even now, though the accepted theory is that of absolute equality. But Roman law never really worked out to democratic results. It did not in the completest sense rest upon the consent of the governed; it was imposed from above and could not be truly representative until it was made by the men it was to govern, and so it had not strength enough to overcome the individualism of the liberty-loving barbarians.

The struggle then centered about this very point, and was marked by the rise of popular parliaments. The first of these sat in Beaune, France, perhaps as early as 921, and certainly in organized parliamentary form as early as 1280. In England the Saxon Wittenagemote marks the beginning of the movement toward a new form of democracy. The only logical result was the far-off and modern resort to the initiative and referendum, the final word in bringing the lawmaking power to the people. In the main, the European struggle was toward the achievement of political democracy. In America the movement received the added impetus toward the achievement of social equality, the doing away of special privilege for caste and class. The means of bringing this about was conceived as that of universal education, free schools, free speech, free press, and free church—and, as supreme aid to the general objective, free land.

These successive aims of Western society, founded on the belief in popular sovereignty, backed by an individualistic philosophy, have more or less been achieved. Their achievement has never, however, been complete, nor met the growing needs of the social order, and has been attended by pessimism and disillusionment.

III. The Overlooked Factors of Civilization

The successive disillusionments that have marked the progress of Western culture have arisen out of overlooked requirements. The achievement of equality before the law, the boast of Roman and of late European, has been made void in a thousand ways. Special privilege seems usually to have been able to nullify and circumvent it. *Justitia* is ever pictured holding the scales of justice with eyes blindfolded to the results, but in actual practice the Western order threatens to collapse because technicalities, erected in multiplying confusion to safeguard the rights of the weak, have become the harbor and refuge of the criminal and greedy. These often dress their nefarious practices in the garb of individual rights. Thus the purpose of law is frequently defeated and is made the means of oppression.

The dream of social equality, so strong in the sturdy and independent American colonists, was measurably achieved in a country where, by the force of circumstances, all had to start equal. In a pioneer country where all were face to face with strenuous toil, where all men were called upon to face hardship and necessity, only the man with wit and physical resource could meet the demands of life. There was small room for leisure of any kind. There was less for the entertainment of luxury and waste. For the first hundred and fifty years of existence on the Western continent it looked as if the dream of social democracy were an actual fact. Then came the wholesale exploitation of natural resources which followed on the days of pioneer settlement and expansion, and with this plunder of what should have been the common resources came the colossal fortunes which raised a moneyed caste and divided a hitherto democratic society into classes, wherein there was little contact between high and low, powerful and weak, rich and poor. Thus the breaking dream of social equality added to the sum of disenchantment.

In a somewhat similar way has ended the dream of political equality. Theoretically, in a land of universal education and equal voting power all the citizens will be intelligent enough to vote for the common interests. Practically, unless there is also moral integrity and patriotism, these generally educated voters may vote unjust laws and bring pressure upon legislators, executives, and judges, in favor of their own special interests. Frequently trading between predatory interests is resorted to in order to insure majorities. Thus the blocs are arrayed against the honest citizen, who finds himself in a helpless minority. And thus we witness the so-called failure of democracy as leadership falls into the hands of the baser elements of society.

One of the expedients calculated to insure the blessings of popular rule was that of free speech and free press. These seem largely to have failed by their very extension to the masses. The Revolutionary fathers never dreamed of special interests in the republic which should become stronger than the government itself and thus be able to temper and interpret the news in an exclusive way—but still worse, they did not dream of influence so strong that they could determine what facts should be given out as news and what suppressed. Under present conditions the chances of the average citizen to learn the facts about men and issues of public life are exceedingly slim. There is a successful effort throughout the West, both in Europe and America, thus to suppress and distort facts. Sometimes it is done in the name of government for the special benefit of the political clique in power; sometimes by financial blocs. The result is the same—the negation of democracy. Along with the movement appear certain self-appointed conservators of the present order who, in the name of patriotism, demand the right to forbid all free expression but their own. Moved by the purity of their own intentions and the results of democracy untested on a national scale the founders were suspicious of majorities that might be moved to disorder and violence through appeals to ignorance, prejudice, or avarice.

Education was likewise depended upon by the fathers of the modern state to balance the caste tendency and to provide the intelligence which, through universal suffrage, would create enlightened government. Under the spur of this intention vast sums have been poured into popular education. The strain of personal greed has, however, too often turned it aside from its real purpose. Education has been too largely conceived as manual and professional training, with the result that, of the millions who enter the public schools, only a few are taught to think or to consider their obligation to the larger unit of society. Above all, that education which is given has been rapidly denuded of all moral and ethical elements in the name of religious tolerance. This has produced a citizenry whose mental training has in too many instances only fitted unmoralized individuals to become more successfully the enemies of society.

In all these it will be seen that there are no safeguards for democracy that can act apart from the moral and good will of the individual citizen. In the last analysis, individualism has this weakness. It cannot be prevented from setting up the individual interest against the common interest. When this feeling becomes widespread and men are no longer restrained by community ideals of patriotism, of integrity, of morals, and of religion, popular sovereignty falls into chaos and anarchy. Democracy is safe only to the degree of the morality, integrity, and self-restraint of a people.

CHAPTER X

THE PASSING OF AUTHORITY IN MORALS

....

WESTERN CULTURE HAS never mastered itself and has never risen fully to belief in and application of its own principle of individualism. This fact has kept alive the old problem, so vital to the Medievalists, between Platonism and Aristotelianism, between realism and nominalism, the doctrine of universals and that of particulars.

Fundamentally, it is the problem of authority. Is truth an absolute, conveyed only by the authority of an infallible institution, Scripture, word or credo which is infallibly imparted? This is the standpoint of authoritarianisms of all kinds. It overlooks, first of all, the fallible nature of human understanding. Is truth, on the contrary, an inner revelation verified by the testimony of the individual soul? Western civilization has never solved this problem implicit in its concept of democracy.

In no field is the dilemma more acute than in that of morals. Has the individual the capacity to discern right moral action apart from authoritative announcements? In case he accepts authority, what is the basis of his judgment as to what is true. Can he forego his inner judgment without the wreckage of his own personality? Synods and councils, exercising the delegated right of private judgment, have tried to answer the question for all times and peoples by silencing the questioners. This method is, however, out of harmony with the basic principle of democracy. The feeling of inconsistency always present has grown with the liberation of thought, the growth of political freedom, and the progress of knowledge. Exponents of democracy have been afraid of the fruits and outcome of popular sovereignty. In the moral realm we have shown an equal timidity. We have proclaimed the right of individual judgment as our dearest ideal, and forthwith have hastened to deny it to all others by the establishment of codes, conventions, and creeds. There has been forever the fear that the average man could not be trusted with the truth, above all that he must not be trusted with an idea of his own.

Here lies the secret of the passing of authority in morals, which constitutes one of the most challenging facts of modern life, and contains the threat of the decline of the West.

1. THE RISE OF AUTHORITY IN MORALS

Recent writers have almost with one voice named the basis of religion as "fear"—which is far from the truth, since fear inhibits all freedom of action and is the arch-enemy of true religion. Where men have been misled is in the confusion of religion with institutionalism, of religion with authority. The promulgation of authority has its basis in fear of individual judgment and is the least reasonable of all methods of moral advance.

The threatened whip of parental authority begins where reasonableness leaves off. It is too frequently the confession of a lazy-minded and too little ingenious parent that arguments are offered that cannot be rationally answered. He then falls back upon the *ipso dixit* of parental authority and the resort to intimidation.

So far in its experiments with democracy, and particularly in the realm of morals and religion, this has been the ill-considered and infantile method of our moral leaders. The truth was something forever settled in Heaven, and not to be understood, even, by the feeble mind of man. Some man's say-so must be received and accepted as an unquestioned authority. To secure this apotheosis, canonization, creedal conformity, have been resorted to, to bolster conventional moralities. Whoever dared to question was, by the very act of questioning, rendered heretical and subject to anathema and persecution. Here seemed the easy solution of the whole moral and social problem—a conventionalized society which would think not for itself but only that which the spiritual leaders and fathers had decided it should think. Individual right of judgment was construed as the right of each individual to agree with the authorities, never to dissent.

A society committed to individualism could not, however, stop with such a conclusion. It was its very genius to go on. There is no point to the claim that authority has been correct in its moral judgments. For the individual, the whole value of a moral judgment lies in the unrestrainedness of its freedom. It is mandatory because it is *his* conviction.

To the man of yesterday it was unthinkable that the moral code of Western society was a construction laboriously arrived at, based in many points on the forms and artificialities of prevailing social and economic practices. It seemed so entirely of the nature of things as to have existed from the earliest period of human history. In reality it was the work of the Jewish prophets, the Greek philosophers and the Christian fathers. It came by degrees and was the result of innumerable changes in the social structure, reforms and insights which followed the progress of a refining civilization. Individualistic morals, the sense of personal responsibility, must look primarily to the Jewish Ezekiel and the Greek Socrates as the great innovators who inaugurated their career in Western culture. This is not to overlook a possible deeper source of both movements in the religion of Egypt which gave direct and insistent emphasis to the matter of personal moral responsibility. Egypt was always near to Judea and Jewish religious thought bore close connection with it from at least the time of Moses who was a high priest of the Egyptian religion. The *tempo* of collaboration arose in strength in the Alexandrian period. Greek thought was profoundly affected by Egyptian Orphism through the Mysteries. From this there grew up that feeling of moral responsibility which set off the individual from his caste, class or nation as accountable for his own acts which could not be glossed over or expiated by the institution, racial or political, of which he was a part. This movement was a dominant factor in the individualism of the West.

Once the question of individualistic morals has been settled however, institutionalism begins to obscure the issue. There is always the tendency to build moral precepts into a system of authority. The more pronounced the convictions, the more rigid the authority becomes. Morals are codified to such an extent as to suspend or remove individual judgment. The identification of morals with a system presents a specious advantage. Teaching the code to the young becomes simplified but loses in character. A similar oversimplification takes place in the mind of the individual. He is relieved of responsibility for personal decisions by the written law. His moral judgments thus become something other than his free and rational decisions; they are automatically decided for him. Such has been the fate of institutionalized morals, in Stoicism, in Judaism, in Scholasticism, in Puritanism. With the decay of the institution, confusion reigns respecting the moral obligations which its rules have laid down.

II. THE WEDGE OF DECADENCE

Any system of morals built into a rigid code and dependent upon established institutions either of church, state or social custom, and accepted by the general public without personal decision is sure to be disrupted by the fall or weakening of institutions or by the inevitable changes of social practice. In Western society the first great disruption began with the advent of Jewish-Mohammedan learning which introduced Aristotelian individualism anew to the little European world that had long been under the spell of Platonic and neo-Platonic authoritarianism. Then began anew the march of a rising individualism which expressed itself in the growth of political democracy in the Free Cities, in the establishment of the universities, in the creations of Gothic architecture, in chivalry, and in the worship of Mary. With the growing individualism thus expressed, and the upset of old social customs, involved artificial codes could not abide the questioning or had no answers for new moral dilemmas. An advancing individualism threatened always to change the seat of moral authority from the institution to the individual judgment. Dependence on the letter of the law is always dangerous, for in removing the right of private judgment it removes likewise the spirit which is essential to morality.

Aristotle had pointed in the direction of the individual as the seat of authority and the whole forward movement of the Revival of Learning and the Renaissance took on that drift. After Protestantism had done what it could to replace papal authority by that of scriptural infallibility, there came the impact of Chinese civilization which opened to question the chief claims of verbal inspiration. They learned that to other times and other men, untouched by Judaism or Christianity, had also come a sufficient revelation to found a law-abiding, non-idolatrous and highly ethical society. The claims for an exclusive Judeo-Christian morality were vacated.

This discovery marked the rise of naturalism and relativity in morals. Moral action must be justified still more by the judg-

ment of the individual. The Chinese influence seemed to point
to the excellence of moral decisions without the aid of church,
Scripture or revelation. The result should have been to deepen
the sense of personal responsibility for moral decisions but it
was not. The immediate effect was libertinism, a feeling of the
unimportance of ethical decisions. Something of the moral relativism of the ancient Sophists was in the air. Whatever one
wished to do had a natural justification. Conscience was looked
upon as an artificiality created by authorities that hoped to profit
by the code, and could thereby be dismissed as prejudiced. The
whole movement was climaxed by behavioristic psychology which
effectively denied the existence of morals. Our animal ancestry
was assumed to have provided us with certain racial instincts
which no restraint of ours could control and yielding to which
was natural and therefore right. Since there was no freedom,
obviously there could be no morals. Such a result could be expected with the overthrow of an ethical system which had already
preferred institutional authority to the right of private judgment.
Old moral codes have collapsed in our time because we have
failed to pay attention to the in..er seat of authority in the consciousness of the person. The old problem of Sophistic relativism
in morals can be met again only as it was met by Socrates with
an appeal to the inner consciousness as the arbiter of right and
wrong.

Confusion has been added to the present situation by rapid
changes in the social order. The multiplication of devices of
living, calling for new habits, new means of social contact, new
luxuries, new responsibility, outvies any set code and reduces
to utter bewilderment the man who has not been taught to trust
his own judgment and to depend upon the underlying and
permanent principles of righteousness. It is possible to sin
against our neighbor, against society, and against ourselves in a
thousand new ways. Neither coded morality nor behaviorism
bear the solution of our moral dilemma.

A further source of confusion has been the rainbow dream
that science could by mechanistic or economic or eugenic processes reform society and build moral character without the
willing co-operation of the individual. All sorts of fantasies,
from cranial to glandular operations, have been proposed to
change the evil wills of men. There has in many cases been

complete oversight of the nature of moral action. A man made good by glandular operation—if that were possible at all—would not thereby become the possessor of moral character. The scheme overlooks the essence of morals, and throws all the emphasis on the physiological. The theory has obtained wide acceptance in the place of greatest possible harm, in popular theories of education. The result has been that large sections of society, especially among the young, have lost the sense of moral responsibility; not only the constraint of conventional moral authority, but the further constraint of a sense of individual moral responsibility for their acts.

III. THE PRESENT CONFUSION IN MORALS

Thus at the present moment the Western world is faced with moral anarchy from two sources. The first of these arises out of the discarding of conventional authority, which is largely the result of a growing popular self-expression and an increasingly complicated society. Humanity as now constituted does not represent homogeneous masses made up of similar faith, training, outlook, education, and traditions. Moral habits have been broken down by rapid transportation, more rapid communication, the denationalizing influence of cinema and daily press. Merely conventional authority cannot stand in the face of such social influences. There are so many men of opposite minds expressing themselves by print and radio that it is no longer possible to protect any one set of ideas from contamination or the inroads of doubt. One must, if an authoritarian, look with serious dismay upon the present moral confusion.

The other source arises from actual disbelief that man is a moral being. This is, of course, the more deadly doubt of the two; for it paralyzes the sinews of action and releases the antisocial forces of society from even the slight restraint of their own consciences, giving them a pseudo-scientific assurance that their vilest action is a part of the course of nature for which they are in nowise responsible. Herein we witness the moral debacle of the West.

IV. MORALS AND DEMOCRACY

We have come in the midst of so much moral uncertainty to take the whole matter of righteousness somewhat lightly. Perhaps we have not even asked ourselves whether there is any connection between morals and democracy. As between democracy and autocracy there seem to be but two general methods on which society can be organized. Organized society calls for orderly processes. These may be obtained in either one of two ways. The way of autocracy is by violent control of the majority by those who command military power. The only alternative to that lies in the self-control of the majority. So soon as power in a democracy passes out of the hands of those who practice a reasonable self-restraint democracy is replaced by chaos or by tyranny. This is merely to say that democracy can take care of only a limited number of antisocial, avaricious and criminal citizens. The citizen who refrains from breaking the law is the backbone of the democratic order, the *sine qua non* of popular sovereignty.

From this it becomes clear that whatever confuses or perverts public or private morals, or conduces to disrespect for morality, becomes an immediate threat to the existence of the democratic state. This is the principle frequently appealed to but more often overlooked when the question arises as to what government may do to protect the moral ideals of its citizens and particularly of the rising generation.

At long last no free government can withstand the moral debacle of its people. The ultimate defense of the state lies in the integrity of its citizens. When this is gone the only alternative is a totalitarian government. Such is the stern and difficult lesson increasingly taught to a morally indifferent age.

CHAPTER XI

THE FAILURE OF LAW

. . . .

ONE OF THE earliest of the thirteen colonies placed on its
shield this motto: "Liberty under law." Large portions of
society seem at present to have lost sight of the fact that general
respect for and obedience to law is the fundamental condition
of organized society. The colonists of Massachusetts Bay were
greatly aided by Puritan public opinion, and even now the government would scarcely be able to summon sufficient police power
were it not for the churches, synagogues, and ethical societies
that help to mold public opinion. We forget in our individualism
that law is the necessary concomitant of a crowded world. The
more there are of us, the more necessary it is to act for the common good. Many things cannot be done in the crowded city
without making life unbearable. In order to have my own
largest measure of freedom, I must give up many things legitimate in themselves which endanger the life, liberty, or even
comfort and welfare of my fellows. It is not at all a question
of what I want; it is a question of the common good. It is the
right of society to prohibit anything which is a menace to the
social order, is against the general welfare, or endangers the
life and freedom of the masses—even to the extent of pro-
hibiting me from living, if my menace is otherwise incurable.
On this basis the law must ultimately rest. It is what was once
known as the majesty of the law. This is sometimes overlooked
even by judges themselves, who mistake majesty of the law
for the majesty of the court, condone and encourage the breaking of laws with which they disagree, and severely punish contempt of court on grounds of personal pique.

This condition has been greatly aggravated in public opinion
by the antiquated system under which we labor, whereby justice
is easily defeated on technicalities. The present administration
of law too often favors the criminal and flouts society. It becomes frequently in practice not a search for reasonable justice

but a study of technicalities for the defeat of justice—a game in dialectic in which the smartest lawyer wins. This in itself leads to disregard for constitutional forms, makes possible court delays that establish a permanent injustice toward the poor, and sets up a government by injunction which in frequent cases favors the violation of the law. Such a condition ought to be impossible in a civilized country, and, unless remedied, must in the end lead to the collapse of democracy. Already there is in the world a trend toward dictatorships made possible through such conditions. It is easier to tolerate a dictatorship than lawlessness. The difficulty arises when an individual citizen desires to feel himself above the law, which he would have enforced on his fellows but not on himself, never seeing nor caring that such an attitude makes free government impossible.

I. LAW FOR THE INDIVIDUAL

Due to the stresses under which it has developed, the wresting of individual rights from successive tyrannies, Western law bears within itself a certain unavoidable conflict. The conflict arises out of the problem whether law is primarily for the individual considered by himself, or for the individual as a part of society. Much popular thought has not gotten beyond this first stage—that law has no right to interfere with personal liberty, that the individual should be free to do whatever he pleases, so long as he does not commit the more extravagant crimes. In fact, the average man contends for his right to commit the most antisocial acts, provided they are committed with a certain finesse, without regard to the social consequences—particularly if these consequences involve only those members of society who have no means of voicing a protest. Sometimes these members of society are minors; sometimes only prospective members of society, the unborn; sometimes the weaker, the ignorant, and the impoverished members of society, against whom are raised the barriers of legal expense and the archaic machinery of the courts. The wide prevalence of this individualistic concept of the law is the factor making most rapidly for the contempt for and breakdown of the law which now threatens the collapse of society. A little reflection will show what a reversal this condition is of the original principle of the protection of the least and weakest member of society. In the name of legal rights, strong individuals, through process of law, are enabled to commit wrongs against the whole of society. Not only are they permitted to do this, but they find the very laws which were aimed at antisocial acts their principal refuge and protection.

Out of this situation has arisen the difficulty of conviction for the most heinous crimes against the persons and property of individuals, to say nothing of wrongs against vaster numbers against which all legal protest is barred. Thus the law finds itself, hedged about with technicalities which repeatedly permit the worst criminals against society to escape. Criminal prosecution has become as erratic as the throw of the dice, with this further proviso, that the dice seem loaded in favor of the criminal and against the interests of society. The archaic nature of modern law shouts to heaven. The meticulous nature of indictments, the pedantic rendering of legal codes, the multiplicity of laws that can be twisted into the semblance of conflict, the willingness of judges to pin decisions upon the frailest pretext of legality, without regard to facts and sense—all these give to the law a doddering sense of futility. The further attack upon law is made through a jury system that chooses without selection and then carefully weeds out all who are the possessors of convictions, or who because of reading show a quicker intelligence. The tendency is further aided by excusing from service the more capable citizens—all these have been the multiplying influences which have brought the law into contempt. Yet all these perversions of justice and right were originally made to protect the accused individual from the unjust tyranny of power. They prove too often to be protection for the powerful criminal; while for the weak, who are despised for their weakness, the power of the prosecuting interests, bent on justifying their job in the statistics, is able to make these protections weaker than water.

II. LAW FOR SOCIETY

The significant oversight in this modern legal dilemma is that the attention of the Western world has been too exclusively turned upon the protection of the individual. As developed in Western society it has been aimed principally at the defense of the individual from governmental tyranny. Protection of society from the selfish usurpation of individuals has been neglected for fear of the invasion of personal liberties. What is forgotten is the fact that no individual stands alone. He is also a member of society, bound up with society in an inseparable way; is nothing, apart from certain social obligations; has no rights which can supersede those obligations. Discussion has run so exclusively to the one theme, the rights of the individual, that the man has become increasingly rare who thinks of his duties to society. He has not yet learned the fundamental truth of a permanent society —that the individual must not only sink his rights in the common good, he must also seek that common good in the higher sacrificial spirit which men learn in days of war, and in which they gladly give all.

There must be a revival of spiritual values if Western culture is to survive. There must be a patriotism which is more than flag waving, more than martial victory, and grounded in a deep-seated reverence for the common good, and a willingness to achieve it at the expense of personal sacrifice. Patriotism of this kind is, in the last analysis, not only moral but spiritual. There will not be a return of respect for law, a purification of the courts, a demise of demagoguery, a new regard for the national welfare without a revival of patriotism having a basically ethical significance.

Society is now too complicated to view the individual by himself. It must take into account the effect and influence of his acts upon society as a whole. All acts which offend against the welfare, happiness, success, and opportunities of any other members of society must come to be viewed as crimes, even if for the individual committing them they seem innocuous enough. Moreover, this influence cannot stop with the adult and competent portions of society, nor even with the living. The weak, the sick, the infantile, and even the unborn, must be taken into consideration. Nor is it possible any longer to confine these considerations to the more or less artificial boundaries of nationality. They cannot rest until they include the whole world. Invention and discovery are hastening the day when the individual must look upon himself as a part of the whole society, or civilization must fall.

III. THE CONFLICT OF FREEDOM WITH LAW

Those individualists to whose lot had come the task of wresting the lawmaking function from tyrannical and autocratic government and putting it into the hands of representatives of the people were sensitively aware of the fact that law was the basis of personal freedom. At the very moment that the lawmaking process has by excessive democratization, as in the initiative and referendum, been pushed to the most popular extent, we witness a vast popular indifference. Here again it seems as if the balance of self-interest so depended upon by the Manchesterian school has failed. Is there a quirk in human nature which leads man to despise all that which seems attained or easily attainable? Paradoxical as it seems, the popularizing of law appears to have wrought its decadence. Possibly, popular sovereignty has given individuals such a sense of control over legislation that they have been led to despise it, as some of our legislators, administrative and executive officers, public officials, judges, and police have shown signs of feeling above the law. Such may be the source of the popular American feeling that law is for other people but must not be applied to oneself. However, it has come about —and no one section of society can be held solely responsible— there is widespread disrespect for law. Not only so, but the basis of individual freedom is lost sight of. Individuals in the name of personal liberty are claiming courses of action as allowable when it is clearly seen that they invade the rights, safety, and welfare of others, born and unborn. Among great multitudes has grown up an indifference to the common good and a wild plunging into unsocial courses of action without regard to the consequences to others.

This is to overlook entirely the natural law of personal liberty, for there can be no personal liberty where there is no personal self-restraint. The truth holds here down to the last item and to all eternity. Self-restraint is the only path to the largest liberty, and the rule applies both to individuals and to nations. The self-controlled man who saves his resources for the work worth doing and the life worth living is the only man that is free. Any going into questionable or immoral paths inevitably commits him to the slavery of evil habits, and toward a sort of half life that deteriorates him mentally and spiritually and prevents the highest self-realization. Neither the citizen nor the nation can come to an acquiescing compromise with wrongdoing and retain sovereignty, once a course of action is seen as immoral or antisocial. The course of many a personal-libertyite is directly toward a physical, moral, and spiritual bondage that removes from him even the power of consistent thought and delicate appreciation of social obligation.

We are free only to the extent that we invade no other rights, and we are free only to the extent of our self-control. The purpose of law is the recognition of these boundaries and limits beyond which the individual should not go. But the power of the law lies in the good will of individual citizens, their ability and willingness to exercise self-restraint in the interests of the general good. Apart from this, no law can ever be enforced and no nation can live. There are not armies and navies enough, police power, guillotines or scaffolds enough, to maintain for long a civilization which does not possess widely among its individual members the good will of self-control in the interests of the wider society. Individual rights can be protected and are consonant only with the existence of individual duties and obligations.

IV. THE MENACE OF INDIVIDUALISM

It becomes very clear in the face of these considerations that democracy has become the keenest foe of what is often assumed as popular right, because democracy cannot survive without self-restraint. If our sense of popular sovereignty leads us to feel that because of position, economic worth, or relation to the social order, we are exempt from the duties that bind other men—if the feeling becomes widespread, then democracy will be at an end. This is indeed the most serious disease that at present afflicts Western society. It was the demand for special privileges which killed the Roman Empire, which wrecked feudalism and monarchy, is wrecking capitalism, and would wreck Communism, Socialism, Technocracy, or any other system of government that ingenuity could devise. There was a deep significance in the prophecy of the angels of "peace on earth to men of good will." The man who, in haste for unfair profits, rides roughshod over the welfare of his fellow men; who uses the technicalities of law as the bulwark of oppression; who is indifferent to the sufferings and the future opportunity of helpless children; or who in ignorant blindness foments the ill-will of class feeling; who is willing to be a leech on society, receiving that for which he makes no honest return—all these, though they were classed as the pillars of society, are its enemies and traitors. The fact that few, very few, of us can qualify as not being in some one or more of these categories is the high tragedy of an age which has learned better but which has not the moral and spiritual stamina to set its house in order—an age which watches the late flare of its setting sun and has not the spiritual vision nor even the faith to hope for a tomorrow. But—perhaps. . . . The perhaps must await the consideration of another chapter.

CHAPTER XII

THE CRUMBLING SAFEGUARDS OF DEMOCRACY

· ·

OUT OF THE struggle of the centuries has arisen a faith in certain safeguards of democracy. These are: equality of opportunity, extension of the suffrage, free education, and free religion, free speech and free press, citizen soldiery, and impartial and accessible courts. These principles have been won in the successive battles of Western civilization for a realized government by the people. The basic philosophy behind the assumption that these were true and proper bulwarks has been the theory of self-interest—that an informed electorate would not vote against its own interests. Theoretically it should not, and these various devices of freedom should be a sufficient guard against oppression and misrule. The fathers certainly felt they were laying deeply the cornerstone of civic liberty. It might be well for us to inquire as to the failure of these principles. Has there been a failure of the principles involved, or have circumstances arisen which have made them void? Where, if any, was the flaw in the theoretic armor of freedom? These are the general questions which we must propose.

I. EQUALITY OF OPPORTUNITY

The burden of proving that "all men are born free and equal" has been one of the standing embarrassments of the West since our fathers, in a moment of strong emotional excitement, gave utterance to a profound belief. The custom has been to tone it down to the less extreme statement of "equality of opportunity." Even this is, under the rigors of our complex civilization, becoming more and more an iridescent dream. We have long seen that differences of birth, education, environment, possession, rendered the first declaration academic. We are beginning to see that the moderated statement is likewise largely in the realm of theory. Until the present there has not been severe strain put

114

upon the theory, for the reason that Western culture has been undergoing rapid expansion to the unoccupied areas of the earth. So long as there was free land to be had for the asking, or for the taking, there was much in favor of the argument of equal opportunity. If one did not find his equality in the old home, there were the entrancing regions of the West or around the world where the peasant might become at least an hereditary landholder, and, with good fortune, a lord of the earth. There seemed no reason except lack of enterprise why any man should not become the equal of any other. In fact, it is this dream of equality brought by the easy turn of fortune which has misled much of the Western world into an indifference toward the deeper liberties which are involved in the principles and processes of government. It is notorious in American political life that political overturn does not take place until conditions have become unbearable to the point of revolution. If the general masses are prosperous, liberties are safely invaded, and the multitudes have little care. Even yet there are great numbers enduring hardship with an unwonted equanimity, because they expect the next turn of circumstance will provide them fortune, luxury, and power.

The era of expansion, which drew off from the crowded portion of the country both the most ambitious and energetic and the most hopeless, setting the more dangerous members of society upon their own absorbing quests—that day of expansion is now closing. Ambitions and despairs, which have no prospect better than slum dwelling, in an organization of society which holds out little hope for advancement, now ferment in the very heart of the commonwealth. The dream of equal opportunity goes by the board in a civilization in which large numbers, by reason of economic inequality, are prevented from education, from making openings for themselves in small businesses, from conducting for themselves small industries, and from access to the living of the land, which assures at least an independent sustenance.

The growth of industry, the god we have been worshiping as success, has been the Moloch that has swallowed up this fact of equality, and we have not yet found our solution to the problem raised.

II. FREE SPEECH AND FREE PRESS

Among the foremost achievements of democracy were the establishment of the rights to freedom of speech and press. Often suppressed, there can be no democratic action unless the voters are able to know the truth. They can never know the whole truth if but one side of any fact or set of facts, historical events, or political happenings, finds expression. As an antidote to both autocracy and demagogy the fathers rightly assumed that the privilege of free speech could not be safely denied to any citizen or party. Free press was but another branch of free speech. These were presumed to be the foundation stones of intelligent and free political action in a democracy. Where they prevailed it was seen that no cabal, clique, autocracy, or tyranny of any kind could long survive. By the same token, no democracy, however complete in name, can long survive where these rights to individual expression of opinion are in any complete way invaded or abrogated.

The amazing invasion of these rights, which include also the right of free assembly, has been one of the most significant developments in Western civilization. The necessity for these prerogatives has been forgotten by large portions of society in fear of social transition. The one evidence of moribundity in any state of society is the fear of change. For life is a constant readaptation of the organism to its environment. When its forms become so stereotyped that they are no longer adaptable, death has already set in. And the same thing is true of society. Only those forms of social organization can permanently survive which can accommodate themselves to new views and changing conditions. In the past half century the altered conditions of living represent a revolution. The stresses and strains upon all organized forms of social control have been vaster than in any similar period. At such a time as this to deny the right of free speech, free press, and free assembly is to confine dynamite. The greater the repression the vaster and more tragic will be the threatened explosion.

Special classes of our people, those who have prospered or who hope to prosper under things as they are, have attempted to abrogate these ancient rights to citizens whose views are in conflict with theirs. Whether it be undertaken by law, or by an illegally directed police force, or by black-listing and innuendo on either side of a labor conflict, the result differs only in degree. It is an act of war upon constitutional rights, a hostility toward democratic institutions which cannot retard but will inevitably hasten the collapse of the system such tactics are intended to preserve.

Half the ills of modern society would be cured if it were ever possible to get the truth to the people. Such a statement seems anomalous in view of the hurrying presses of millions of print shops, the widespread hookups of millions of radios. It would seem as if no corner of the world could be dark or lacking in full information about any essential interest of mankind. Such is unfortunately not the case. In most of the Western world the newspapers are under the control of the government, which means they are under the control of political blocs. These political blocs are frequently the most grafting, greedy, and dangerous that exist. Everywhere the politicians withhold the truth from the people and nearly everywhere there is concerted effort to deceive. Great syndicated newspapers cover the lands, and through debauchery of public taste, by dishing up scandal in a false yet interesting way, by misconstruing public events, imbue millions of people with false political information. In many countries only such interpretations of news as seem good to the ruling class ever reach the common people. Furthermore, the news is gathered from the far corners of the earth by a few agencies under direct central control. Reporters naturally furnish such stories as will find ready printing by the agencies they represent. This unforeseen result of a changed world has put the power of the voting masses into the hands of men who in most cases have been unable to resist using them for their selfish interests. Even the latest organ of general information, the radio, is often controlled by political interests. There are multiplying evidences that such stations as imperil the political future of our most dangerous politicians will find it impossible to continue, while others highly favored will be continued though they start financial panic and bring widespread distress. Thus the forces that were depended on to save democracy can be made the instruments of its destruction.

III. Free Courts, Free Education, Free Religion

As the great supports of free speech and free press, the pioneers of representative government placed free courts, free education, and free religion. The ravaging tooth of special privilege has not yet bitten so deeply into these institutions, but it is attacking them. Here again the attack is concealed under the pretense of friendliness to democracy. The courts have for the most part the deserved confidence of the people. If that confidence fails there will hardly be left the semblance of an organized society. The moral confusion which has fallen upon the Western world through the breakup of institutions and traditions representing moral authority has fallen upon the legal profession likewise. Unfortunately, to put on the juristic robe is not to endow with new moral attitudes or juster opinions. The resulting confusion is seen here and there in judicial decisions which justify inequity upon legal technicalities and apparently have not the moral stamina to press through these to equitable decision. In the name of democracy the election of judges has been turned over to the people, with the result that if the jurist withstands the bribery of the few, he may yet fall before the misinformation and prejudice of the many. In spite of all our legal forms, trial by misinformed public opinion becomes more and more common. Further, the prohibitive cost of court redress has closed in many cases, the avenues of appeal. Free education has likewise been attacked. The Scopes trial in Tennessee which had for its object the prevention of the teaching of evolution, while it attracted world-wide attention, is not by any means the most flagrant case of attempted interference with free education. Even evolution can be taught with a narrowness of opinion and belligerence of design which deprive it of all claim to being scientific. There is much difference between teaching it as the most reasonable scientific hypothesis and driving it, with dogmatic insistence, down the throat as the demonstrated fact of a wholly mechanistic universe what is at best only theory. Possibly the reason for revolt lay more in the use of scientific dogma as a weapon against religion, than against the dissemination of ascertained fact. If one were compelled to choose between the fundamentalistic dogmatists and the scientific dogmatists one might be at a loss where to take his stand.

The most serious invasion of education lies possibly in the manipulation of courses, the waste of time in matters extraneous to education, the endeavor to demoralize and despiritualize the machinelike product of mass education, the compulsions which silence individual expression and repress genius into the given molds of tests, which seem desirable only to the overcredulous educational doctrinaire. Free education will sometime be judged less by those who survive in spite of it and more by its cast-off products—those upon whom it has failed to take effect.

Upon the subject of free church there is at present great controversy. There is little doubt that with the founders of American democracy free church meant freedom of worship according to any desired form. It also looked to the church for moral and spiritual leadership—that untrammeled by state interference it might train the citizenship in moral idealism. The present generation has witnessed the rise of a new theory in Western political life—that the moral teaching of the church must be rendered subservient to national policies. This idea is so repugnant to all the principles upon which Western civilization has been founded that it cannot be considered as more than a reactionary movement which must soon subside. However, it is at present offering serious impediment in many places to the right of free religion.

IV. EXTENSION OF SUFFRAGE

In the long struggle for democracy one of the chief means looked to for betterment of conditions has been the extension of suffrage. Begun as a gift to the few, limited by heredity, or wealth, or caste, or sex, the suffrage has only in our own time and in some countries approached a universal character. It was presumed that the ills of democracy might be cured by more democracy. Each extension has been bitterly opposed, winning its way only gradually. It has been presumed that the new bloc of voters would vote their own interests en masse. Behind the whole suffrage movement has been the philosophy that voters could be relied upon to protect their own rights.

The result has been disappointing, for it has been found that the electorate cannot always be aroused to express itself. Furthermore, such expression is frequently motivated by a venal press, which distills misinformation in the interests of action whose real aim is a personal selfishness which is carefully concealed. Even direct legislation, presumed to be the last word in democracy, has shown itself capable of grave misuse by designing politicians. Referenda are so written that their real object is contrary to their seeming import, and they are attended by other referenda which add to the confusion, or they are written in such a way as to deny the voter an unequivocal choice. He is by indirection kept from any choice save the one laid down for him by the predatory interests, and must choose between two evils which he considers the less or the worse. Knowing this in advance, he is discouraged from voting at all, and an apparent majority is had for a measure that is really carried by a negligible minority of all electors. This becomes the particular weapon of evil and antisocial interests, since they are ever ready to employ means that the friends of society would disdain. This method of indirection has been recently illustrated in the handling of the repeal of the Eighteenth Amendment in the United States.

One by one we have in a time of great social change seen fall the trusted supports of democracy before the onslaughts of the avaricious enemies of the common good. The battle is pressed to the wall. No wonder that many have lost heart and are appealing for dictators to pull them out of the political morass of misgovernment, in which every man's hand is against all others, and every man seeks some special privilege. The movement parallels in many ways the struggle of the robber barons, who, taking advantage of some exclusive possession, and growing in wealth and power, became stronger than the king himself. At the present time the appropriation of such power comes only to those who are strong enough to control the ordinary means of information such as newspapers, radios, and cinemas, for without true and accurate information democracy becomes impossible. The pioneering fathers of liberty never dreamed of the possibility of such wide influence falling into individual human hands. It would seem that with universal suffrage an accomplished fact, the battle for freedom is all to fight over again. As it is so in every age, for still "eternal vigilance is the price of liberty."

CHAPTER XIII

EDUCATING EDUCATION

. . . .

THE WESTERN WORLD has for a long time been under the dominance of the educational philosophy of Rousseau. While this is the case throughout the Occident, it has been particularly emphasized and developed in America. The theory is consistent with the philosophical individualism out of which it arose, and, perhaps more clearly than any other development, indicates the underlying principle of Western progress. It began as a protest against methods of education which left no initiative to the child either as to what he should learn or how. He became the parrot-like receptacle of instruction. Information had been handed down upon authority, and there was no room for questioning and no pretense at intellectual liberty. As action is followed by reaction, it is quite probable that we are now at the extreme of the arc away from the old type of education. It is quite probable, too, that this extreme position cannot be permanently retained. In the revolt from authority the child has been conceived as by nature the possessor of faculties that are themselves to be drawn out by rational exercise, rather than containers to be filled with facts. Furthermore, it was the dream of Rousseau that the natural interests and capacities of the child should take a hand in directing its own education. The contact of the French *voyageurs* with the American Indian, and the exaggerated tales they had carried back concerning the idyllic freedom and happiness the Indians enjoyed, did undoubtedly play a part in Rousseau's nature theory. Of even greater importance was the contact of Rousseau's generation with China. The nature theory of education may easily have resulted from the indirect influence of Lao-tse. Formative for Rousseau may have been Diderot's advice that his best chance of winning the Dijon prize was to oppose the common belief that moral achievement was enhanced by the arts and letters. Nature was the kindly mother who would do her own work perfectly if left alone. The mental life of the

121

child should take its own directions, like the growth of the tree, assimilating the sustenance which it naturally acquired. It showed the extreme confidence of the then prevailing intoxication of democracy, but it was a wholesome break from the educational yoke that had bound the centuries.

Meeting with bitter hostility at first, the once despised theory of Rousseau has become the head of the educational corner. It is to be doubted whether any other educationalist ever lived who has wielded a tithe of the influence of this doctrinaire Genevan. There is question whether there has been any real advance in principle from the time of Rousseau's *Émile* to Montessori, or whoever may be the current educational faddist. The "progressive" schools are but the echo of that now distant day. Though there has been little change in theory, there has been much in practice, and we may be permitted to investigate the weaknesses and point out the shortcomings of a system that has arisen to such completeness. To do so will, of course, draw down upon our heads educational anathema from the dogmatists, who will resent all criticism. Nevertheless a little friendly inspection may result in common good. Unfortunately, making education natural has been confused with making it easy. Much of educational effort has gone to waste by presuming that the child could acquire an education unconsciously, or without knowing it. If this means that the driving interest shall be impulsion rather than compulsion, well and good; but if it means a mere dillydallying, a mere playing with knowledge, an intellectual and moral flabbiness is the certain result. There is such a thing as intellectual integrity, and very few cultures can be realized without effort. Any education which overlooks the value of mental discipline is sure to fail. Thus the perversion of education must stand its share of blame for the decline of Western culture.

1. NATURE METHOD, DISCIPLINE, AND SOCIETY

We have already mentioned one of the main weaknesses of Western education—the attempt to make education painless, so painless that there shall be no conscious effort. There is a palpable error in this assumption, however. The physical educationist does not find it expedient in training bodily strength to leave entirely to the pupil the choice of exercises. Under such a system the individual would perpetuate all sorts of physical defects. For he likes to do what is easy to do, and the stronger his dislike of whatever involves effort, the more certain it is that he should be trained in the direction of his dislikes. What is true of corporeal health is equally true of mental health. Left to his own choice from our ever-expanding elective curricula, the student in most cases chooses to train himself to intellectual deformity of some kind. This is not due to innate depravity but rather to ignorance, a lack of experience, and a failure to understand his own needs. The consciousness of need is far less certain to be apprehended in the mental than in the physical realm. The intellectual discipline that the student needs is something about which he knows nothing, which presents no particular appeal to him, and whose benefits he is not prepared to understand. In such a case, to throw away all discipline and direction, to indicate no required courses, is to do an irreparable injury to the mental development of a student, and, in most instances, to shut out future prospects of ever achieving it. As a matter of fact, many of our men now eminent in special lines of learning were directed into their elementary investigations against their inclinations. Their later enthusiasm became intense in the very proportion of their early disinclinations, as they were captured by the unfolding truth and beauty in a discipline which they presumed at first had nothing worthy of their effort.

The unfortunate effect of all this has been to push ahead the period in which final commitments toward special intellectual interests were made into the period of adolescence, when the individual is quite unprepared to judge what his special interest should be. An admired and favorite teacher, an early facility, which would not command the enduring respect of adulthood—these have been most often the incidents determining the future career. No wonder that later life has in so many cases brought disillusionment and life-weariness. The whole tendency has been signalized by the schools in offering pre-professional training and giving in the secondary schools a miserable smattering, without a real background of culture, that only led the graduate to despise the profession about which he knew nothing except the shallowest technique; or, in proportion to his ignorance, to assume himself the master of a profession. The tragedy lies in the after years, when a student so trained is incapable of rising in his profession and lapses into bitterness against society, not realizing the sources of his own weakness.

The general effect of this lack of discipline and this absence of foundation culture is baneful to society. Already mentioned is the effect upon the individual of this trashy and speedy type of education, which turns out the ill-prepared with a diploma, and "a swelled head," as being certain they are completely educated; but the result in society is even worse. The general feeling is created of free and easy living—that the rewards of life can come by bluff and trickery; and the whole basis of success is shifted in the minds of the common people to the money basis. There being no discipline in such education, we acquire a growing body of citizens who are taught to resent discipline in society even as they were able successfully to avoid it in the school. They believe in success without work, governmental protection and support without obligation, and individual desires without social restraint. The present disintegration of Western society must in large measure be traced to the theories and practices of our present educational system.

II. THE HODGEPODGE OF MODERN CURRICULA

The net result of the present tendency toward free election of studies has been the multiplication of courses without corresponding content on one hand, and on the other a complete confusion in the student's mind as to the relative importance of the courses offered. Any course which promises "units" seems to the unwary as important as any other offering a similar number of units. If, in addition, he learns that a certain course is easy and will obtain high grades, thus making possible the achievement of honors or membership in scholarship societies without too much draft on mentality or the curtailment of the social or athletic schedule, the case is already settled in many student minds. The outmoded system of "required courses" which put all the educational grist through the same hopper had at least this that could be said for it: everyone willy-nilly got a taste of a fundamental culture. Much outcry was raised against history, philosophy, Greek, and Latin, but most of the students at least learned what an education *might* mean. Under the present practice they do not often get even that. Attention was recently called to a high school student who earned a portion of her "units" toward a diploma by a course in manicuring. The worst consequence of all is in the turning aside from education of numbers of our young people who, with a different under-standing of the meaning of education, could become more valu-able members of society.

Every year many young people enter the universities in the expectation that a college course will be merely a continuance of what they have had in high school—which it too often turns out to be, because they come so poorly prepared for any serious work that many of them can get through only by choosing "snap" courses. The college kindly caters to the situation by a system of free or nearly free electives, or according to a newer mode does away with freedom of electives in order to force youthful minds into channels of so-called "practical" education. The method makes it possible for a student to acquire athletic ability, social standing, self-assurance, and a life of self-satisfaction, without having at any time been within speaking distance of an edu-cation.

III. The Oversight of Moral Education

The most serious defect in Western education must, however, be placed on the moral side. The lack of moral education has grown out of conditions that have arisen with the growth of our cities, the suburbanization of the country districts, and the influx of foreign population alien to the earlier American spirit. Com-ing from lands in which education has been principally in the hands of the church, and where the public school has not the status and development known here, these populations have well-nigh driven out the teaching of morals in the fear their children may absorb some religious views not quite in keeping with the views of the hereditary sect. The result has been not only toward breaking the bond with the given churches, but to make the whole matter of religion and morals seem hostile to learning. When this view is participated in by the teacher, the alienation is often complete. The absence of ethical training from the school or its relegation to odd times and places makes it seem to the child a matter of minor importance. The public school used to be the great moral bulwark of the democracy, but can scarcely be called so any longer. Nor is the device of religious training out of school hours more than a weak makeshift. The mind is not a compartment affair, and to separate religion and morals from the common processes of education is to make them seem something less important and less authoritative than the school curriculum. Nothing can bridge this fatal gap in a child's education but the combining of the moral with the mental discipline. All the churches and all right-minded people have enough in common without infringing on special faiths and creeds to give this fundamental training in the public schools and leave the children still enthusiastic for the hereditary faith. But the policy of mutual jealousy between faiths is driving the youth from all religious, and even moral, loyalties.

Not all of the results can be laid at the door of the school. Much of the fault lies in the selfishness of conflicting faiths; even more, in the indifference of the home to moral and religious training. Where parents indulge in questionable business practice, excusing the less than honest with success of business or social achievement, not all the schools that ever existed could overcome that deeper training in immorality, which is absorbed from birth in many of our "best" homes.

The tendency is further abetted by the educational theory that the child must never be thwarted in any scheme. The Montessori-trained child is for the most part impossible, because he is taught to consider his own designs as supreme. We are so fearful of thwarting some budding genius that the child is not learning that he has an obligation to society quite as profound as any obligation for self-expression. The weakness of the whole Rousseauan theory lies in the assumption that "whatever is in him" ought to find expression regardless. There are many things "in us" that are not worth expression, and some few that are worse than that. The citizen of a civilized community is constantly called upon to practice self-restraint. In fact, there can never be power in self-expression until there is restraint in expression. A recent illustration has been called to attention. When asked if a certain child had ever been made acquainted with any of the great poetry of our literature, the answer was: "Oh no! Clarabelle is encouraged to read her own little poems to us." No wonder an unfeeling pupil of the other sex characterized poetry as "rot." We may foolishly dream we are bringing up a race of artists, geniuses, and inventors by teaching the immediate expression of whims and idiosyncracies, but artists, geniuses, and inventors are never the result of such methods. Our modern trained children are, some of them, too much like Lincoln's Mississippi steamboat, whose engine stopped whenever the whistle was blown. The moral delinquency and antisocial habits which naturally follow such a course should be obvious to everybody, and have not a little to do with the present lack of restraint in morals and in social and political life.

IV. THE DEBACLE OF UNIVERSAL EDUCATION

It must be freely admitted that the debacle of the noble dream of universal education is one of the most disconcerting factors in any view of the present situation. A system designed to give opportunity for the fullest individual self-expression has become, in the judgment of many, a machine which deftly subdues individuality and because of the mechanization of our school procedure reduces many to the dead level of mediocrity. This drift has taken place at the very moment that professional educators have tried to foster individualism by the multiplication of elective courses and the introduction of manual arts. Before this confusing array of good things the youthful student stands in utter perplexity. Instead of being encouraged to provide himself with a body of sound learning which would be a secure basis from which to build any special field of activity, he is incited to specialize. Thus he comes through the schools with many courses to his credit but with little fundamental education. Like a child exercising free will at a feast, he goes for the desserts with frosting, first, and so has no room left for the fundamentals of diet. Many of our graduates suffer from a sort of intellectual stomachache. In the meantime, an increasing number of Doctors of Philosophy cannot spell nor write with cultured consistency, others are totally innocent of the history of the race, still others will never be able to read a book in any other language than their own. That there are mental concepts which lie at the base of the present state of scientific achievement would be news to many of them. Teachers are actually going into the schools unprepared for the subjects to which they are assigned because the greater portion of their effort has been required for official courses in pedagogy, that could easily have been mastered in one-fourth the time demanded. To such a state we have been reduced by professionalism and the blind following of untempered educational theories, against which no one would any more dare to rail out than to tamper with the sacred cow. While professing to foster individualism we have erected a "free" system developed, as we think, along scientific lines which is nearly as bad as the old tyranny because while requiring so much in the pursuit of educational fads, it eventually leaves the student without the fundamentals of a truly cultured life. Who will essay to educate education?

CHAPTER XIV

THE FRANKENSTEIN OF RELIGIOUS FREEDOM

....

As THE PHILOSOPHY of Plato, prevalent in the early Christian Church, established the certainty of universals, and with it the authority of the universal Church, depository of absolute truth, so Aristotelianism, with its doctrine that only the particular and the concrete is real, could but have the result of disintegrating the seamless fabric of authority. This development of individualism has been a long process. Its early outcome was the formation within the Roman communion of the various brotherhoods or orders. It was as much individualism as was allowable within the pale of supreme authority. But the strife between Dominican and Franciscan prepared the way for the greater break which came with the Protestant Reformation. Protestantism itself, however, could not easily find common ground of action and belief, and, as soon as the pressure of common peril was relieved, began to break up into ever more and more organizations.

There seemed no limit to the divisive positions that could be taken. The contest hinged largely upon the question of the seat of authority in religion. Was it from above, or outside, or from within? Protestantism answered with true Aristotelianism that it was from within, and rejected the authority of the papacy. But the break was too great for people behind whom were centuries of respect for external authority. Protestantism, untrue to its primal principle, dared not trust the inner authority, and so set up an external one of its own, a certain portion of the Jewish and Christian Scriptures. That the spirit of individualism should eventually question this substitute for papal authority was inevitable. As democracy has never yet dared to be true to its fundamental principles, so Protestantism has by credo, confession, and rite attempted to protect the individual against the issue of his own judgment.

It was the task of biblical scholarship, the so-called Higher

129

Criticism, to break the yoke of this new compulsion. There is confusion today in many minds, but out of it is emerging the consciousness that religious constraints must come from within, must flow out of individual judgments. The result is the disparagement of the old divisive interpretations, a demand for new and natural alignments not of creeds but of world service. If every man is to be protected in his individual beliefs, then his co-operation with others must be on some broader lines than mental or creedal assents.

This movement causes great distress to many devout and intelligent minds. Much of the old seems going by the boards with dizzying swiftness, and it is not evident what is to come in to take its place. Again we are frightened at the principles which we have evoked. Can Christianity save itself, or is it one of those phases of thought arising only to be outgrown by the march of the centuries? Christians have quite generally come to the conviction that energies hitherto spent in fighting each other over creedal differences have been energies misspent. Is there anything else to fight that is worth while?

I. The Modern Attack upon Authority

The roots of the Protestant Reformation were laid far back in the history of the Christian Church. They represent a movement at least as old as the *Glosses* of Porphyry on the *Predicamenta* of Aristotle. They could not be smothered, because they were really indigenous to the spirit of the Gospel itself. These expressions of individualism as opposed to authority of an external nature formed the undertone of medieval life, were carried into it by Boëthius' revival of Porphyry and of Aristotle, and brought to the surface in nominalism and the work of the early Franciscans. Had the political situation of the church been less involved, and had the Franciscans officially won the famous controversy over Universals, it is safe to say there would have been no Protestant Reformation. Possibly there would have been no divided church, though it is not probable, since individualism is in its nature divisive.

The general essence of the nominalistic movement was rightly interpreted by the ecclesiastical leaders as hostile to external authority. Even the Franciscan system began with the exaltation of individual experience, the possibility of direct communication with God through the mystic experience of ecstasy, dream, and vision. There was no need for an intermediary of an official kind, but such communication was the right and possibility of the individual soul. And this was the great bulwark of Reformation doctrine until at least a portion of it proved untrue to its own principles of protest and hardened down into the external authority of scriptural legalism, and even resumed the once discarded institutionalism. The reaction of Roman Christianity was to move from the authority of church councils to that of the Pope. In either case the sad confession must be made that Christianity has never yet been tried except by individuals. But free ideas, once liberated, cannot be got back to the old confines. This spirit of free inquiry and of the right of individual judgment of religious truth cannot be stopped at any point convenient for any of the institutionalized forms of religion that make creedal belief or authority the basis of their organization. Wherever mysticism is encouraged, or where it exists, there is always a point of danger to set forms.

Just as the reformers attacked the authority which had gathered about the claims of the papacy, it was inevitable that their own claims of verbal inspiration and infallibility for the Protestant portion of the Scriptures should eventually be attacked in the name of truth and of free inquiry. It is only as she has been untrue to her basic Protestant principles that a portion of the church has presented hostility to such inquiry. What is known as the Higher Criticism was due to come to free the minds of men from an authority which was being interpreted in a way to prevent the right of individual judgment. The evil in the situation has been that such investigation was ever opposed; for while it did undermine the authority of unwarranted dogma, it reopened the Scriptures to new understanding and, if encouraged, would have led to a great popular revival of interest in the Bible and in religion. Opposed, those churches which chose to stand by external authority and tradition now find themselves discredited among the intelligent classes of the community. Their real mission to the community is imperiled, and the essential truth which they still represent has been discounted by their opposition to the Protestant principle of free inquiry and private judgment.

In the meantime, while the right of untrammeled investigation has so many times been institutionally denied by the church, another authority has been growing up which has made the free pursuit of knowledge its basic dogma. This authority is that of science. There is no reason why moral and spiritual progress should not have kept pace with scientific progress, but for this innate conservatism which exalts religious dogma above religious fact. Science took over the Protestant right of individual judgment, and now proceeds to claim final authority for herself in a bold, dogmatic way reminiscent of the days of ecclesiastical power. In many places, in an attempt to stem the tide, the church has herself, in an effort to share the profits of scientific popularity, given hostages to the mathematical method of science, thus not only abrogating the prestige of her ancient dogmas but likewise surrendering the warrant of the moral and spiritual voices of the inner spirit of man.

The former authority she could bravely lose, but not the latter. Thus it can be seen that the church is now threatened by that very spirit of inquiry which she once invoked on the pathway to freedom. She now finds the type of authority which she preached and upon which she had depended for her moral mandates, falling on deaf and incredulous ears, because she has been untrue to her own basic principles.

II. The Decline of Sacerdotalism

One effect of the dominance of scientific research has been the decline of sacerdotalism. Revolting from a widespread belief in the magical and the mystical, the populace have arrived at a complete distrust of all things which bear those marks. While their incredulity regarding the mysteries of religion has been growing, it has been marked by a preposterous credulity regarding all predictions that are tabbed with the name of science. Some scientific notoriety seeker has but to announce through the press that he has been able, expects to be able, or will be able to raise the dead, and the happy word is passed among the multitudes that science has already achieved a resurrection. The existence of countless fakes and false alarms and cheating promises in no wise seems to dull the faith of the multitudes. Exploited in every paper that falls from our presses, they continue to believe the impossible, with all the dogmatic certainty with which the medieval throngs believed the miracles of the saints, or in the physical apparition of the dead.

It is not strange under such circumstances that sacerdotalism is lost on the multitude, nor that it is resorted to by the panicky few who are frightened at or see the hollowness for religion in this new credulity and flee for refuge to the older.

Thus the Christian world finds itself torn between belief and disbelief, shorn of its long dependable authority, afraid to strike out boldly with an appeal to that authoritative judgment which lurks in the soul of every man, distrusting "the light that lighteth every man that cometh into the world."

III. THE TRANSITION TO SOCIAL SALVATION

The shift from Platonic to Aristotelian philosophy brought about a distinct change of emphasis upon the meaning and place of salvation. So long as the individual was conceived as existing only for the institution, the institution was forever settled, and it only behooved him to adjust himself to it. Individual salvation was man's only task. So soon as the Aristotelian dominated, and the *ecclesia* was conceived as made up of and existing for individuals, a process of growth, of institutional and doctrinal advance was indicated. Consequently it was only to be expected that, with the passing of external authority, men could no longer be satisfied with a concept of salvation purely personal. The social redemption of society became the importunate demand. Not that the salvation of society had not hitherto been dreamed of, but it was dreamed of differently. Instead of the adaptation of all men to the power and creed of the church, salvation was conceived as the reformation of all society, the removal of social wrong, the advance to higher planes of physical living, the universalizing of education. There was a new sense of individual responsibility for the world order. The institution was not something imposed by divine right; it was something which individuals were building up and were under obligations to make better. The individual himself was responsible for the social fabric under which he lived.

It cannot be denied that the introduction of such a principle in a widespread way was diverting and divisive. Its presence in the Western world has been much deplored by those who would like to see one undivided religious, social, and political authority. But its chances for real progress are in proportion to the number and untrammeled freedom of its leaders. One of the most frequent charges against Protestantism has been against its immediate breaking up into "sects," but this was one of the supreme evidences of life and the result of the introduction of the new principle. It is true that the early impulse lost itself in the emphasis on nonessential and unimportant articles of theological belief. Breaking from external authority, the early reformers wasted too much effort in bolstering up a new authority. Some, indeed, caught no social vision at all, and it has remained almost to our own day to find institutional religion concerned with social welfare. At present this is the revolution through which Protestantism is passing and through which the Greek and Roman communions will eventually pass in spite of all boasts of changelessness. Indeed, the Roman communion is not outclassed by any in the number and effectiveness of its social services.

The changing emphasis is, however, undermining the old appeal of the church as a refuge from an individual damnation. It is shifting the problem from the life after death and is placing it in this present world and condition. The church faces social obligation as it has never appeared before, and the question is whether she has living power to rise up and meet it. She is tempted on the one hand to seek retreat in the refuge of fundamentalism, with a weakening grasp upon the minds and consciences of men. On the other hand, she will hear the alluring voices of a social order which conceives the welfare of men solely in terms of material prosperity. If she succumbs to the first temptation, she will lose her power over the minds of men. If to the second, she will abdicate her spiritual leadership. Just now organized religion is in the dilemma of having forsaken the one point and of not having yet fully adjusted herself to the social vision. In the meantime her enemies hasten to proclaim her aridity and defeat.

IV. The Repercussion of the Missionary Movement

Nowhere has the transition from the individual to the social standpoint been more marked than in its effect upon the missionary movement. Christian missions sprang out of a profound conviction of the efficacy of personal acceptance of religious dogma. They summoned to the crusade the most intense religious convictions, combined with a spirit of the most absolute altruism and self-sacrifice. Such a spirit could not go unrewarded even under social, religious, and political conditions the most impervious to change. It seems quite the popular pastime to cast aspersion upon the missionary effort and to view its results as negligible. Its direct result has been the modernization of the Orient, and making it a part of the civilization of the West. However narrowly conceived it may have been at particular times and places, it has nevertheless interpreted the highest and most ideal achievement of Western life to the East. To Christian missionaries is mostly due the present enlightened participation of China in world affairs.

No sooner was the missionary on the ground, than he began the modification of his own narrower outlook. He found a reception for his message through hospital and school that no amount of preaching could give him. The broader his own intellectual sympathies, the more was borne in to him the lurking excellencies and beneficent truths of other faiths and cultures.

In the *Layman's Missionary Report of 1932* we have the open acknowledgment of the revolution of practice that has taken place in the missionary enterprise. So vast a change demands a complete practical readjustment to the whole problem. Meanwhile the transition from old to new has sorely cut down missionary support and is putting the Christian enterprise in the Orient upon its own feet and upon its responsibility. It will reach the zenith of influence only when it is fully taken over, organized, directed and supported by its native converts.

Not the least result of the nineteenth century crusade for missions has, however, been at home. Just as in the Middle Ages the Crusades wrought a new respect for the Moslems and an avidity for their learning, this last crusade has come to modify the whole Protestant position regarding its own in relation to other faiths. Not only so, the missionary movement has been one of the determining factors in the new conception of the social responsibility of religion. At the present, many minds wander in darkness between the new and the old, and find no resting place. The doubt which first assailed the missionary enterprise has crossed the Oriental sea to abide at home. Men, East and West, view the situation with white-faced perplexity, praying for the salvation which must eventually come from within.

v. The Effect of Religious Relativity

The refinement of astronomical instruments, and the improved mathematical technique of the twentieth century disclosed to the scientific world the necessity of choosing a plane of reference for each of its calculations, out of a multitude of possibilities. Time and space, which had been conceived as absolute, were seen to be the relations under which we attempt the correlation and mastery of a world of relations. In a somewhat similar way the old religious world, with absolute truths, absolute ethics, absolute dogmas, and absolute authorities has vanished, with some noise and with great heat.

The result has been one of pronounced confusion among all the literalists. Absolute commandments must be replaced by individual and specific ethical judgments in given cases, and the task and responsibility seem too much for many people. The intellectually and morally lazy prefer written rules to individual moral decisions and personal responsibility. The crisis had been forced by the changed conditions of living, by domestic invention and socal innovations which, within a century, have been greater than in all the centuries that have preceded. The effect has been to compel individual judgments, since only the most general principles rather than specific rules could give guidance in such an hour of confusion. We have suddenly been pushed from a more or less static moral world into one full of activity and confusion. Moreover, this world has grown so small in space and time that deeds ethical enough in a sparsely inhabited world become unethical in a crowded society as they impinge upon the rights, needs, and welfare of others. A type of ethical action once considered legitimate is now shown to be unethical.

The resulting confusion is displayed on the side of faint-hearted religionists by a clamor that all religion, all sense of ethical and moral values, is being lost, and that nothing looms before the world more certain than perdition. That portion of society on the other side which welcomes looseness of morals joyfully proclaims that all moral and ethical values have vanished and that it is the business of each individual to live only according to the heart's desire. Much scorn is cast upon the reformers who still nurse a lingering sense of social responsibility.

There is an appeal that might be made on the basis of scientific fact, namely, the law of atrophy of unused powers; the self-destructive character of all evil, violence, and wrong; the cooperative assistance of world forces toward all earthly efforts which make for life and improvement. But half the religious community chooses more loudly to cry its outworn authority, and the other half is so insistent on popularity that it comes near joining the common disdain for the eternal principles of righteousness. The age has become one of both religious and moral confusion, because of the absence of deep convictions.

CHAPTER XV

SCIENTIFIC INDIVIDUALISM AND RELATIVITY

. . . .

W E HAVE SEEN how the progress of Western culture has so far hinged about the theory of the individual in his relation to society. The progress of our science has been molded to the same form. The inductive method in science is as individualistic as any other of the applications we have been discovering. Universal laws are built up by the observation of concrete facts. Under the general movement of thought it was inevitable that science should take the way of mathematics, the point-to-point correspondence, the advance by quantitative measurement. The device has served us well, for it has laid at our feet vast new worlds where our ancestors "moved about in worlds unrealized."

We have been living in the very heyday and apparent youth of science. The voices of its prophets still re-echo among the promontories, predicting that science shall bring the perfect day, the perfect condition, the perfect emancipation of man. But already the tang of frost is in the air. There is even now a sense of disillusionment. As Spengler has declared, our scientific conclusions even as our religious beliefs depend at last upon an inner certitude.[1]

Spengler goes on to show that the scientific claim to free itself from the personal, the anthropomorphic standpoint is only self-deception.

We can never achieve an absolute truth, free from and independent of our human outlooks. This is quite as true of science as it is of religion. If the religionist can be accused of making a God in his own image it is no less true that the scientist constructs an external world after the patterns and concepts of his own mind, whatever the reputed basis in fact.[2]

Of our endeavor to reduce all social and personal experience to quantitative and mathematical expression, by statistics, he

[1] *Decline of the West*, Vol. I, p. 381.
[2] *Ibid.*, p. 381.

declares that we end by finding that "the object of understanding is ourselves."

The actual result achieved is a sort of grammar of scientific interpretation by which the human mind hopes to seize the realities of nature. But this proves to be but the fabric woven from our own inner understandings and is at last the revelation of man himself. The less of anthropomorphism science may claim to possess, the more anthropomorphic it really is.[3]

I. THE QUANTITATIVE CHARACTER OF MODERN SCIENCE

The main genius of present-day science lies in its use of numbers, and would have been impossible but for the modern development of mathematics. The method depends upon the discovery or assignment of a quantitative measurement or unit in a given field of research. It then becomes possible to compare mass with mass, and to extract quantitative facts. Obviously this is an appropriate method to use in the quantitative sciences, though in some of these there are sharp limits to the conclusions that can be drawn. The facts of chemistry, for instance, have to do primarily with quantities and the possible relations that exist between quantitative differences and qualitative changes. Yet the analogy and the information are not complete, since there is also the unexplained fact of isomerism,[4] where the quantities are identical and the qualities differ. The numerical or quantitative method is also the main dependence in physics and astronomy, and gives results that are accurate and certain for the numerical or quantitative facts.

The difficulty with the mathematical method of science is that there are facts which escape quantitative measurement. For too long it has been the practice of science to ignore the existence of such facts. No special harm is done, however, until we approach the pseudo sciences which try to apply quantitative measures to facts that are not chiefly quantitative or even not at all quantitative. Such examples are readily found in the so-called sciences of psychology, sociology, anthropology, and some portions of economics, not to mention others. In general, these are the sciences which attempt to apply the method of number in a

[3] *Ibid.*, p. 427
[4] The logical inconsistency remains under the projected solution of isotopism, though we seem close to the secret of the vexing problem, in the recent discovery of "heavy water."

mechanical way to relations into which either chance or personal volition enter. At best sciences so complicated can give nothing more than an approximation of probability based upon observation of an exhaustive number of cases, and as such it has a very great value. It cannot, always, predict the result in any individual case, and for that reason falls short of exactness. This applies to all sorts of vital statistics which furnish valuable working approximations but which can never be accurate.[5]

Even in such cases no difficulty would be encountered were not the scientific claim set up to bolster what is no more than dogmatic opinion. Every newspaper bears daily the ludicrous vaporings of pseudo scientists who make claims of epoch-changing discoveries based frequently on personal whims, enthusiasms, interests, or, in some cases, no more than desire for personal publicity. These claims are swallowed by a credulous public as the latest scientific advance. Frequently in the attempt to create numerical or quantitative analogies, one to one correspondences, the essential facts are overlooked. The first of these is the qualitative character of the given fact, the second is that the quantitative correspondences are *not explanatory*.

For instance, in the first case, social surveys are made to determine the housing conditions of a crowded city. Certain assumptions have previously been made regarding the social results of absence of bathrooms, toilets, separate sleeping apartments, and other details. Then the statistics are used to draw conclusions regarding the morals of the section involved, and to throw moral discredit even upon individual families within the area. The facts depend upon the generalization and are true of the generalization only, and when proved by specific cases. People may and do keep their moral integrity in many, if not most, cases in spite of temptation to the contrary. Most statistics of this kind, applied to our pioneer ancestors and even to the Pilgrim Fathers, would prove early American society a hotbed of social delinquency—as no doubt it was, in spots. The factor overlooked in such cases is that morals and religion are maintained by individuals and by families in spite of adverse conditions. At the most it can only be affirmed that crowded conditions favor moral laxity—but the same might be said of abnormal sparsity of population. The misleading character of such statistics appears

---

[5] Heisenberg's discovery of the Principle of Uncertainty indicates only approximation *on a large scale* to the predictable activity of a single atom.

when we try to reverse them and argue from the presence of bath-tubs and luxury a pure and superior moral character. The fact is, we are trying to give fictitious numerical value to non-quantitative facts.

But there is a still further weakness. In every instance the numerical judgment set up is no stronger nor better than the frequently prejudiced and faulty judgment that sets it up. A good illustration of this is the attempt to reduce to scale the results of psychological or mental tests. As approximations they have value, but they are wanting the accuracy which seems to be given by numbers and decimal points. Any wide-awake instructor, a part of whose task has been to grade examination papers, must have been impressed with the futility of his 90's, 80's, and 70's, or his A's, B's, and C's, as a real gauge to the ability of his pupils. In general the system provides a valuable though variable judgment, and no one has seemed to discover a way that is better. But the individual instructor, if he have any sense of humor at all, must frequently realize the faultiness of his own findings when he is overpowered by sleep, or boredom, or a long succession of poor papers followed by a good one. Not only so, but personal predilections enter into that evaluation involving his own views, mental outlook, social and religious training, which may unconsciously pervert just judgment. Even a group may in general have their conclusions warped by class views or educational enthusiasms, or the objectives they have in mind. Once these estimates, however, are reduced to scale and assigned to their percentiles, they have all the convincing falsity of the ancient proverb that "figures never lie." The fact is that figures are no more than symbols of oft-erring appraisals and never tell the essential truth.

A great deal of this factitious science passes as coin of the realm and has hardened into dogmatic forms for which its protégés will fight in unconscious ignorance with all the ardor of a holy war. We are sorely in need in many places of logical and philosophical criticism, but woe to the scientific popularity of the man whose fortitude proclaims it.

II. THE ANTHROPOMORPHISM OF SCIENCE

Most of the misleading tendencies in latter-day science may be traced to oversight of the part that individual judgment plays in conclusions from scientific fact. One of the supreme charges which the mechanistic scientist has hurled against religion has been the, to him, dreadful anthropomorphism which has characterized the concept of God. Religion is accused of conceiving God in man's own image. Since the days of Xenophanes this has been considered a fatal thrust at religion, and it survives in modern literature with all its pristine self-assurance. The one notable exception to this anthropomorphizing tendency of the human mind has popularly supposed to have been science. Here it is presumed that we come down to the solid basis of fact without human imagination or human interpretation, facts which no individual judgment can warp.

Let us inquire to what extent this judgment may be true respecting scientific claims. It will probably be admitted that there is no field freer from anthropomorphic tendencies than that of astronomy. Here we have instruments of the most delicate accuracy, yet designed by the hand and mind of man. Still we dare not trust the single reading of the moment at which a stellar body touches the fine line across the transit instrument. Why? Because of the personal equation. Into the event which the astronomer observes enters inevitably his enthusiasm or his scientific caution; hence several observers are needed to verify the fact. But most scientific observations lack the simplicity of the transit of a star across the telescope, and many of them are loaded down with personal viewpoints, prejudices, faiths, theories, which mock professions of the white light of unprejudiced fact in many cases. It is exactly the anthropomorphism of modern science which gives rise to the extravagant magazine and newspaper claims with which investigators rush into print. The situation is even worse than that. The scientific graveyard is full of headstones which mark the sepulture of generally accepted theories which at one time ruled with unquestioned acceptance. The chief task of the science of the past twenty-five years has been to get some of these scientific "brass tacks" decently buried, such as the "ether," "continuous energy," "material atoms," "absolute space and time," and many others besides. Such situations arise in the progress of science not because the facts of the natural world change but because the anthropomorphizing tendencies in all human judgments can only gradually be amended. To be sure, certain of the sciences are more prone than others to drop into this tendency. Pure mathematics is perhaps least tempted, since the purer it is the less meaning it has beyond one of simple relation of nothing to nothing, a logic of undefined units whose conclusions are true provided the premises are true. The very moment meaning is attached to its units and their relations, "pure" mathematics becomes anthropomorphic and begins "seein' things." The most susceptible science is modern psychology, which, under the title of animal psychology, has written all the reactions of human organism, mind, and spirit, into its interpretation of animal actions, where obviously they have no place, being merely the psychology of the observer and not of the observed. The gap between human and animal psychology is made by the presence of reflective consciousness in the one case, and its absence in the other.

III. SCIENCE AND THE EMANCIPATION OF MAN

That is an affecting moment in the Gospels when the men of Emmaus recount to their strange companion the story of their broken hopes, closing with the words, "and we trusted it had been he which should have restored again the Kingdom to Israel." Somewhat similar to that has been the disillusionment of the Western world respecting the gifts and powers of science for social amelioration. For at least a half century the world has been looking to science for the control of disease, for the wiping out of hard conditions of labor, and the ending of industrial slavery, for the bringing of well-being and leisure to all classes of society, for the spread of happiness and of knowledge. All these benefits have arisen along the horizon of our hopes. They included nothing less than the complete emancipation of man both physically and mentally. Until almost the present moment there has been no thought but that science would fulfil the program. Now great numbers of people are discovering the incapacity of science to perform the task unaided by moral integrity.

As to the first objective, the emancipation of man from unremitting toil, we discover that the ethical and social factors are as important as the physical. Means have been found to multiply the output of a single hand to hundreds, but ways are found by which the extra profits are passed on to the consumer in small measure, to the employer in large measure, to the worker very little. His situation is indeed rendered worse and even more precarious since but one workman is now needed where a hundred were needed before. Moreover, machinery has robbed him of that slight individuality, intelligence, and pride in work which was his under the old non-factory system. He is now only a part of the machine which he feeds. In fact, the machine now commands his intelligence for him, and in many cases a child or a moron could feed the machine quite as readily as himself. There is no longer in his work much scope for individual intelligence, skill, or invention. The product is deprived of that individuality through which artifacts rise to art. The net result is toward denser ignorance and deeper slavery, or, if the spirit in him is not quite submerged, toward social unrest and revolution. In the meantime, absentee bondholders, whose much-watered stock frequently represents several times the amount invested, are inexorable in their demands for profits. The immediate employer finds himself wedged between conflicting interests, his concern for his workmen and the necessity to produce profits. Without earnings he must close his shop. The stockholders are themselves often widows and orphans. Nevertheless it is evident that a social structure has been reared as detrimental to the welfare of the whole as the fortified castles of the robber barons. There is no question but that the system will of necessity be changed, but it can be changed safely only by the renewal of social sympathy. The ideal condition can never come about through the arraying of class against class in industrial war. A social conversion on the part of the "haves" would bring a bloodless revolution that would yield good to all. The danger lies in the avarice and lack of social consciousness on the part of some holders of great possessions.

The failure of science to emancipate the minds of men has already been touched upon. Tending a machine for long hours is deadening to the intellect. A wearied body is not consonant with an acquiring mind. There is little outlet for the human spirit save in such excesses as form a grave danger to society and complete the ruin of the individual.

Thus the modern world stands disillusioned and confused before the system which it has created and seems unable to summon that moral and spiritual power which alone can raise it from the grave of its scientific slavery. It is discovered that science is quite as much the handmaid of slavery and of ignorance as she is presumed to be of freedom and intelligence. Our clever machines threaten to destroy us. It is obvious that we shall have to bow in again the religion we have so lightly bowed out, or, if not that, some type of religion which devotes itself less to the salvation of elect souls than to the reclamation of society.

IV. SCIENCE WITHOUT MORALS

It thus appears that science without morals is the aide and abetter of anarchy. Every one of the more recent great inventions intended for the general benefit has been allowed to become the weapon of the criminal. By the telephone he widens the net of his conspiracy against society, by the automobile and the airplane he makes his getaway and establishes his alibi. The possession of high-powered weapons puts every citizen and even the scanty officers of the law at his mercy. Banditry, robbery, kidnaping, murder, and all sorts of anti-social acts are, through the discoveries of modern science, made easy. What cannot be accomplished by the weapons named can be completed with time bomb and poison gas.

The weapons which society has forged for protection against its enemies it suddenly finds in the possession of its enemies. Unfortunately the use of these weapons does not demand the same intelligence as their invention. The world is put in the position of having armed its moron criminals, both as individuals and as nationals, with power to bring about the collapse of civilization. The frantic invention of new arms, of new means of destruction, the enlargement of fleets and armies, is but piling up the resources of general destruction and making the end more certain and more near. The reason for this is that we have no assurance that our weapons are going to be placed in the hands either of intelligent or of moral people. In fact, the more intelligence without moral character, the more ingenious and complete the forces of destruction. The race for armaments around the world was but the inevitable prelude to the catastrophe which is now upon us. A generation into whose hands were placed the greatest resources for recovery, peace, international understanding, the welfare of all men, irrespective of race, creed, or nation, is the generation which with faster *tempo* achieves its own destruction.

One potent reason for this arises out of our complete confidence that a science devoid of religion or morality should save us from our woes. Even science itself, as commonly received and taught, has done its best again and again to contribute to this result. But the fault belongs on both sides—both the hostility of religious people and the self-sufficiency and moral obtuseness of the scientific have led to this result. Science and morals have been put too often in opposing camps. Science has found itself execrated by the pious—but, on the other hand, has frequently gone out of its field to show hostility to religion. Whose ever the fault, the tragic denouement is upon us. The two disciplines which should be forever allied are in too many cases hostile. Such a condition, so long as it continues, will make impossible the reclamation of mankind.

CHAPTER XVI

THE QUAGMIRE OF PHILOSOPHY

THE POPULAR CONTEMPT for philosophy is commonly
expressed in the old saw about its being the search of a
blind man in a dark cellar for a black cat that is not there; or in
the oft-credited assertion that philosophy, instead of being the
source of history, is rather the alibi that is offered after the events
have taken place. The reason for the deplorable situation is
double—the arrogance that has held sway in the camp of scientific hangers-on, and the foolishness of the philosophers themselves.

When philosophy is true to her tasks, she should furnish
light and leading to society, but seldom has she done this, and
then not in the institution of her official and dominating schools.
These have been as futile for the reform of society as the great
and dominating systems of theology. If one wishes to study the
philosophy which has wrought itself into social fact, he must
nearly always hunt out the subsidiary streams that run under
the surface of thought and that burrow deep within the common mental attitudes. These streams of thought are seldom
dominant or accepted until their vitality is exhausted and the
movement, so far as its influence is concerned, is practically over.
History has afforded repeated illustrations of the power of
rejected doctrines to command popular thought. It is the old story
of the rejected stone becoming the head of the corner. New
ideas, if they are important, have always the characteristic of
being violently disapproved. This is because they threaten change,
and institutions having vested interests are always hostile to
change, fearing any disturbance of the *status quo.*

For this reason the ruling philosophy of a given period is sure
to reflect the dominant interests, while the philosophy which
rules the future will likely be found upon the scaffold rather
than upon the throne. Such was the case with Socrates before
the Stoic movement arose to give him the dominance of a

147

civilization, and such the case when Hobbes more or less represented the official philosophy while Rousseau the despised was
laying down the outlines for modern education. Numerous parallels might be drawn from the whole course of human thought.
The more dominating and official a philosophy in one period,
the less likely is it to appear important in the next. Only inter-
mittently has speculation arisen against the spirit of the age—
and then to the age in question it has seemed unimportant. This
condition is one source of the popular distrust of philosophy.
Nevertheless no age can free itself from its philosophy, since no
age and no man is without a controlling, even though unconscious, ideology which lays down the pattern of his thought and
determines his reactions to society. Such is the basis of the
apparent illusiveness of philosophical theory to the men of the
present or of any given era. Thus it is but natural that the field
of present-day reflection should be justly characterized as a quagmire. It is easy to point out the shortcomings, and, laying finger
here or there, to indicate the lack of logic; but who has the
wisdom to discover the ideology which even now is preparing
to take over the future as its kingdom?

1. The Reign of Materialism

Though not at first recognized, the governing mood in un-
official philosophy since the appearance of Darwin's *Origin of
Species* has been that of mechanistic materialism, or, perhaps
more latterly, naturalism. Beginning as an undercurrent, and
assisted to birth by the whole Enlightenment movement, it has
for the last fifty years dominated thought. Probably no system in
history has so commanded popular attention save only the individualism of Socrates. The source of the infatuated following
may be easily found in the great fertility of the quantitative
theories on which science has gained its triumphs. Not until our
own day has there been any real check upon this movement, any
questioning of its validity, nor will there be in common thinking
for a long time to come unless certain forces now working beneath the surface of our modern life should come to violent and
swift expression. The leaders in scientific thought, the genuine
scientists, are mainly the ones who find themselves puzzled as to
future directions. At the present moment there is no real disturbance of the faith of the common or garden variety of scien-

tist in the efficacy of naturalistic salvation. It seems as easily comprehensible to this era as did the doctrine of Divine Election to another age. The present popular scientific intoxication allows neither for unbelief nor distrust. It is easily assumed that, provided we can arrange the distribution of material goods so that there will be no want—and we should insist on nothing less, in all morality—the whole moral problem will be solved. It is assumed that the progress of invention will give man control over toil, provide his leisure, and assure his happiness. Only one thing is commonly overlooked: neither happiness nor social justice can be secured by the distribution or possession of goods. The unhappiest members of society at the present are not for the most part those that have the least, but those that have the most, or at any rate whose chief care is the acquisition of material possessions. The love for and the hope of gain has not even power to construct a cohesive society, since those who are moved by such motives easily drop into selfish and internecine warfare. Spiritual ideals are the only enduring cement of a well-ordered and just society.

The genius of scientific invention has laid at the feet of the modern world the great gifts of luxury and leisure and has made unnecessary the stalking forces of starvation, disease, and untimely death—and yet so great is its devotion to the false gods of materialism that society lacks the moral power and the spiritual vision to achieve its own deliverance.

II. THE IMPASSE OF IMPERSONALISM

The persistent undertone of scientific philosophy has been a contempt for man. That such has been the case has been the result of a curious reaction against a theology which too conspicuously considered man apart from his social and mundane relations. It was partly due to the imaginative mood of such men as Giordano Bruno, who in early reaction from a narrowed concept of the universe fled to the opposite extreme of infinite worlds and spaces, with man insignificant and negligible in a cosmos conceived chiefly as quantitative. The Brunonian mood still holds us. One can scarcely pick up a general scientific work of the last half century which does not speak of man with contempt, matching him against the vastness of space or the colossal powers of nature. This type of thinking, assuming itself to issue from modesty, proceeds rather from a certain materialistic arrogance that is willing to assume the nothingness of the mental and spiritual, and in order to do so is driven to a mock humility and a denial of its own intelligence. By this method, it lays claim to a higher importance, shocking the galleries, and dominating arguments for which its logic is inadequate.

Wherever this impersonal mood has gone, it has worked havoc with the highest interests of society, and it is everywhere rampant, in philosophy, in education, in politics, in business, in society. Everywhere we witness the worship of the colossal, which triumphs universally over the rights and welfare of individuals like some holy juggernaut. Everywhere we observe the depreciation of man. The practical conclusion we have unconsciously drawn from the verification of the evolutionary theory has been not an insistence upon the higher nature and value of man but upon the extermination of the unfit.

In the realm of psychology a pseudo science has had the effrontery to rid the psychologist of his own field. The popular saying that "psychology first lost its soul, then its mind, and has now lost consciousness" does not tell half the pathetic tale. The final tragedy is that psychology has lost its sense of humor. This has removed from it the power of self-criticism, so that it goes on lugubriously taking itself seriously while it has in actuality, without the frankness of admitting it, reduced itself to a small branch of neural physiology. This abject abdication of its own domain of inquiry could only have occurred in the attempt of psychology to prove itself a science, and a science which believed that all that exists is matter and all that occurs is motion. The social effect of widespread and popular acceptance of a doctrine that has not been received by a considerable portion of the psychological profession has been disastrous to the belief in individual responsibility. It has filled the minds of many with a feeling that there is no freedom and hence no morals—that the so-called instincts are not only natural but mandatory and to be followed without restraint and without sense of moral turpitude.

Not only must what has passed for psychology be held responsible for this antisocial state of affairs, but it has also managed to cast doubt on the reality of knowledge and the power of the mind to reach any tenable convictions. Its mistrust of man has led it into a mistrust of mind, and with it a denial of the norms of value, of freedom, of morals, and of religion. All these, under the claims of scientific procedure, are made to appear as extraneous to reality. The writer is quite aware that these strictures apply primarily to the now discredited system of behaviorism. But this unfortunately has been the type of psychology which has gotten itself written conspicuously into modern theories of education and thus has been widely taken up and taught to the rising generation as scientific fact by teachers who had no powers of critical judgment but only a credulous belief in whatever was taught them as "scientific" and as the "latest discovery."

The impersonalism that has characterized much modern philosophy has led also to a concept of a universe hostile to man and hence to man's highest interests. If it be assumed that the universe is in reality only matter, and that matter is self-grounded rather than the act of an underlying intelligence, the universe is immediately erected into something hostile to the mental and spiritual interests. Mentality and spirituality do not then belong to the cosmic system; man is himself the only good and the only God. He is likewise a forlorn and inexplicable excrescence on the face of nature. The inconsistency is that such a system can in no wise account for the appearance in us of mentality or of spirituality. If it could ever be logical, such a naturalism would proceed to deny its own knowledge, in which case its opponents' faith would be shown as in every way superior to its own knowledge, and quite as true. The attempt to rule out the kingdom of morals and spirituality has too much the character of a special pleading that would have it so in spite of the facts, and to cover its own unwillingness to assume moral responsibility. The upshot of such a system is to prove the unreality not only of the things that naturalism desires to be rid of but also the unreality of all things of worth in practical life. Nature is seen as a machine as terrible as a Frankenstein monster which crushes all our hopes and our nobilities. Professing itself no longer to believe in God, and discarding lightly the old theological concept of the Devil, it proceeds to erect a supreme devil who, as a hostile cosmic force, becomes the sole arbiter of life and death. It conceives a devil that makes the medieval thing of horns and hoofs seem a jocose travesty upon the fact. Denying a hell to come, it insists in the present on an all-embracing hell for the living, from which there is no escape. Any place or state without faith in the reality of the supreme values of love, truth, righteousness and moral integrity becomes the great void, the sea of ice, which is Malebolge, or hell. Any mind living in such unfaith is already damned.

One of the most significant developments in the Western world has been the invasion of religion itself by the thought, mood, and temper of naturalism. Not even religion has been able to stand without shame the easy charge of being unscientific. It overlooks the fact that science cannot absolutely command the whole field of man's interests. And so we have the dreary spectacle of an apologetic religion which dare not even affirm the reality of the great moral and spiritual laws unless it is able to discover some so-called scientific groups for them. Finding a scientific basis means in such a case reduction to quantitative measurement. The evidence most often adduced for the reality and vitality of the church is not the purity of its ethical ideals and achievement, but its statistics of membership and attendance. This demand for the application of the mathematical method to whatever claims to be real has led to the depersonalizing of the cosmos. Even God is held to be incapable of personality because personality is held to be such a contemptible thing in the cosmic order. It is presumed that only the vague, the indefinite, the unrestrained can be either perfect or powerful. Such a religion is but the attempt to extend the quantitative method into the qualitative realm, where it has neither application nor meaning. It is not seen that to remove personality from the Divine Being is to remove the possibility of moral character in him and to do away with the concept of God altogether. Some who are determined desperately to cling to the notion of God and yet claim to be scientific have hastened to affirm a God who is not the Master of his world but whose will is ever blocked from realization.

Here is the last desperate attempt to save scientific face and give hostages for good behavior. A God who becomes the prey of matter, whatever else he may be, is the slave of evil. One arrives at a universe which is hostile to goodness and to intelligence. Everywhere the reign of the mathematical method has shown its incapacity to deal with or explain life, vitality, or movement. It has set the hand of death upon all it has touched, reducing all to the static and the dead in order to analyze it and bring it within the range of scientific understanding. This is legitimate enough when accepted as a method or even an hypothesis if its purely provisional character is recognized. The effect upon religion of the reduction to scientific explanation has not been essentially different from that in other realms of inquiry.

III. THE RISE OF PRAGMATIC RELATIVISM

So complete has been the subservience to the impersonal and quantitative method that for a time it looked as if philosophy might either be compelled to divorce itself from all practical questions or else voluntarily commit *hara-kiri* and leave the whole field of man's interest to an illogical and dogmatic science. The situation was akin to that in the fairy tale where two specially good salesmen persuaded the king to reject clothes for the gossamer tissue of words which they would supply. All went well so long as no one dared, against the king's orders, to raise the charge of nakedness. It remained for a little child to utter the charge, upon which the whole spell was dissolved. What we have lacked in the present instance has been someone with the fortitude to expose the nakedness of the scientific philosophy.

While the spell was on, the best philosophy could do was to call attention to certain practical issues concerning which it was permitted to assert reality. Soon these effective issues were seen to be values, and the judgment of values was seen to involve persons. Thus, by a certain indirection, philosophy has managed to stay in the field until the temper of men's thoughts should change. This would appear to have been a clever counterattack to the all-pervading materialism which threatened. For as soon as we admit that there are values for which men may worthily live, and which are of equal or even greater significance to them than meaningless quantities—that moment, wittingly or unwittingly, the reality of man's mental and spiritual life leaps back into the reckoning. Once more through the gloom arises the ghost of Protagorean relativism: "Man is the measure of all things: of things that are that they are; of things that are not, that they are not." It may seem to some, and doubtless will appear to the future metaphysician, the sign of the abjectness of philosophy that it could thus find standing ground for itself only through the appeal to practical interests. It is a measurable repetition of the bulwark which Socrates raised against the Sophists, the appeal to personal judgment and the person as a necessary part of cosmic reality. This was the only escape, then, now, and always, from a skepticism which involves even the denial of knowledge.

There have been many objections: from science, which feels safe only with impersonal quantities; from those forms of philosophy which dare not be unscientific whatever the cost to intellectual self-respect; and to certain others who hopelessly cling to an Absolute because they feel there is no place to go. The difficulty with its opponents is the introduction of insecurity into their various systems which pragmatism brings. It is a method sure to be anathema to safety seeking souls, scientific, philosophical, or religious. However, it does accord with life, with movement, and with change, hence with reality. There is nothing about it that is static or made to order. It is perilous in that it requires the individual to forsake formulas and to exercise a continuous judgment. It places the responsibility upon the person in an age which seeks to escape personal responsibility. Whether humanity will avail itself of the proffered freedom is concealed behind the sphinx-like gaze of fate.

IV. A PHILOSOPHY OF SHREDS AND PATCHES

The outcome of a temper of thought to which masses were more significant than minds, units than organisms, things than persons, objects than meanings, has been to create an unreasoning philosophy of shreds and patches. Its metaphysics, in attempting to be scientific became a predetermined materialism. This laid the burden of philosophic speculation on epistemology, and it is not strange that at times philosophy has threatened to do away with itself by denying the validity of all knowledge, nor that it has been the laughingstock of a self-assured and unreflective science. Its final stand was that we *do* think, and that our thoughts have some relevance to the facts, a certain pragmatic value for us if not for the universe. Thus has philosophy hungered for the husks which the swine did eat. Systematic philosophy became a source of shame. It was presumed that an epistemology could be built up out of experience and experiment and so accord with scientific demands. But a "system" of philosophy demands a metaphysics, and metaphysics is a leap in the dark. Our naturalistic conclusions have been for the most part a dodge to avoid the fundamental questions of metaphysics. But the whole system has been made to depend upon a system of causality which until most recently has not been questioned, and this system is essentially, though not so recognized, a metaphysics. What has been overlooked is that there is no consistent thinking, either philosophic or scientific, in which there is not an implied metaphysics. Some of my friends who wish not to be annoyed with such problems raise the eyebrow here, for to them an hypothesis does not necessarily imply a metaphysics. But if we allow the common definition as given in the dictionary, how can such implication be avoided? "Metaphysics is the reasoned doctrine of the essential nature and fundamental relations of all that is real."[1] We cannot carry systematic hypotheses about the relation of things without making inferences concerning the nature of things. The Protagorean assurance that "man is the measure of all things" is one of the most metaphysical assumptions in the history of philosophy. If human perception can measure the universe, there is an implied commensurability with the nature of the universe. To assume under such a dictum the absence of intelligence from the "things" or their source is to be plunged at once into a denial of the possibility of knowledge. Thought and reality are held together only by a metaphysical assumption. It was the metaphysical assumption with regard to the place of mind in a world of reality that gave potency to the famous formula. Any effort to escape the metaphysical implication lurking in every systematic hypothesis concerning knowledge, life, thought, or reality is as futile as would be the effort to elevate one's self by pulling at one's bootstraps. We can study a cloud, but we cannot utterly ignore the sky.

Our experiments with nature herself are based upon some presumption of her ground. There is not the least nor last experiment in the laboratory which does not rest on some acknowledged or concealed metaphysical foundation, some hypothesis regarding the nature of reality. It is there whether or not the experimenter is conscious of it. It is there whether or not he is able to formulate and explain it. It exists in the presuppositions which lead him to experiment. So long as a stark materialism held sway in science there was no way of detecting this unseen metaphysics, this unconscious influence which was warping scientific con-

[1] *Standard Dictionary*: Funk & Wagnalls Company, New York.

clusions. Only the scientific developments of the last two decades have been able to disclose it and to put science once more in a humble mood.

The tragedy of the present philosophic situation lies here, that philosophers have so long disavowed their interest in "systems" that they can meet the present challenge of science with only a philosophy of shreds and patches. What is needed is a system which will indicate the relative place in nature of both minds and objects, and which will present the world as a whole. For such it undoubtedly is. Philosophers who boast "no system" become the easy victims of what someone has called "the delusive clarities of detached expressions." Our specialization, which enables the little following of a particular science to "high-hat" in its parochialism all other disciplines, has well-nigh reduced us to intellectual impotence. We have witnessed the profession of an Einstein, made by him or for him, that but a dozen men could understand his system. If this meant any more than the capacity to demonstrate the mathematics of the theory of relativity, it was the sign of a widespread mental poverty—the modern specialized incapacity to understand or to allow a foothold for worth or meaning outside one's own specialty.

The most conspicuous lack of our times, in spite of our intellectual prides and self-sufficiency, is a dire mental incapacity, an inability for continuous or profound thought, an incapacity for mastery of many complementary facts. We suffer from the provincialisms of overspecialization. This is discoverable in the growing innocuousness of our educational curricula, in the meaninglessness of our amusements, in the journalistic reign of our mob psychology, in the overflooded presses issuing the latest fiction, in the detonations of our jazz orchestras, the popular crooning of the radio, in the newspaper exploitation of those who seek a cheap and easy notoriety as scientists and in the popular connotation of the word "Philosophy." This lost intellectual leadership is the philosophical quagmire of today.

SECTION III
THE SCIENTIFIC REVOLUTION AND THE NEW DAY

CHAPTER XVII

THE SEARCH FOR REALITY

. . . .

INTRODUCTION

THERE ARE MANY aspects as there are many approaches to reality. It matters little with what self-consistent or rational theory we approach nature, she is certain to answer back in kind with some knowledge. All approaches have to be made, however, through the experiences of human consciousness and all, however varied in result, are stamped with the hallmark of the interpreter. It may well be a source of wonder that with such diverse fundamental assumptions nature should appear so accommodating in informing us, but not if we reflect upon the fact that the human mind itself is a part of that nature which it essays to interpret. As itself a product of nature its normal workings insure its capacity to achieve some truth no matter by what means or in what direction it seeks. In the realm of human thought we are never free from its implications and when all is said and done can never be more sure of our universe than we are of ourselves, of our own existence, of the validity of our own experience. Many men have pretended to escape the shadow of their own minds to find refuge in some Absolute, but in vain. Neither the absolutes of space, time nor matter with which the scientist has beguiled himself, nor the Absolute Idea or reason of the philosopher, nor the infallibilities of revelation of a Divine Absolute by which the theologian has driven home his dogma; none of these has cleared himself of this fateful "shadow that walks by him still," the necessity for individual judgment. Each in its own field has at one time or another laid exclusive claim to enlightenment. Each has been at some time denied by the others.

Not only is the approach to reality bound in some sense to be personal, one in which the observer must be reckoned a part. There is a variety of reals which can be apprehended only by diverse methods. Some facts are disclosed by one method which

159

successful methods in other fields cannot touch. To get facts one must discover and use methods appropriate to the facts he seeks. It would be quite useless to drag the speedometer in from the automobile to take the pressure of the air because it looks like a barometer. So in the world of realities some are subject to temporal measurement, some to spatial, some to material, some to mental, or psychic. Certain values, and these the most important to human life and happiness are immeasurable and incomputable like love, heroism, honesty, good will. Such realities possess no commensurable degrees of any kind. We need then in the approach to reality to have a mind to the appropriateness of the method we employ. Failure to stress this point has led to much misunderstanding and even recrimination between the three main endeavors to get at reality, the scientific, the philosophical, and the religious. The conflict has arisen out of the insistence of the disciples of the one that his method is supreme and even in some cases the sole judgment of all truth and reality.

Let us discuss the various aspects of the approach to reality, for truths appear to be of many kinds. There are facts of the material world as substantial at least as the rock by which Dr. Johnson in contemptuous misunderstanding disproved the philosophy of Bishop Berkeley; there are facts which Plotinus declared to provide the field of philosophy, "the things that matter most"; and there are facts like righteousness, love, and self-sacrifice in the tenuous-considered realm of religion which however immaterial have changed the direction and aspirations of human society and of individuals without number.

As to reality, our standpoint shall be the pragmatic one, that anything is real which may be said to make a discernible difference. Whatever falls outside this falls outside our human purview.

One frequently overlooked factor in such discussions must be set forward as the starting dogma in all fields, unproved, undemonstrable as some think of demonstration, and received by faith. That dogma and that faith are namely these, that we assume the validity of human intelligence and the intelligibility of what any of us may call reality. The fact that we employ them uncritically does not keep them from being tremendous assumptions.

I. THE SCIENTIFIC SEARCH FOR REALITY

Science approaches reality through the medium of temporal and spatial measurement. This is a legitimate limitation of its field which science makes in the interest of clarity. It asks the question: What may we know of physical reality about us from the standpoint of physical relations and measurements? It should not be condemned for sticking to its field and keeping silence with respect to philosophy and religion. As in the case of both philosophy and religion, science starts with an essential dogma or dogmas. It presumes first the intelligibility of the world it seeks to know, assuming at a stroke the whole problem of epistemology. The second dogma is a metaphysical one. Science presupposes the existence of universal laws of nature of which it seeks examples. To a certain extent, it is thus confined to a *petitio principii* argument, or begging the question. It accepts such facts as sustain the initial hypothesis. This renders it particularly vulnerable in face of any examples of contingency. Both these scientific dogmas, we now discover, are under fire within the ranks of the scientists themselves who for the first time in scientific history seem called upon to examine their primary assumptions. Science now shows dissatisfaction with its former dogmas as in its examination of the atom it trembles precariously on the brink of metaphysics, the consideration of factors which lie outside of or back of matter. In fact, physics has for a long time resorted to metaphysics without being aware of it. This has been true particularly of the assumption of an invisible atom and of an Unknowable ground of being. Perhaps the best defense that may be made in the future for these unprovable scientific dogmas will be like the best defense of philosophical and theological dogmas, the pragmatic one, true according to their practical or working values.

Under the circumstances of its own limitations we cannot expect science on the physical basis to yield us anything more than physical explanation. It confessedly sets out to discover all facts of a material or sensuous nature. Its method is measurement, its tool is mathematics and its test is predictability of physical events. So long as it remains within its own avowed field science, both in methods and results, is above all criticism from either philosophy or religion. Neither can it be placed on trial for its demonstrated findings. Whoever falls upon this rock will be broken to pieces. The most telling criticisms of science arise when it goes outside its field, forgets the limitations under which it has chosen to work, and without philosophical acumen or religious insight adopts the unjustifiable dogma that no reality exists outside of its own prescribed limits. Such an assertion is not only dogmatic but likewise arrogant and has brought some scientists into just and well-earned disrepute. It is like insisting there is no sea beyond the measure of my pint cup. Scientific fulminations that it alone holds the key to reality are on a par with those of the philosophic subjectivist or of the theological intuitionist who denounces verified scientific facts.

Science meets with three insuperable difficulties which are respectively the metaphysical, the epistemological, and the religious. In the case of metaphysics if the scientist assumes the autonomy of nature, his mechanistic explanation cannot hold since he posits an inner magic by which the unique "emerges," i.e. $2 + 2 = 5$. On the basis of weights and measurements he can only describe those uniformities which he sees. When as in the case of evolution new factors appear which never before existed he can afford no explanation of why in a given case adding two and two seems to make something more than four. Scientifically he is under obligation to account for the increment and apart from such a finding does not speak as a scientist. To say that new qualities "emerge" may describe what happens but as explanation only begs the question. An autonomous nature is not one that achieves results by reaction to external forces alone. On the question of epistemology he is even more at sea. Science has done and can do nothing to clear up the field of how we must think reality in the physical world. The more it has actually discovered about physical reality, the less certain has it been of the terms under which it could describe it until now we have the open confession that present scientific descriptions of ultimate reality are only mental constructs, imaginative attempts at picturing certain experiences or what more recent physics might be inclined to describe as unpicturable notions of the understanding. On the third count science has failed to tell us anything about "the things that matter most," so that if we were to miss the whole of scientific reality we should still remain in secure possession of the things most worth while for human life.

Under these circumstances the present modesty of science is fitting and in striking contrast to the claims made for it by its less enlightened members or its philosophical camp followers. This is not to depreciate its values nor to deny its facts but simply to call attention to the limitations of the space-time phenomena which provide the charter under which it has chosen to work. Since in its world of investigation it has elected sometimes to act as if the spectator did not exist it is now embarrassed by a world in which the spectator is seen to be a factor.

There is no wish to diminish or depreciate the importance of scientific knowledge. It has a significance far beyond the gathering of scientific facts. It has a salutary and restraining influence upon the excesses of both philosophy and religion. Its contributions to democracy and the freedom of the human spirit are incalculable. Within its proper limits it speaks with authority. All we wish to emphasize here is the fact that it is a special approach to knowledge and limited by the method itself has adopted.

II. The Philosophical Search for Reality

Philosophy is not universally granted to be a window from which we may look out upon or into reality. Certainly not by any such as deny the validity of values or cast doubt upon the operations of the human mind. That this is so must be held as largely the fault of the materialistic and naturalistic philosophers who for some time past have been industriously engaged in sawing off the philosophical limb on which they are sitting.

It must perhaps be admitted that we have happened upon a time when the market for rational coherence, the demand for reason is at low ebb. The man of the street seems in some way to imagine that humbug can furnish a platform for success and his credulity regarding irrational measures verges on the pathetic. For this he can scarcely be blamed when even in the seats of philosophy there has been so much deprecation of systematic thinking, so much encouragement given to fragmentary self-canceling concepts that cannot hold together.

Philosophy, like science, starts with the dogma of the intelligibility of the world. It presumes that the outlook, previous education, or prejudice of the observer make a difference with the observer's concept of reality. Philosophy therefore believes that we should apply the test of coherence to our concepts. This is done, of course, on the assumption that the universe is coherent, just as science assumes universal law. The philosopher proposes to approach reality from the standpoint of what is coherent, unless indeed he be altogether a skeptic. The only real charter he has for such an approach lies in the assumption which the scientist had previously left out of his, namely, the existence of the spectator as himself a portion of the phenomena of nature needing also to be accounted for. Since the interpreting mind is a portion of nature he declares himself on the dogma that science has often assumed without question, namely, that the intelligent mind truly apprehends an intelligible reality. In other words, he bases the intelligibility of nature on intelligence in man, or vice versa. Both man and nature arising from the same source and forming a part of the same process cannot be assumed as a fundamental contradiction or disagreement. If this be true, coherence has a meaning and provides a ground for philosophical speculation.

It may be said that this approach is purely epistemological and in no way involves metaphysics. Reflection will show, however, that our answer to the problems of thought will depend upon our metaphysical assumption. Is the external world amenable to thought or does it simply produce thought on the empty tablet of the mind? This is of course the crucial question in philosophy. If we adopt the first alternative we have still a charter for philosophy; if the second we have none, since the spectator is again left out of the picture. This conclusion will not be obvious to either absolutist or monist since each is habituated to a life of inconsistencies. The first is committed to a divine experience out of keeping with the divine character, faced by the problem of evil, the second with the problem of error. The latter is set about to explain errors in understanding that are caused by the same basic experiences.

How shall the philosopher maintain his importance and justify his philosophic existence in the face of the popular impression that he is committed to a search in the darkest corner of the coal cellar for the black cat which is not there. In reply he can only say that the way they look on their world makes a vital difference in the conduct and happiness of men. If they consider it a meaning-less chaos there is bound to be something chaotic and irrespon-sible about their response to it and to the social order in which they live. Organized and coherent thinking bears a part in every well-ordered life. As Plato makes Socrates say: "The unconsid-ered life is not worth living." Our minds call out for reasons with as much insistence as our bodies call out for food. Philos-ophy attempts to meet this need by the presentation of coherent thinking about the basic relations in which we live.

Nor can the metaphysical problem be avoided. Coherence in thought without anything corresponding to it in the physical world would render philosophy only a silly dream or illusion. Coherence of thought in an incoherent world would be impos-sible. This is so because our minds are always a portion of that world of external reality into which we look. Our own minds are among the phenomena we seek. Unless they are part and parcel of the whole universe of reality there is no justification for us to assume we can know anything at all. The assumption of the unity of our minds with that of nature is a metaphysical assump-tion and necessary to all understanding. The task of philosophy is then to ascertain what it can of the conditions of human knowl-edge, the laws of the human mind, the relations which we as thinking beings bear to the physical world. All these facts are to be gathered into a unitary coherence of meaning through philosophy. For this reason philosophy has been called and is the Queen of the Sciences since she must make evident that charter of coherence which justifies the scientific assumption of the universality of natural law, which is itself metaphysical.

III. THE RELIGIOUS SEARCH FOR REALITY

The average person of intelligence is not satisfied with seeing the world of reality through the windows of science and philos-ophy alone. Even the most rabid opponents of religion instead of neglecting what they declare to be a myth, a superstition, an ultimate futility, spend a great deal of time and energy in reiter-ation of what, if their theories were true, would be obvious to all. One who attends many philosophical meetings cannot, if reflective, but be amazed at the time and energy spent in this negative way in attempting to disprove the existence of God. It would be only natural to think the idea of God so easily disproved would quickly fail to command the minds of men, yet the great effort of some philosophic lives seems to be the renewed slaughter of what they describe as an effete or dead God. Of course their weapons of attack are philosophical or scientific and have no relation to the method by which religion can be proved or disproved. Because religion is not amenable to either scientific or philosophic method they declare it unreal. They feel themselves called upon to daily battle against these specters that never down. The average man is convinced that so far he has been scientifically shown not more than half of the world of reality, and that for him it is the least important half. He sees certain great values that are not measurable by sense arithmetic, certain facts that are more than simple knowledge; these are those deeper facts for which and by which he lives.

Thus the inquiring mind is inevitably, whether for or against, brought into the field of religion. If *for* it, he can justly claim to be talking about reality, if *against* it he can only make the negative excuse that he is willing to talk about nothing but a persistent and pernicious illusion. To the normal man the supreme realities of life spring from love, loyalty, honesty, integrity, altruism, high-mindedness, fortitude, reverence for what is greater or better than one's self, duty, obligation, social responsibility, respect for the rights of others, faith in the practicability and value of the good life, confidence in the friendliness of the universe and an utter devotion of one's powers to the life of values. All these one acknowledges as religious without claiming them to be a complete definition of religion. These form the field of religion, of all religions alike. This will, of course, be violently denied by such as are habituated to slur religion as only the escape mechanism of people who fear hellfire. The religious man is not however under compulsion to accept as a basis of discussion the caricature of religion which is the inevitable resort of his opponent. As a matter of fact, there is no religion where there is not love of values for themselves. Wherever a man loves these values however protesting his irreligion, there is religion. However faulty in accomplishment, however perverse in methods, the aim of religion everywhere is the same, the cultivation of the good life as the supremely worthwhile reality.

Men have discovered that to this end the assertion of a dogma

gets the best results. As the scientist proceeds on the undemonstrable dogma of universal law, even though it be of statistics,
and the mathematician on the elusive dogma of infinite divisibility, convenient mental fictions as Vaihinger calls them, so the
religionist assumes a universe in which moral and spiritual values
matter, are at home, are reals. He symbolizes this concept under
the term God, believing that these values are the highest form
of reality. The test here again is a pragmatic one. If it turns out
that belief in, and devotion to these higher concepts or values
leads to a better life, to a larger achievement of those values, to
a growing appreciation of them, then he is justified in his belief
in God. The cogency of this belief is denied by some who do
not see that fundamentally theism is a confidence in the moral
nature of the universe. If we resort to the scientific expedient of
statistical verification, we shall, I think, have to admit that for
the general run of men the concept God is of supreme pragmatic
value. It is simply a working proposition in an endeavor for a
good life and should be applauded by every lover of mankind.

We have here a field of reality which is and cannot be proved
or disproved by scientific measurement. Index pointers of emotional psychology can be here of little avail because they can
speak only of intensity of physical reactions and have nothing
at all to say of moral quality or value. We have not invented
a pointer that can distinguish between love and hate or indicate
the mental and spiritual sources of the aberrations behind the
needle of the lie detector.

While religion is emotional or gives rise to emotions it is not
purely emotional nor can it be measured by its emotional effects.
Religion is attended by feeling but is not fundamentally a feeling but a result. Its real measurement is its capacity to produce
ethical values. If it does not produce ethical values it remains
a physical or mental experience but not a religious one. Neither
can religious values be said to lie mainly in the field of rationality for here we are in the region of paradox. Such paradoxes
as these are common: the presence of extreme physical suffering
with extreme joy as in the martyrs; the concomitance of external
shame with inner self-assurance; the sense of external loss with
the assurance of inner gain. Here we have the whole realm of
tragedy as represented in art and music. Why does the darkness
of the background in the picture bring satisfaction by exposing

the high lights? Why do the minors and even the discords in the music bring a satisfying fullness of expression, without which our minds grope unsatisfied? The introduction of minor chords and half-steps or even of disharmony seems to speak of a higher harmony in which the dissonances of grief, loss, and misfortune are dissolved in the larger whole. It is because in the region of values the paradoxical finds expression which neither scientific measurement nor philosophical coherence can deal with. One has to be endowed with a point of view, a platform of appreciation, a power of insight, to press through the world of casual appearances to the deeper reality. At this point, the fact that the believer in the phenomena of external senses alone, or in rationality alone can say to me "I do not see it," has no weight at all. He is like the man used as an illustration recently by one of my mechanistic colleagues who criticized the person who hoped to get the reality of an oil painting only by rubbing his nose against it. The nose-rubbing order of scientist and philosopher is apt to miss altogether the very meaning of religion.

CONCLUSION

The conclusion of these considerations might be summarized in certain likenesses and differences found in the exponents of the three realms of reality. All are compelled to make the fundamental assumption of the intelligibility of the universe. Each sets before himself a goal which is inconsistent with his present achievement and which if taken literally could only be considered preposterous. These are the various absolutes, the convenient mental fictions by which we are enabled to advance. With science, of course, it is an absolute space-time world of universal law and predictability, with philosophy it is absolute truth or logical coherence, with religion an Absolute person or God. All these terms are obviously unattainable or unintelligible to a space-time bound creature such as man. On the other hand, if he were altogether the creature of space and time such questions could not torment him.

Each discipline has at times claimed for itself exclusive insights into reality and yet each leaves its devotees inwardly unsatisfied by reason of a consciousness that something has by this claim of exclusiveness been left out of the picture. For this reason each has attempted to go beyond its fundamental assumptions, to speak for the others, to condemn conclusions it considered inconsistent with its own. It is as if three groups of children playing at three windows should claim their own perspective to be the only true one and that their view could be maintained only by denying all others. This situation arises from the fact that reality is approached by three distinct methods, each of which is legitimate for the realities it seeks but can arrive only at such realities as lie legitimately within the scope of its own rule. In the use of its method there is a necessary orientation if there is to be understanding. This has led to a certain cocksureness by the employer of a given approach and to contempt by proponents of the other two realms. Orientation, mathematical and observational, is necessary to the scientist. With the philosopher it is logical and dialectical, with the religionist it is an insight into spiritual values and realities that requires an orientation. The trouble arises from the fact that however much we trichotomize our world for purposes of observation, the division is only academic and none of us can be exclusively scientific, exclusively philosophical, or exclusively religious. We are looking at one reality, the universe, under three aspects, the better to understand it.

There is no point therefore to the claim that our opponent has not grasped reality because it doesn't fall in with our own scientific, or philosophic, or religious approach. There is no value to our prejudice toward each other. No one can consistently hold that truths in one realm are at war with truth in another without abrogating his own fundamental thesis. How futile then it is for either philosophy or religion to catch at the coattails of passing scientific methods, or for science to deny religious facts because they cannot be measured and weighed, or for religion to anathematize science or philosophy. We should fit the method to the field of inquiry. Logical coherence is not to be judged by time-space measurement, nor are the upward reaches of the soul after a new life in God to be condemned as unreal because they are neither altogether coherent nor space filling.

However various the methods by which we approach reality there is one inevitable factor in all which has been resolutely overlooked. However much science, in the interest of complete disinterestedness, may have desired a universe without a spectator, "himself from self he can not free." The same fact has beset the most perfect syllogism of the philosopher. Coherence is always relative to himself. The absolutes of religion have after all been something less than absolute in the understandings and interpretation of very human and fallible individuals. Each man in the last analysis sees and interprets the world through his own experience. And here he will see and understand the most, who keeps open and clean the windows of his own soul with a minimum of arrogance regarding his own understanding, not denying the understanding of others but anxious to profit by whatever of value they may bring.

To the wise man in search of reality nothing human can be alien.

CHAPTER XVIII

THE USE AND ABUSE OF ABSOLUTES IN THE SEARCH
FOR REALITY

PERHAPS NO PROBLEM has been more persistent in Western
thought than that of the seeming contradiction between universal and particular, the absolute and the concrete, totalitarianism and democracy. The genius of the West is particularly
typified in the raising of this question, and the query has been
one source of Western progress. Since the paradoxical belief in
both universals and particulars has been so permanent though so
contradictory it becomes impossible to dismiss the problem without assuming the presence of an important truth. They may
in fact come to be seen as complementary and necessary phases
of the same general truth. The name which John Wright Buckham has chosen to represent this fact is "contraplete." If the
existence of contrapletes can be sustained it may offer relief
to our dilemma.

Why should human beings be forever worshiping and pur-
suing perfection when there is nothing perfect under the sun?
We speak of the perfect life, the perfect political or social organization, perfect knowledge, perfect science, perfect ideals,
when at the very moment we feel them unachievable. There is
always an interfering contingency which keeps us back from
actual accomplishment, or makes it appear as unreal as Plato
represents the objective world as being, but the shadow of a
deeper reality. Always, however, there is something about the
dream of perfection which has a religious or an ennobling cast,
from the aspiration for absolute moral goodness or holiness to
the dream of perfection in scientific method and knowledge.

The danger that lurks in religious or scientific absolutes is in
considering them as something apart from their practical application. The ideal seems so perfect and so important that it is
easily worshiped to the neglect of practical achievement. The
religious dogma thus becomes more important than religious

practice, since it seems to be the source of all. The dream of an ideal social or political state outweighs to its proponents the actual safeguarding of individual liberties and rights. Such scientific dogmas as the absolutes of time, space, motion and matter, blind men to the recognition of specific realities of contingency and uncertainty. They overlook the fact because it conflicts with the accepted hypothesis.

Both theological and philosophical thought have been an effort to resolve and to rationalize the paradoxical. The whole history of European and American reflection shows an attempted mediation between absolutes and particulars, idea and substance, mind and matter. Science has been the one discipline that has laid claim to being free from paradox. To it, the paradoxical is irrational. From all irrationality it hopes like philosophy to free itself. Based on the principles of non-contradiction and predictability, these promised to save science from all taint of paradox. But science has not been so free from paradox as it has wished to think. Busy with experimentation and discovery so long as the deeper issues were not called in question science has remained unaware of philosophical inconsistencies in its fundamental assumptions. The background of scientific dogma has been a belief in materialistic monism, an absolutism of matter, space, time, and motion. These absolutisms are the sources of scientific paradox and embarrassments in present-day scientific theory. Among others the old certainties are gone under the ruthless attack of experimentation and their places taken by "the principle of uncertainty," discontinuous energy replaces the ancient axiom of continuity, and even the suggestion has been made that "matter," whatever that may now signify, is in process of creation rather than "eternal." We waver between a substantial Daltonian atom which we conceived to be the ultimate lump of reality, and an atom which is only a mental construct to account for an event in a space-time continuum; between corpuscular and undulatory light. We admit ignorance of the meaning of causality, while the theory of gravitation takes on a new appearance under the light of the theory of relativity.

It may be of little comfort in this melee of conflicting ideas to be reminded that our present chaos is a hang-over from an earlier trust in absolutes. Modern realists will gladly admit that absolute idealism has been philosophy's "Old Man of the Sea," liberal theologians that a similar principle is hidden in the contentions of fundamentalists, but few scientists realize that the demand for a scientific absolute is their heritage not only from Greek science but from Medievalism as well. Just because the demand is so necessitous they even yet labor with an obstinacy as persistent as that of some theologians to recapture an all-embracing equation, some universal formula, some absolute of scientific expression upon which to depend.

The real reason for this wasted energy, this sense of frustration, is the unwillingness of the human mind to admit the paradoxical. Yet life and reality are full of paradoxes. If we examine closely and with insight we shall see that in most cases the contradictions come by viewing events out of their proper settings. We try to reduce everything to a single standard of measurement. We want our diverse realities to be of a piece. The all-mastering aim of our science has been a theoretic monism which could classify all varieties of phenomena under a single head or law. What can be evaluated upon one plane, however, refuses the measurements of another. Out of this fact arise the seeming contradictions between science and philosophy and religion and even within these varieties of explanation themselves.

Philosophy at least should have sufficient insight to analyze the paradox and show its necessity for practical living without being stampeded by it. This is a plea not for obscurantism but for realism. First of all, philosophy should recognize the human character of the problems raised. Their persistence indicates a necessity of human thinking. The recorded history of human thought shows the need for affirming absolutes in every realm. Yet the practice of life displays everywhere the fact that from the standpoint of human understanding and achievement, absolutes are academic illusions. "The need for illusion" may itself be taken as a paradoxical statement, but there is something in the nature of human thought and achievement which makes it less absurd than it seems.

I. ABSOLUTES IN THE REALM OF SCIENCE

Zeno first called attention to the paradoxical nature of the spatial infinite or mathematical absolute, hoping by presenting the absurdity to establish an idealistic monism. It was not merely fortuitous that over against the Eleatics were the Heraclitans appealing to the same contradictions to establish a monistic materialism. Just as the Eleatics appealed to an unknowable, all-embracing static Mind for the solution of philosophic problems, the Heraclitans, from an opposite quarter, appealed to an unknowable, unseen reality of change to establish their viewpoint. Heraclitus in particular believed in the reduction of qualitative values to quantitative measurement. It took the work of both Zeno and Democritus to bring this absolutism to the point where it could claim that the incommensurable could on occasion become the commensurable if there were enough of it. The multiplication of an unextended point, for instance, could become an extended line. A qualityless, homogeneous atom multiplied indefinitely could become laden with qualities. One could both eat his cake and keep it. The pure *hocus-pocus* in this procedure has not sufficiently distressed the mind of scientific thinkers even to our own times. The present revolt in physics arises out of the belated comprehension that there is some discrepancy between facts and announced absolutes. The difficulty arises from the unwillingness to surrender absolutes. In theology this persistence is called fundamentalism. That the character of the contradiction has not earlier been apparent to scientific thought was due to the successful pursuit of its formulas and its indifference to rationality in its theories. Any notion that seemed to approximate explanation of facts was thoughtlessly seized upon or as carelessly invented (like Lord Kelvin's "wooden models") and set forth as fact.

Science now discovers that its fundamentalistic and theoretical absolutes were the invention of its own mind. In a more primary sense they were the invention of the Greek philosophical mind and late scientific discovery is beginning to disclose the tentative and purely hypothetical character of numerous scientific theses.

It is anomalous that Zeno's famous paradoxes setting forth the contradictory nature of the spatial infinite should have remained only a "joke" for more than twenty-five centuries. That this was so is due doubtless to the fact that science cannot get along without the concept of the infinite divisibility of space in order to carry on many if not most mathematical operations. Yet the dogma of infinite divisibility reduces actual space to meaningless jargon and illusion in which short and long are degraded to an equally incomprehensible number of unextended points. The practical usefulness of the concept cannot be doubted, the meaning of the concept can never be rationalized.

The illustration in mathematics is obvious but there can be little doubt about a like condition elsewhere. Many of the working hypotheses of science are in a similar case, useful in the organization and furtherance of knowledge but equally illusory in any individual and factual particular. The Daltonian atom which science has not for twenty-five years been able to get along with or without is now disclosed as merely an intellectual construct. The latest, though by no means the last, description of the atom is that it is "an event in a space-time continuum." This definition may endure as long as it can be used practically, but the distance between it and Dalton measures a revolution in scientific concepts. In somewhat similar fashion, we have now to put copious question marks, or even negations, behind such absolutes as the "conservation of energy" which becomes a relative term, as it always has been in practice, the second law of thermodynamics, the Newtonian concept of gravitation, and causality. The doctrine of continuity of energy is superseded by Planck's Quantum Theory. Evolution, emergent or otherwise, is seen as wholly doctrinaire and untenable without a self-existent and self-identifying Mind, involving purpose, as its ground and support. What has been used for several generations as an argument to bow God out of the universe has turned out to be the main reason for suspecting his presence *in* it. With respect to the problem of causality, Max Planck has recently declared that any true notion of causality demands the assumption of an ideal and omniscient Spirit enduring above the whole physical process.[1]

II. Absolutes in the Realm of Philosophy

It must be admitted that the expedition on which we are at present engaged must seem to some a considerable attempt to rummage among the specters of a dead past, and no more so perhaps than in philosophy. Yet the ghosts are not dead enough to be without friends and therein lies our difficulty. In spite of the centuries that have passed in which the fallacies of the abstract and of the universal have been exposed, these children of time continue to be left unfathered upon the philosophical doorstep. Nothing is quite so easy perhaps as to erect a particular fact into a universal concept. Despite the danger of backfire, for a single exception can overthrow it, these fallacies are the common

[1] *The Philosophy of Physics.* W. W. Norton & Co., Inc., New York, p. 79.

resort of debaters, philosophers, cultists, demagogues, social and political writers, ministers, atheists, or what-have-you. The tyranny of extreme statement is powerful with the unreflective and with partisans of every kind. The despotism of words becomes the source and power of movements, no less in philosophy than in more mundane (if there are any such) spheres.

It was the Eleatics who introduced in striking significance the absolutes into philosophy as a means of organizing metaphysical thought and then affirmed the principle as the supreme reality. This was carried out to beautiful symmetry in the Platonic and Neoplatonic systems. Nearly every one is now ready to damn this idealistic type of monism because it makes demands upon our thinking capacities and our sense of moral responsibility which we are unwilling to admit. Despite the vagueness and visionary character with which it is charged by our so-called practical and efficient friends, and notwithstanding that it is morally irksome to us, yet most would concede the extreme beauty and grandeur of the system. This transcendental grandeur is however its shortcoming since it effectually removes its spiritual Absolute so far from the world of events that it can no longer have part in it. What such an Absolute would mean for the human mind becomes as tenuous as the non-extended point which can be multiplied into extension.

It is incorrect however to imagine that the idealists have been the sole beneficiaries of absolutism in philosophy. That greatest absolutist of all, Spinoza, is claimed both by materialists and idealists. It matters little whether the Spinozean Substance be considered material or spiritual, the result is equally unsatisfying. If one chooses the high road it leads to an incomprehensible God and if one takes the low road there is no stopping short of unknowable substance and universal skepticism. Some minds can survive and flourish on universal skepticism because they unconsciously reserve their own consciousness and experience from the application of their theory. As always, the twin specters of mind and values stand athwart their way and cannot be passed, being only ignored.

III. ABSOLUTES IN THE REALM OF RELIGION

The problem of absolutes in religion is no less serious than in other realms of thought and experience. Here they are invested with a sacrosanctity that involves the questioner in a charge if irreligion quite comparable to the anathema of ignorance cast upon the questioner of scientific absolutes. The unhappy state of that intrepid spirit that dares to question both is indicated by attacks from religious quarters for being a scientific atheist, while the scientific pronounce him a bigoted and ignorant religionist. He does, it is true, have the comfort of thinking that both charges cannot be true.

Just as in mathematics, the mathematical infinite presents a working principle exceedingly useful in achieving results, so there is an inner demand that morally and spiritually one must aim at perfection. The perfection aimed at can have no flaw, it must appear superhuman. These superhuman perfections are demanded as the attributes of God, the supreme reality. That superhuman perfections put a strain not only on human achievement but likewise on human understanding makes no whit less necessary the demand. Thus the religionist resorts to a system of words of which he cannot know the meaning, not as the measure of his understanding of God but as an appraisal of his ignorance. For in the endeavor to understand the Infinite he has only a very finite mind and experience to help him. He is exceedingly limited in time and space, and tries to grasp the meaning of the unlimited. His knowledge is at best but a fragment and he tries to contemplate the meaning of all knowledge. It is comparable to the attempt a native of Dahomey might make to reconstruct from a single drive shaft in his possession a complete locomotive which he has never seen. All concepts of God are necessarily very human and very limited. The words by which theology attempts this understanding are generally the *omni* words. In spite of their affirmative and constructive appearance, they are really negatives. When the theologian ascribes to God, omnipotence, omniscience, omnipresence, omnificence, he endows God with powers and understandings that are beyond his own human capacity and comprehension. He means to assume that God is everything good, powerful, and perfect that man is not, and God must be this because the human mind can worship only perfection. For this reason the religionist finds it hard to tolerate any imperfection. He clings to ideals, and must, even though they are not attained, thus laying himself open to the undeserved arraignment of inconsistency. The fact that his reach must exceed his grasp exposes him to the hostile and unreflective charge of hypocrisy. It would be quite as just to condemn the scientist for his failure in the search for truth. Of insincerity the religious man may be no more chargeable than would be the mathematician who plays around with unextended points or an infinite divisibility he can never achieve. The religious man's dream of absolutely perfect moral conduct, unachieved, is no more reprehensible than the scientific search for absolute reality or the philosophical one of absolute truth. The only moral requirement is that he should honestly strive after it. The illusory character of these absolutes in practice is no evidence that they are not necessary. They will be until partial knowledge becomes complete, faith becomes sight and all hypotheses are either demonstrated or disproved.

Unfortunately the tentative and pragmatic nature of absolutes has never been sufficiently realized in any realm and in religion absolutes have been raised to the highest power. This has made theology unfriendly to any research or dialectic which seemed in the remotest way to question or threaten belief in the absolutes of doctrine, authority, institutions or Scriptures. Devotees cling to the absolutes as saving dogmas without attendant holiness, while opponents on the other hand charge them with wishful thinking. Failure to achieve in practice what he sets forth as his aim leads the anti-religionist to dismiss the whole matter of religion as negligible and unimportant. Because the religionist himself has not given sufficient thought to his postulates, his dream of perfection has become stereotyped and meaningless. This accounts for the outcry against the concept of a changing and growing God, as if growth, the pursuit of an ideal, were itself a sign of imperfection. Neither growth nor limitation, if it be self-limitation for desired ends, can be held to be preventive of divine perfection unless we desire to consider the soil more perfect than the flower that springs from it.

IV. The Paradox of Absolutes Can Be Resolved Only in Persons

Enough has now been written to make clear the contradictions involved in the affirmation of absolutes. Like the Daltonian atom, or the man that married a wife, we can neither get along with them nor without them. What should be evident to all is that these universal paradoxes display something about the nature of the human mind. They may as in Platonic concepts be but the shadows cast upon us by a larger and more perfect world. Of one thing we may be certain, without the entertainment of as yet unachieved ideals the world would be turned back to the bestiality of the pigsty. The lapsing of these spiritual and religious ideals is apparent in the present state of society at home and abroad. Without them all will agree there could be no true religion but it is equally true that without them there could be neither philosophy nor science.

In science, in philosophy and in religion nothing could be easier than to make the proponent of absolutes appear silly. The opponent of religion glibly announces the overthrow or the falsity of all religion by pointing out that religionists never achieve the ideals they profess. In similar manner Aristophanes ridiculed the idealism of Socrates by representing him as praying to an Absolute, the Great Vortex. Where there is the mood of criticism, the most respectable generalizations of science are open to the same ludicrous treatment. Why will the mathematician never discover the paradoxical character of an imaginary point which has no extension and which on any useful occasion can be multiplied into length? The reason in every case is plain: the imaginary mental construct or fiction, if one must use so base a word, is assumed as a working hypothesis to achieve the best possible practical results. We can never reach any goal by assuming that there is no goal or no possibility of reaching it. For human beings the whole of knowledge and the creativity of experience lies in setting up what seems unachievable, and then approximating it as closely as possible. The pursuit of absolutes is not a cause for shame. To be without them is the greater shame. But to hold them as other than tentative constructs, subject to growing knowledge and advancing experience is to use them to defeat their own end.

Seen in true relations the emergence of absolutes in human thought represents the difference between ideal and achievement. They betoken the long road of scientific, philosophical, and religious accomplishment which is the making of man, and it may be the goal of evolution and the task of God. But the answer to our problem can never be an impersonal one. To man alone, so far as it is given us to know, is given the rare privilege of entertaining unachieved ideals, and of holding fast to them until his dreams come true. Such capacity can be had only in a creature not quite absorbed in the temporal and material; one who is something more than the world in which he lives; one who transcends both time and matter and is himself creative. In personality the contradictory notions of immanence and transcendence, of essence and reality, find common ground. Whenever they coincide in man or God, we have personality.

Ideal and achievement, however imperfectly understood and illusory, are yet the necessities of a changing, living world. Since all practical knowledge depends on putting individual informations into a universal frame of relations, they are discovered as necessary for every advance in knowledge, rationality, or value. As actual achievement they are never completely realized or fade into some larger demand of duty. This is however the dilemma of a personal world, a living process of growth. The paradox is one of human thought and circumstance which arises from the conflict between what is and what should be.

CHAPTER XIX

THE MATHEMATICAL BASIS OF WESTERN CULTURE

. . . .

To SUGGEST THAT the progress of Western civilization has been a struggle between arithmetic and geometry seems a fantastic proposition until we examine more closely the underlying facts of history. Mathematics was the peculiar development of the West. The successive migrations westward fostered the linear concept of history. Advances toward the new land, the perfect society, were to be made step by step. History was progress: it was arithmetical progression. There is a sense in which Western mathematics originated both arithmetic and geometry, but with a certain difference. Geometry was influenced by the Orient and comes tingéd with the Oriental love of form of which a cyclic order of time and history are expressions. In Greek philosophy mathematics arose among the Pythagoreans and partook of a metaphysical character. The reason for this is more or less of a commonplace. In a primitive system of notation an integer can be represented by a dot, two by a line, three by a triangle, four by a square, five by a pentagon, and so on. It was an easy deduction from this to the assumption of triangularity as a character in all triads, and to establish for the form of each figure a numerical quality. In this way structure and number became identified, simple numerology was soon erected into a system and gave rise to the geometrical concept as representing the character of individuals, institutions, and societies. The numerical index of quality was further accentuated by such discoveries as that of the relation of the length and vibrations of the string to the place of the musical note in the scale. Thus was inaugurated the search for numerical equivalents to qualitative values which still goes merrily on. With the Pythagoreans it became not only metaphysical but religious, taking on the structure of absolute form. Its emphasis on form has made it the facile expression of the imagination, of deduction as the means to knowledge, of the superior and absolute gifts of the mind and of vision and magic and esoteric insight into the nature of things. Under its dominance there are assumed to be an enlightened few who alone can possess the mandates of learning, of government and of religion. It is autocratic, hierarchic, and totalitarian in its sympathies and outcomes. It is invariably fearful of and opposed to democracy.

Arithmetic on the other hand has quite a different face and outcome. It depends not at all on form and it grows by accretion of units. To it the unit is essential and primary. If this may be said to be particularly true of the cardinal numbers such as one, two, and three, it is likewise illustrated in the ordinals. Though as first, second, third, and so forth, they contemplate a place in a series or process, yet no individual could be left out without falsifying the whole. Any institution worked out under the arithmetical concept must take account of the individual, for from these its importance springs. Individual integers give it its authority and upon the existence of each the whole depends. In this way it is essentially democratic.

The arithmetical rather than the geometrical ideology represents the genius of Western progress and is the source of its scientific achievement.

A study of these contrasting ideologies will disclose the essentially unsatisfactory nature and ultimate breakdown of each as it stands alone and in contrast. It demands a unifying principle which it has not yet found in history, at least of which it is not yet sufficiently aware. The failure of each, in so far as they have failed depends on a property which they have in common, namely, their impersonalism. It is the purpose here to inquire into this source of failure, and from the examination to learn, if possible, the direction of a true solution of the dilemma raised by the conflict. This dilemma has now become of world-wide significance in civilization and is one source of present world discord. To point out the facts then becomes a task of the utmost importance.

I. THE MATHEMATICS OF THE LOWLY

Arithmetic can be called the mathematics of the lowly for two reasons. The first is its simplicity and accessibility to the meanest intellects. The second is the emphasis which it puts upon the units which comprise its sums. All the integers of a given whole must either be exactly like every other, or the qualities which would differentiate them must be neglected as unessential. The temptation to oversimplification is very great since it is easy to treat units as if they had reality apart from their qualities. The qualities of any given thing lend it a certain character of uniqueness, which is overlooked in all abstractions. Abstraction itself respecting any series of facts or events would be impossible except to a continuing self-identifying subject of experience which transcends the whole process. This personal element in every series of facts, events, or postulates is most often overlooked because we are more conscious of the external world of phenomena than we are of our own mental processes and contributions to the interpretation of facts. This is as true of the arithmetical concept of men as it is of things, and is a devastating fact in the interpretation of statistics which can take no account of differences within its aggregates. An arithmetical aggregation of any kind is an essential democracy in its equality of emphasis on each constituent of its wholes. The discovery of the democratic ideal was the supreme invention of the Western world. It began in Greek thought with the Milesian philosopher-scientists who began a period more significant for the demarcation of West from East than the division of the Roman Empire. When Thales, Anaximander, and Anaximenes set out to discover the nature of reality they not only made the first step toward modern science, they were inaugurating the peculiar features of Western civilization. The scientific achievements of these men from Thales down through Heraclitus, Anaxagoras, Empedocles, Leucippus, and Democritus was astonishingly great and wonderfully true to modern scientific method. They were the early proponents and practitioners of the empirical method some two thousand years before Lord Bacon. The accuracy of their predictions of such sidereal phenomena as eclipses and conjunctions of planets was surprising. Tradition accords to Thales prognostication of an earthquake, which, if true, would argue seismological knowledge now unknown. These facts were gained by observation and induction, presenting a contrast to the methods of Oriental geometry.

The aim of the Greek scientists was twofold. First, there was the desire by investigation to come to grips with reality. Second, they employed their faith in themselves and in their method of investigation to rid the world of its dominating myths, traditions, fears, and magic, which held the masses of the time in bondage. They believed and they sought to establish their belief, that natural phenomena instead of being the erratic and irresponsible acts of the gods, were due to the functioning of natural laws. It was thus that they represented the movements of the heavenly bodies, conjunctions of planets, eclipses, and earthquakes, to a world that was terrified by all intermittent natural phenomena, and which sought to ward them off with incantations and prayers.

It is impossible for us in this far-off time to appreciate the depth of these fears or the release to the human spirit which came with their overthrow. The moving figure of this new day who kept the scientific spirit alive in the midst of prevailing superstition was Epicurus. There was nothing peculiar about the undeservedly unsavory reputation that attached itself to him. The extant writings of Epicurus do not substantiate the charge of an unconsidered search for pleasure on his part. He sought happiness not by the indulgence but by the limitation of desires. As one has put it: "Epicurus was no Epicure." He welcomed to his garden for the high emprise of philosophy such as were content with common black bread and pure water from the spring. An echo of this is given centuries later in Rome in a little verse addressed by Philodemus, the Gadarene poet, to Piso the father-in-law of Julius Caesar inviting him into the Epicurean fellowship:

> Tomorrow, Dearest Piso, one will come
> To guide you to a philosophic home,
> Where, Epicurus's disciples, we
> Observe our master's anniversary.
> Song have we, and sincerity of soul,
> But look not, Piso, for the Chian bowl,
> Or sumptuous dishes, or aught exquisite,
> Except thine own urbanity and wit.[1]

The bad reputation of Epicurus arose from two sources. The first was the hostility of the established religion. To religious devotees, the denial of the efficacy of their idols and of the validity of their oracles, was atheism. Deeper than this was the further fact, that the religion of the age had a political signifi-

---

[1] Translation by Richard Garnett, inscribed in author's copy of first English edition of *Epicurus' Morals*.

cance. The state religion was kept in the hands of the ruling class, the better to awe the common man into unmurmuring acquiescence with a lot which was for him everywhere, slavery. The "first families" claimed to be under the special protection of heaven because they declared themselves to be descended from the gods. In their presence the common man had only to tremble and obey. The lower level of society could not even approach Zeus or Apollo except through the official mediation of members of the ruling class. Here it may be appropriate to recall the frequently overlooked fact that the charge of atheism made against Socrates was primarily political. The Athenian Demos was not principally concerned with religious sensibilities. The corruption of youth meant the instillation of democratic ideas. If the helots of Athens should learn about an inner *daemonium* which each man possessed and upon which each could rely for moral direction, the power of the oligarchy which ruled Athens would be gone. Direct access to the Divine Spirit was too dangerous a possession to be entrusted to the common man, who must be kept in his place. Any assumption that knowledge was something to which anyone had direct access by consultation with his own inner consciousness, or by an experimental approach to nature unleashed a deadly threat of too much democracy. It destroyed at a stroke, political, educational and religious monopolies. And through the long years of history when has this not been true, from the days of Anaxagoras and Socrates in Athens to those of Galileo, Bruno, and Darwin?

II. THE GODS GEOMETRIZE

Geometry by contrast with arithmetic favored esotericism and absolutism. An ancient saying in philosophy calls God the Great Geometer. The saying is appropriate, since in geometry the lower proceeds from the higher, the simple is but an aspect of the all-important whole. The axiom with which one begins in geometry must be assumed as a universal, an absolute, which contains all that is later to be deduced from it. All that is discovered or discoverable must be in and verified by the original axiom. Can there be any doubt that this is the way of authoritarianism? If then one can discover or have revealed to him the most universal of all truths, this will include all lesser truths, will embrace the whole realm of knowledge, now and forever. Historically this was the outcome of Plato's doctrine of Ideas. For it the objective world of events was only a shadow, the passing and transient panorama of illusion. To this concept Epicurus with all his might and enthusiasm opposed his scientific method of learning, not by the oracles of the gods but by investigation of such facts as lay open to every inquiring mind. The appeal was to that knowledge which anyone could verify, an essentially democratic principle, but the world was not yet ripe to receive it. A long period of tutelage was yet necessary. Real democracy was far away. Slavery was universal. Only the occasional man had the hardihood, the opportunity or the leisure for intellectual culture. So long as such a condition existed there was reason for intellectual, political and religious dictatorship. Philosophy was limited by world conditions more or less necessary. Upon the models of geometry, the structural concept, were reared the great and ruling institutions of society. Primary attention was paid to form. The individual must fit himself in some appropriate way into the general picture which was assumed to represent an a priori and eternal Idea. He must be warned by such a philosopher as Plato that all men were not equal. There were clay and silver as well as golden men, and while there was occasional transference from one class to the other, this was unusual, not to be expected, and unaccountable. Each must take willingly the place in life assigned to him under the divine sanctions. If it chanced to be that of a slave, any rebellion against his lot or dissatisfaction with it was an act of impiety or even of atheism which the gods would certainly not overlook, and a treason against the nation.

The political use made of the absolutist philosophy found ample illustration in the following centuries. All authority lay in the supreme or universal axioms of church and state. These axioms were thought to be divine, were revealed, and became masters of all human rights and opinions. In the kingdom, it was embodied in the theory of the divine right. The king was the state. He could do no wrong. He was the source of all political authority. The time came when the church contested in its own name absolute sovereignty. Sure enough, did it not represent a higher and therefore more universal truth than any political authority, since spiritual must be considered higher than secular truths? On the basis of such a philosophic or geometric concept, if you will, the church laid claim to world sovereignty. Spiritual axioms would seem to be superior to all material postulates whatever. While such maxims prevailed, scientism must bide its time and could receive no hearing. The individual and his interests were lost in contemplation of the perfect, or nearly perfect, geometric forms which men reared on the theory of deduction. These were forms of state and church, of theological and philosophical systems and the inventions of political and social doctrinaires.

III. THE ABSOLUTIST DREAM OF CHURCH AND STATE

Perhaps the most significant fact about the absolutist dream has been its quest for the unchanging. We deride the mathematical illustrations by which the early absolutists in philosophy, the men of Elea, sought to prove that change was an illusion. Geometrically considered, the footsteps of Achilles could never overtake the infinitesimal progress of the tortoise, therefore change was but a phantasm of the mind. In such manner did they try to persuade themselves of the validity of their own ideas. If one possesses the universal axiom, if he is the recipient of an infallible revelation, what further can he ask? From this must flow as in Euclidean geometry all other figures and solutions. The suggestion of progress under those conditions seems not only incredible, but impious in religion, and treasonable in the state.

Such a doctrine could never have dominated the multitudes except for the inertia of common minds. Humanity takes to infallible dogmas in religion, in politics, and in science, because of mental laziness, the love of undisturbed security in unshakeable convictions. We grow inevitably angry at the man who disturbs our certainties. Our wrath against him is multiplied the more surely he is proved to be correct. Our indignation approaches the proportion of geometrical progression if we discover him unsettling dogmas of social, religious, or political faith upon which our selfish interests depend.

The new, or modern, tyrannies, whether of Fascism, Nazism, or Communism are in each case an appeal to a sense of security: national security as opposed to other nations or races; social security as opposed to other classes, high or low; and all based upon such absolutistic axioms as those of Hegel, Marx, Hitler, or Mussolini. It is not strange that such absolutisms should feel it necessary to drive from the field all differing ideologies. They must be total in their wars as in their philosophies, since the existence of any other system than their own gives them feelings of insecurity and frustration. If one's whole world of reality is formed on the geometrical pattern of the Idea or doctrine, its only safety lies in driving out contrasting ideas.

One important consideration arrays itself against the success of this type of dogmatism; it has marshaled against it the fact of life. Life is a process of continuous change. An institution which ceases to adapt itself to the changing environments of time can survive only by the suppression of its own intellectual processes. Such inhibition, tried many times in history can succeed only in such a case as that among the Chinese when a whole nation was in its political and social philosophy convinced that progress was an illusion. Even there the unavoidable breakup came with real contact with Western ideas. No political absolutism can succeed except by reducing the conquered people to abject slavery. This slavery cannot stop with physical intimidation; it must reduce the mind also to a kind of idiocy if it is not to fail. The world should be possessed of no illusions as to the eventual terms of peace if such dominations succeed. The peace as well as the war would be "totalitarian." This is truly a colossal undertaking but the alternative is that idiocy itself is contagious and will eventually attack the conquerors. We have a significant illustration of this in the reported conclusion of the totalitarian government in France that the new order calls for "the de-intellectualizing" of the people. The first step as reported in the press was to demand the discontinuance of the teaching of philosophy. More potent than any other is the truth, however, that life has its own way of lording it over death and staticism. Absolutism must as surely give way at last before the forces of life as it is certain that last season's oak leaves will succumb to the rising sap of spring. Such is the end of Absolute axioms, authoritarianisms, dictatorships, or totalitarianisms of any kind, in a living world.

IV. SCIENCE AND DEMOCRACY

If we ask ourselves certain questions about the progress of Western thought we become aware of unmistakable contradictions and paradoxes that have lived so long together that most men are blind to the inherent and lurking oppositions. For instance, we think of Plato as the world's supreme idealist. His concepts were developed into Neoplatonism and taken over into Christian theology by the fathers of the church. Plato himself was advanced in Western thought to a standing little short of sainthood and his philosophy provided the frame for the theological structure of ecclesiastical authoritarianism. At first glance all seems committed to a pure and noble idealism and spiritualism. Then comes a historian of philosophy who by quoting Plato's *Republic* makes him out a practical materialist. If we push the matter further we find a score or so of utopias bearing the significant peculiarities of *The Republic*. One utopian has already been advanced to sainthood,—St. Thomas More, but his utopia has the main characteristics of current Communistic doctrine. The list of utopians also includes Karl Marx. His work maintains the same old resemblances and is surely materialistic. The world has but recently been startled by the discovery of mutuality between two great totalitarianisms—Nazism and Communism. Where is the answer to that problem to be found if not in the identity of their ideologies?

Looking into Greek philosophy we come upon even more incongruities. The Milesians while they were materialists were yet genuinely scientific in the modern sense of the word. They sought to free men from superstition by referring physical events to natural law, but so long as Platonism with its eternal and a priori concepts was in the ascendant, scientism was in eclipse. When at last science returned to recognition in the European scene it came under the aegis of Platonic-Aristotelianism. This tradition loaded the scales in the direction of the absolutes of space, time, and matter that came as a Neoplatonic heritage to lead science to a new authoritarianism. Science reappears in the field then burdened with a double monism, an absolute monism of matter which it inherited from the more distant scientific past, and a monism of ideas as exacting as the absolutes of Zeno. This is the reason perhaps that the point to point correspondences of Zeno have seemed so baffling to some modern thinkers. Zeno's paradoxes were invented to confute Heraclitus' claim for a living and changing reality and the substitution for it of an absolute and changeless Mind. These ought to be contradictory theories, yet we find them sitting together. When Epicurean scientism again revived it became a great arouser of the democratic spirit, a new ally and herald of democracy. Why have these contrasting ideas become so inextricably mixed in our concepts? Do they possess some common feature which hides the incongruity?

Whatever answer we make to these questions there has been a strange concurrence in the history of the Western world between the scientific method of arriving at knowledge by experiment and the upsurge of the democratic spirit. It is abundantly illustrated in the annals of the West from the time of Milesian science to Socrates and Epicurus, from Marcus Brutus to the French Enlightenment and Revolution. Empiricism puts every experimenter on a common level, ruling out authoritarian revelations that cannot be verified by experience. No fact can be considered inconsequential or omitted. Individual data which cry out against the hypothesis cannot be long suppressed. There is democracy among scientific data even for the unwelcome facts. Consequently science is found on the side of democracy.

v. The Common Thread of Failure

The proponents of the respective ideologies of arithmetic and geometry will neither of them be likely to admit failure. The inextricable blending of these contradictory systems, however, in the history of Western culture would seem to indicate that by neither alone can satisfactory solutions be found. If we catch our greatest idealist, Plato, in the role of a materialist, and the greatest materialist of our times, Marx, in the character of an idealist, what strange congeries of ideas seem to be interpenetrative in spite of themselves and the logicians. Such a mixture could never occur but for some common menstruum. If in the contradictory propositions we can find something that is held in common, that may suggest the reason why neither concept alone presents us with a solution.

If we note the reaction of the two systems upon each other we may recall that the Milesians laid down an essential axiom, the monism of substance, which was later incorporated into the fundamental doctrine of absolutism by the Eleatics. If as the Milesians stated it, there is one primary substance from which all things arise, and it should become necessary to consider mind and mental activities as real, then that one substance must account for mind. They jumped to the extreme conclusion that it was exclusively mental, or spiritual. Similarly the absolutists neglected the problem of matter and landed in subjectivism, just as the scientists had neglected the problem of mind and thereby became materialists. But their opposition to idealistic absolutism led them into a materialistic absolutism. In denying that mind is all, they affirmed that matter is all. The great controversies of Western philosophy have raged about this contradiction.

When with its revival in modern times science again began to dominate thought, it took over this unconscious heritage from absolutism. It makes little difference whether we describe the pedigree of these scientific absolutes—Milesian, Epicurean, and Lucretian—whose impenetrable, indivisible, and eternal substance was pictured in the Democritan atom, or whether we lay the burden on the absolutism inherited from scholasticism in which modern science arose. The result is the same in either case. We have in each dependence on an absolutistic dogma. The deadlock is between a monistic world which is spiritual and mental in character or one which is purely material. Spiritualistic monism finds itself worshiping an Absolute or God who by its own definition could take no part in the creation or ongoing of a material world. Materialistic monists must on the other hand, if logical, deny the possibility of knowledge altogether since their world has no place for mind as a reality. This is the meaning of the affirmation by Herbert Spencer and others of an Unknowable as the ultimate reality. Some modern physicists are frank in the matter and boldly confess their inability to make any affirmation about anything whatever.

It becomes apparent that the common source of this dilemma resides in this common absolutism. If the absolute idealist must concoct a God so unlike man as to have no part nor lot with him, and the materialist has erected a world which is out of reach of human interpretation perhaps the solution of the dilemma is to be found in man himself. Since he is both the subject and the interpreter of experience, a sort of dweller in two worlds of mind and matter, perhaps he is the menstruum in which the age-long contradiction is solved. We may make a great show of learning by denying this, and we may say that we do not know *how* it can be done, but we practice it with every decision we make and with every interpretation which we give to the world of experience. We cannot deny *that* it is done. Doubtless we would like some stronger demonstration of the nature of reality, but doubtless we shall never have it. When we get to the self or person, we are at the end of the rope of experience and can go no farther. What we call personality may be and is the nexus of thought and thing, mysterious to be sure, but nevertheless experienceable by all. This nexus of thought and thing which is a person, *is* reality, and the only kind of reality we can know.

VI. NEW TRENDS FOR NEW TIMES

It should now have become clear that a close relationship exists between the histories of peoples and their ruling concepts. Such a relationship existed between the empirical method of early science and democracy, between the absolutistic ideals of Plato and the neoplatonists and the development of autocratic institutions in Western life. If we discover a change of any moment in basic ideals or concepts we may look for corresponding changes in the direction of human history. For three hundred years absolutism has been losing out in one field after another. The battles against autocracy in the state went on simultaneously with those in the church. In religion the latest phase has been the assertion of the autocracy of theological absolutes, infallible doctrines or Scriptures. Last of all to yield have been the absolutes of science: absolute substance, time, and space, energy, light and gravitation. These are now seen under the theory of relativity as linked to particular moments and situations. Thus in our own time science has come to free itself from the geometrical absolutes. For instance, space is not now seen as a vast geometrical form to hold things that may not be there. It is rather a relation between things that are there. Though we speak of them as gone, and for serious minds certainly their day is numbered, yet the old confusions will still remain confused for many who do not see their way to think implications through to their only conclusion. Science in clearing itself from its inherited absolutism may be on the threshold of a new freedom and development for the service of humanity of which it is at present unaware. It might under certain conditions remake the world. Absolutism is now making its final stand around the earth which is like the struggle of some gigantic Titan in the grip of death. There are many incentives to the fear that democracy may perish in the storm. But there should be now no misunderstanding of the nature of the present world crisis. It is a death battle between absolutism and individualism, between authoritarianism and democracy. The contest is so widely waged, so universal that it gathers into its periphery all nations and races and tongues of men. The issue must now be won and that without equivocation. The new democracy must be without the taint of the old special privilege of absolutism. It can only become so when it rises to the full recognition of the supreme and inestimable value of every human person; when it discovers that governments, churches, creeds and educational institutions exist primarily to secure the highest values in every person. The time seems propitious for this recognition since it has long been preparing in state and church and in scientific thought. We are already in the bending circle of a changing direction in history.

CHAPTER XX

THE CHANGING DIRECTION OF HISTORY

. . . .

THE OBJECTION HAS been raised that the redefinition of the atom cannot be considered a sufficient basis for the assumption that a religious, social, or political revolution may rest in it as hidden cause. The presentation of such an assumption must be admitted as arguing the existence of a certain hardihood in the claimant. To some minds it will not even be clear that in the last twenty years or so we have changed from the concept of the atom as an inert space-filling mass to something essentially different. If, however, we are to admit that the ultimate unit of matter, instead of being a lump that has to be moved from the outside, is rather to be pictured as a multiple of many energies from the activities of which we interpret lumpishness, we are taking up concepts that bear revolutionary proportions. Our concepts of reality in the past have certainly changed the face of human thought and history, and there is reason at least to suspect that they may continue to affect the future.

After all our concept of inertia in the atom may be more or less the reflection of the torpor of the human mind which finds itself averse to the mental effort of readjustment to new ideas. The argument against change seems always to bear with it the dignity of good sense, sound thinking, and traditional respectability. "Since the fathers died have not all things remained the same" seems like a counsel of perfection. The span of a human life is so short and the front of civilization is so extended that, to the perspective of any one life, changes do not carry with them the credentials of their own importance. Perhaps no society has ever yet discovered itself to be in the throes of revolution until that revolution was already an accomplished fact. Only the insights of history and philosophy can give intimation of events to come, and discover for us the relation of the initial concept to its outworking in human affairs.

If the concept of arithmetic, as presented in the preceding discussion, with its summation of integers has led to an emphasis in Western society upon the individual and this in turn has favored the inductive method in science; if the faithful multiplication of individual experiments which science has held essential to the establishment of truth, has had any effect upon how we see our modern world; if the emphasis upon the importance of every item in the experiment which characterizes the scientific mood, has had any influence upon other fields of our thinking, we must then admit the new possibilities that face us. The method of science has undoubtedly favored democratic concepts, because of its insistence upon every item of truth as necessary to the whole result. On the other hand the geometrical method of deduction quite as surely neglected the individual items in the dream of the perfect and completed figure, of hypothesis, society, state, or church in such a way as to lead to fifteen centuries of autocracy. This is the plain speech of history. We shall therefore contend that it is worth while to investigate any new theory of reality that threatens to become a ruling idea in man's vision of nature, with a certainty that it is loaded with implications for the future of human society. If the thought of reality as matter has disclosed iself as important it may be no less important if that notion has been transferred to something else. The transfer may be quite as important in its implication as the original concept itself. We have exchanged a lumpish and inert atom that could move only as it was moved from without, for one whose very essence is activity. It is not too much to say that with that change of concept we have traded off an inert and lumpish world for a world of reality that moves from within. Under this notion our universe is seen as a living self-acting reality. The ultimate effect of this change of view is difficult to visualize. We stand now to get rid of many myths. Among these, the materialistic models of reality that we have summoned to our aid disappear. As for instance we have spoken of the attraction of gravitation as if it were an invisible rope that bound planet to sun, or of an ether which was necessary to provide a material medium for the transmission of light. We have sought in chromosome and gene some material aspect for the transmission of qualities quite immaterial, and which were assumed to be present and not present at the same time and place. All this was due to the overriding myth of materialism which would yield no reality unless it was assumed to be primarily material, after the ancient traditions. Our former efforts at constructing wooden models of reality which Lord Kelvin declared necessary to understanding, begin to appear fantastic. One might much more easily imagine a wooden model of a football game which would account for all possible combinations of players both in attack and defense; yes, and for the psychology of the players as well. This dilemma of confusing content with organism is disclosed by discovery of the Principle of Uncertainty. Here there is no place for either intellectual indifference or scientific smugness. We suddenly become conscious of more problems than it seems any generation can solve.

There is nothing discrediting to science in saying that, in main, its working concepts are as fictional as the x, y, and z, of mathematics. These fictions or mental constructs are as necessary as the irrational *infinity* of mathematics, and they are valuable so long as they can respond to the relationships they attempt to symbolize. As soon as new facts come over the horizon, new symbols must be invented if better can be found. Sometimes we cling to the old when we are aware of their inadequacy. For more than a hundred years the Daltonian atom has continued in physics though for many years it has been known to be non-descriptive. The nineteenth century found it impossible of belief, and not discovering how to do without it, maintained it with sheer dogmatic persistence until the new concept of electrical atomic structure came to take its place. Even "being dead it yet speaketh" in the common parlance as if nothing had happened to it. How quickly these changes have taken place is shown by the late date at which physicists were contending for the "pellet" atom of Dalton. It was the working hypothesis of Bray and Branch in 1913; of Sir William Bragg in 1920; of Aston in 1922, who wrote of it that it was no longer a working hypothesis but an established fact. Bohr in 1923 considered it proved beyond all doubt, while Desch in 1925 was assuring the British Association that atoms (the Daltonian) were proved realities, now they had been exploded. By 1928 Eddington was referring to them as mere "pointer readings." Today they are being described in terms of electrical force, the seat not of inertia but of inconceivably great activities. One modern description of the atom, as well as of reality is "an event in a space-time continuum."

Our former atomic world has been one that to our way of thinking was ruled by external circumstance somewhat like the God of the deists who could break into the world only by some sort of miracle. So, in science, we have nursed in the interests of materialism a concept that was wholly incongruous with natural activity. Even psychology in the endeavor to prove itself scientific has bogged itself in the same mire. In society we have dreamed that man could be saved by the amount of his material possessions or made happy by social security without regard to the status of his inner life. We now face in a new science the implications of a dynamic world. The new patterns of science which have resulted in a complete reversal of its ancient metaphysics and have turned its material real into an event real may in the progress of development revolutionize the world in ways that now seem improbable.

Perhaps we can now consider one by one some of these possible developments and ask what results may flow out of these changed concepts. In doing this we should keep in mind the fact that these scientific models of today are to be viewed only as tentative hypotheses which discoveries of tomorrow may outmode. We should therefore avoid dogmatism or excessive emphasis.

1. Relativity and New World Concepts

The doctrine of relativity does much more than break down the old absolutes of space and time. A relational world is one which emphasizes the importance which each factor bears to the whole. It is essentially arithmetical rather than geometrical. The whole is dependent upon the parts as in a mathematical sum.

First of all, relativity calls for a "frame of reference." This introduces an element which has hitherto been foreign to scientific theory, at least in any thoroughgoing way. It would perhaps be more exact to say that it has always been present but hitherto unrecognized. The motions of the heavenly bodies cannot be measured with the exactitude that present-day science demands without naming the specific point or plane to which they are to be compared. This point or plane of reference may be relative to the position of the observer, and it must be relative to a fixed imaginary plane. For the first time in history man finds himself consciously involved in his observation of the external world. He discovers that the world he sees is not entirely independent of himself and his own standpoint. He is seen now for the first time as an integer in his own sum. Even his geometrical absolute is discovered as less than absolute because it bears discoverable relations to himself and must be considered from the standpoint of relativity.

Such a concept most certainly has implications that will eventually find expression in the social and political as well as the scientific order. It should greatly reinforce the democratic impetus of modern society. If arithmetical concepts have aided democracy in the past by calling attention to the individual, the doctrine of relativity puts new emphasis on the person. He is no longer a mere integer. He is a chooser of frames of reference. The world of knowledge depends more or less upon that choice. Things are what they are to him as seen from his chosen position, and though what he sees is somehow relative to the whole, his own viewpoint has a validity which cannot be denied. The new democracy which relativity encourages will be a democracy of quality where in the past we have emphasized the democracy of quantity. How will that differ from an aristocracy? In the demand that every citizen be given an opportunity to develop the quality which is potential to him. The new democracy will realize the importance of getting the most and best out of the least and feeblest. The least of reasons for this is any personal satisfaction to the individual though this is of high value in an ordered society. From the standpoint of society there are other great reasons. Any person has a unique contribution to make to the whole which cannot be neglected without loss to every part of the community. Still more, the foremost citizen with all his powers is something less than his best unless all those beneath him are contributing their own peculiar gifts to the community. Society like the universe around us is relational, and the result of society is also relational.

This principle is as applicable to international politics as to national. Tyrannies, slaveries, and areas of unenlightenment, in a relational world, can be seen only as plague spots that retard and threaten the welfare of the whole. Applying the same principle to education, we see not only the importance of encouraging all types of learning which can add to the richness of human experience, but likewise the necessity of bringing all types of education within the reach of all classes of the people. Every citizen is entitled to the highest cultivation of his unique ability not more from the standpoint of personal enjoyment and self-expression than from the enhanced values with which he endows society as a whole. Society is entitled to his best.

Under the relational concept religion, too, would take on enhanced meaning and importance. Its universal presence in and appeal to persons will be recognized as a proof of its importance to social relations. Here the judgment of religious values would be subjected to the pragmatic and ethical tests. Thus religion must be measured, not by claims of creed and opinion but by its works. On such a basis all religions would be called upon to demonstrate their value in life.

II. CONTINGENCY AND FREEDOM

Professor C. G. Darwin insists that there is no escape from the Uncertainty Principle,[1] and declares that this must revolutionize our ideas about one of the long-accepted and fundamental doctrines of science, the principle of causality. If he is correct, events must be seen as portions or manifestations of a vast relationship, and predictability is based upon the statistics of probability. Darwin would like to believe that the Principle of Uncertainty still leaves no opening for free will but the only conclusive argument against free will in the past has been just this scientific claim of absolute predictability. What philosophy has long pointed out now becomes the working basis of science, namely that the affirmation of causality is meaningless apart from personal will and purpose, either human or divine.

Whether or not Heisenberg's Principle of Uncertainty obtains a permanent place in scientific thought, it directs new attention to the position and importance of the subject of experience. The observer must be considered along with the phenomena. This remains in spite of the fact that science is charged with assuming that it may discover the discrepancy that appears in the unaccountable jump of the electron from an inner to an outer orbit. The duty of science is to attempt to reduce to exactitude

[1] *The New Conceptions of Matter*, The Macmillan Company, New York, pp. 116 ff.

and predictability every known phenomenon. If it stops short of that attempt it is untrue to itself and ceases to be science. The special charter of science is the reduction of mysteries, and it is nothing against it that it has revealed the existence of greater mysteries than it has solved. The discovery of the Principle of Uncertainty has a bearing on many more things than the activity of the atom, for it is here dealing with the very nature of reality. The upshot cannot help leading us to the fact that we, our thoughts and acts, are as much a part of the system of nature as the atom itself. As go atoms, so may go men. If the atom is an activity, a not altogether predictable event, and these activities work toward certain definite and co-ordinated results, the old block universe of inertias and mechanisms must pass from the scientific picture. If events which may or may not occur, do take place to produce certain relational ends in a series, they cannot be considered the result of a mechanical determinism. The alternative of such determinism is freedom. Such contingency or freedom, however, need not be considered to imply lawlessness. The law of a given activity is only an expected uniformity of action, and if it acts toward ends it may very likely spring from the uniformity of a freely willing person. In fact, it needs a personal will and intelligence behind it to invest it with any meaning. Freedom is never synonymous with lawlessless and disorder. It comports only with intelligence and self-restraint. Uncontrolled action, not in conformity with nature and natural functions, can never be free. Nature is never chaotic. The relations she achieves are very complicated, and she fits part to part with a minute exactness. The flower is fitted in advance for the honeybee, while the bumblebee finds his wants equally well supplied by varying species. The fig tree trusts the climax of her functioning to the wasp, without which she would be unable to produce either fruit or seed. These facts which could be multiplied endlessly present too much of a burden of explanation for the cleverest materialist to meet. In a world of contingent events which rise and pass, the relation between events can be foreseen and prepared only by some factor which itself does not rise and pass and to which the whole series has a meaning. If we cannot have a mechanical or physical continuity, and this seems no longer tenable in the new physics, we must have an intelligent and personal one.

These are the conditions in a contingent world by which we can account for uniformity in nature. Only a choosing subject of experience and a director can be assumed to act uniformly in the pursuit of rational ends in a reality consisting of events. The rationality of the end has a relation to the uniformity, which is willed rather than necessitated.

The true basis of freedom is often overlooked in society as well as in the world of physical phenomena. The free man works purposefully and the uniformity of the results is not due to mechanical necessity but to the rational expression of his will toward the end he seeks. Any deviation from the life of reason makes him a slave of circumstance, of unworthy ends, of evil passions which prevent the free and natural functioning of life. He must exercise his freedom in the pursuit of rational and normal ends or he loses it. It is only by self-control that he can direct his energy to the fulfilling of his highest functions and so realize freedom. Tree and bird and beast and man lose freedom and set the universe against them when they stray from the high path of natural functioning, which means only to be true to one's highest possibilities. Nature has set a reward upon purposive freedom.

III. QUANTA AND THE DOMINANCE OF MIND

If the establishment of Heisenberg's Principle of Uncertainty has dealt a blow to the old theory of causality, and is confirmed by other physicists who declare that there is nothing more certain in physics, we may be sure that we have hit more than one bird with the self-same stone. Gone is the smug complacency of a La Place who could answer King Louis' objection that there was no room in the great astronomer's system for God, with the reply that God was not needed. With La Place a knowledge of the initial cell would embrace all the happenings of the universe, and all the events of history, since all were therein contained. La Place's Cell has a standing alongside of Plato's Idea, and both should be recognized as concepts of the same order. In addition to the passing of the mechanical notion of causality, Heisenberg's Principle is linked up with the Quantum Theory. What is true of causality is likewise true of the presumed con-tinuity of nature. Continuity is a mental not a physical aspect of nature, and cannot be known apart from a perceiving mind whose unique characteristic is its immanence in and transcendence of the space-time order. Continuity is a part of the meaning which mind gives to the kaleidoscopic events and multiple relations which are active in time. But the continuity is one of meaning and not dependent for validity on physical contact. When this is apprehended, the difficulty about discontinuity in nature vanishes along with Zeno's paradoxes for the discontinuity may depend upon a higher causal continuity which is intelligent and purposive. So far, mind has been treated as if it were foreign to nature and therefore negligible. We shall eventually discover it to be not only in and of nature, but the highest expression and the most cogent power in nature. This light could never dawn, however, so long as lumpishness was considered the prime characteristic of reality. The time has come when, if we are to have a satisfying explanation of the universe, we must consider not time and space occupancy the highest reality but the transcendence of time and space by living personality. In this privileged spot lies the clue to successful explanation.

Planck has clearly shown that in nature we have not a continuous but an intermittent energy. These discontinuous impulses he calls *quanta*. If this is true it could be that *quanta* "are issued as needed." Their activity may spring out of or in accordance with a rational requirement. They may issue in response to a demand made by the general system of relations which calls them into being. But to get such a result we must endow nature with intelligence and personality in either a pantheistic or a theistic way. The pantheistic notion would call for an equal intelligence and self-direction in every separate cell. It is less difficult to assume that the presence of intelligence is the result of a higher personality capable of reviewing the whole process. In other words, the universal order may be dependent upon a supervising Mind more than upon a continuously uniform energy. We must admit that such a concept is difficult to describe and doubly difficult to visualize. But it is no more difficult of understanding and description than the activity of a human will in the manual production of these pages, or of the mysterious connection between the will and the muscles of the man who lifts a stone. Our stumbling block, again is our absolutistic materialism. We are afraid to accord reality to our own mental decisions unless we can bolster them by some reference to material reality. We should long ago have realized that physical continuity is not necessary to action and reaction. We have in our scientific thinking been beset by the feeling of necessity of dragging in some material container for immaterial and invisible quantities to make the reality of those quantities seem more certain. If only we can imagine the spot in chromosome or gene where lies the quality blue eyes or yellow hair and mark it X we feel we have accomplished something scientific. We overlook the black, brown or hazel eyes of ancestry that may also lurk undiscernibly in the same spot to upset our calculations since they also are "inherited." If, in accordance with the Quantum Theory, physical phenomena need not be continuous and are not of necessity the result of physical contact, they may very well be due to the presence in nature of an Intelligence which is mindful of the whole process. A nature whose energies move in *quanta*, and not as "something always there," existing quite independent of meaning is a nature whose rational explanation requires an indwelling intelligence or a supervising Personality. Such indeed is the latest conclusion of Planck himself. Changing from a former extremely materialistic, mechanistic, and atheistic standpoint, he has of late, in his work, *The Philosophy of Physics*, arrived at the affirmation of the theistic position.[2]

IV. DURATION, LIFE AND PERSONALITY

The greatest significance of all in the changing ideologies of science lies perhaps in the definition of reality as an event in a space-time continuum. A continuum requires not only a before and after but a continuing self-referring subject of the persisting experience, for experiences persist only in meaning. That is, a continuum of any kind calls for an observer who can grasp a unity of meaning past, present and future. We are all accustomed to the ancient treatment of time as a flowing stream. The past no longer exists and cannot return. The future does not yet exist. All that we seem to have is an eternal now which forever eludes us since it is gone before we can reflect upon its meaning. Thus analyzed, time seems to be the least of all our possessions, and this is the futile result of our attempt to define time as a reality apart from meaning. Time is really but the form under which we relate events. But passing events cannot be related except by

[2] W. W. Norton & Company, Inc., New York, p. 79.

something which keeps its identity through the events and gathers their manifold relations into a meaningful sequence.

Providing this fact means anything at all it means that an order of evolution is possible only to a unitary self-referring subject which itself does not rise and pass away with the events which it contemplates and brings to pass. An *élan vital*, initial force or Prime Mover, must then be something beside an accidental upset of the *status quo*. It is really the continuing source of a closely interrelated series of events. If these events are to have meaning, as when for instance conceived as a part of an evolutionary process, they will have such meaning because of an Intelligence in or behind them. This is a logical conclusion since the theory of evolution is a meaning we have constructed out of events long since past and dead. All the items of knowledge, both experiential and analogical, point to a certain rational form in the appearance of species. Hence the theory of evolution is the most rational construct we can assume for what has happened. This could have no meaning apart from the assumption that if there had been a self-referring Intelligence present the unfolding order of evolution would have been what it would have experienced. Since no human being has been able to survey the process, and since it is represented as occurring in an orderly continuum, the presence of a supreme Creative Intelligence working in or through nature becomes a rational supposition.

What is true respecting the time continuum of an evolutionary order is equally true for any event in time. It applies likewise to the human observer. The human subject of experience is thus raised to a new dignity, since he is capable of gathering the discrete events into a meaningful whole. In that sense he can be said to transcend time. This transcendence of time is bound up with self-recognition or self-consciousness. Living in a relational world then means living in a world whose reality consists of meaning for persons.

This fact, again, is full of significance for democracy, because the person is important for a world whose realities consist of events. Science is now free to move away from the old absolutes of impersonal realities to realize the fullness of its arithmetical tendencies as a voice of freedom. It must move in this direction as a strategy of self-preservation, for science can flourish only in a free society. No governmental forms, save those of freedom, will dare to give to science a free range for its activities and discoveries, and to put every discoverer on an equal footing of validity. Where tyranny flourishes science languishes or dies, for science is a potent threat to autocracy, and a menace to revolution. This is the fact that renders the present crisis of such moment to civilization. The new "Enlightenment" of science brings with it the opportunity to become a leading factor in a new birth of freedom by being true to itself and its own principles.

These are some of the considerations which lead us to believe that the new theories of science can portend a new and better day in human history. If belief in the inert atom brought on the mechanical age of the world why should not belief in an atom of inherent activity bring on a new age of the spirit?

CHAPTER XXI

DEMOCRACY AND THE PERSON

....

THE POSSIBILITIES OF a renewed and outstanding contribution of science to democracy have already received mention but these potentialities are obscured by the present condition of the world. Mankind is now undergoing a great disillusionment. From a state of mind in which science seemed to promise a near approach to the millenium; the early solution of economic and social problems; the reign of peace, plenty, and intelligence, we have in a few brief years been brought face to face with the fact that scientific knowledge without moral integrity may lead us only to a new Dark Age, the destruction of civilization. Such a crisis calls for philosophic consideration and particularly for any light which may be shed by a philosophy of history.

It may well be that a frank consideration of the conflict which is contemporary with the rise and development of Western culture will indicate the new direction which science may take toward human betterment.

As we review the history of Western civilization we become aware of a certain persistent antagonism which has characterized its progress. This enmity is typified in the argumentative conflicts of the Middle Ages over universals and particulars. As we have seen, this was really a struggle between the geometrical and the arithmetical concepts of social organization. In a very true sense it has been a contest between Eastern and Western ideology as the West has attempted to clear itself from Eastern absolutisms of every kind. Into this conflict has been woven one continuing thread from the struggle between Xerxes and the Greeks to our own time. This war of ideas has been the recurring fugue and undertone of the whole movement. Present at Thermopylae as at Marathon, at Pharsalia or at Tours. The conflict is between authoritarianism and democracy and is now reaching a new world climax. The democracy of the West has never really clarified itself either in practice or in theory, never having fully separated itself from the Oriental concepts out of which it arose. This influence has been potent in religion and art, in politics, and economic theory, in philosophy and in science. Science is now at a new point of departure where it need no longer be ruled by absolutistic theory. Moreover, its own future progress is now at stake, for the ultimate triumph of democracy is as vital to the future existence of science as it is to the future of civilization.

I. CLARIFYING THE ISSUES OF DEMOCRACY

The present handicap of Western genius is due to the uncertainty which arises from the infiltration of absolutistic ideas. Democracy has never defined its objectives with sufficient definiteness, nor has it properly estimated the relation between practice and ideals. This has been due to the fact that it was a new venture which was in process of growth. At first the Greek cities conceived of democracy as a participation in public affairs by a very restricted class of citizens whose livelihood was provided by a voiceless and numerous slave caste. In the Free Cities of Europe democracy grew to the wider participation in government by the craftsmen who had through apprenticeship been admitted to the guilds. Not until the rise of the American Commonwealth was it deemed advisable to grant the suffrage to all classes of citizens. Even here the founding fathers were overwhelmed by their own boldness and immediately took steps to keep the results of popular suffrage under safe control by constitutional checks and balances. A long period had to elapse before the abolition of slavery and the granting of suffrage to women.

There is with all the progress made to date a great surviving uncertainty as to what democracy means. Democracy has been made more or less identical with universal suffrage, or with universal education or with equality of economic opportunity or with equality before the law. Selfish and designing elements of society have often been able to circumvent these objectives. Weakness has developed through the sentiment for freedom, the unwillingness to interfere with the privileges of individuals even when they become antisocial and against the common interests. The remembrance of ancient tyrannies has yielded a tolerance toward individuals incompatible with the progress and security of all. Through this tolerance the enemy of the common welfare too often goes unchecked.

The saying used to run: "The cure for democracy is more democracy." The supposition was that the good sense of the citizen would lead him to vote for the common interest. But too often in practice his care is preeminently for his special interest. Democracy possesses no power to give insight or honesty. It cannot altogether purge or restrain the work of avarice which is its chief enemy. The rights of the individual have been over-emphasized, while his obligations and responsibilities to society have been too often forgotten. The most serious oversight has perhaps been the reversion to a blind trust in the efficacy of Democracy spelled with a capital D. This is only a recurrence of the old absolutisms under another name. We have returned to the worship of institutionalism as if that could save us. Thus men are led to repeat democratic formulas that have lost their meaning to the modern world and to assume that if we can retain these forms we are necessarily preserving democracy. True democracy is a thing of the spirit which cannot be guaranteed by oaths, however severe, or compulsions of any kind. Promises do not insure the fulfilling of a contract on the part of any man who has not the will and the spirit to fulfil it not only in the letter but in the spirit. The serious deficiencies in democratic practice have thus been due not to failure to acknowledge outwardly democratic principles but to personal abrogation of them in practice. Each man is eager to have the law apply to his neighbor but feels himself in some strange manner released from strict observance. Thus is built up a practice and a theory of special privilege that is inimical to real democracy and which sufficiently prevalent will overthrow democratic institutions.

Because democracy is a thing of the spirit it cannot be preserved by embalming it in laws, institutions, or constitutions or any of the given forms of organization because it is never impossible for selfish and designing men who gain control by one means or another to turn the institution into authoritative and absolutistic forms. Dependent as it is upon the spirit of men, democracy alone has the power of readjustment to social and political change. Like the living organism of the plant so long as it is wedded to living issues, and is fed by a common earnestness it will have power to accommodate itself to social and industrial changes such as cannot be accorded to any autocratic institution. The only power that can kill it is the indifference, avarice, or the undemocratic attitude, of citizens who live under it and would profit by its protection without themselves recognizing any personal obligation toward the common welfare. Perhaps the now-discarded proverb that "the cure for democracy is more democracy" has a deeper meaning and cogency than has yet been generally recognized.

Democracy can survive only through the widespread belief in the ultimate and supreme worth of the person. It was this conviction which made possible the inception of democratic ideas, it has been some resurgence of this conviction which has under-girded every advance of Western culture. This is a conviction which no caste or class system can achieve. If democracy is to survive we must have a renewal of belief in the possible worth to society of every human being. Here must be discovered the supreme value for which all societies, organizations and governments exist. True democracy holds that every person has capacities which are of moment to the state, that these capacities can be realized and developed only under freedom. This means that none is so poor or so low in the scale, nor so high and independent as to be overlooked. His life and his capacity have a worth and meaning by which all are entitled to profit. To find his true place in society is likewise to find his own highest development, self-expression and happiness. The greatest good to the greatest number means not merely a passive receptivity. It is not merely a right but is also an obligation. Repression is considered justifiable only to prevent action hostile to the common welfare. Unless this conviction governs, universal suffrage, universal education, the common advantages of democracy themselves may become a menace.

It will not do for the present age to falter before so vast and impractical a dream where our pioneering fathers stepped boldly forth. Let us proceed to a new and more perfect clarification of objectives as we live under the light of more extended experience.

II. The New Appreciation of the Person

The various absolutisms ignore or depreciate the person. Thus it becomes possible for institutional religion to appear anti-democratic and authoritarian. The chief consideration being the survival of the institution, or the creed, or the scripture, or the formularies, the person can only adapt himself to what is considered changeless and infallible. The effort to restore the person to his proper place and function in religion has been agelong, an important part of the struggle for democracy.

While the conflict within philosophy has been less grim in results it has been no less real. As Augustine once said: "Men go to admire the peaks of mountains and the vast floods of the sea and they neglect themselves." There has always been something scandalous—ever calling for philosophical anathema—in a philosopher who contended for the reality of the interpreting person. Such have for centuries been the butt of laughter for materialistically inclined minds. Humanity is only beginning to arrive at an appreciation of the key to reality which resides in the person and his experience.

More than any other in its importance as an influence is the new appreciation of the person which is coming over the scientific world. A cosmos of relations calling for frames of reference, which are to be chosen from many possibilities demands a person who chooses, and his interpretations are seen as dependent upon his point of view. Absolute truths and absolute interpretations become impossible or inconceivable. Man no longer can be thought of as looking out on a world of fact from which he is quite divorced. The most important fact may be the interpreter himself.

We have already seen how natural is this newer view of the world to a science which proceeds upon the arithmetical concept. No integer in the mathematical sum may be lost or omitted without changing the result. The important thing is not the hypothesis or the geometrical figure to which facts must conform but the facts themselves. This is the spirit of ancient Greek science and it is the spirit after which modern empirical science has striven in the method of induction. But in spite of this, modern science has almost to the present given itself to the verification of hypotheses to such an extent that its progress has been hampered. As one scientist has recently put it, it is much more easy to assume an error in the experiment than to imagine a discrepancy in a generally accepted hypothesis. This is only the hang-over in scientific practice of the old absolutistic dogmatism.

The new temper of science is to return to that freedom from dogmatism in which it took its rise. This new temper includes the person as an item, a necessary item, in scientific knowledge. With such a turn science can advance to a new freedom. As she does she will also become a new instrument of democracy. The common habit of depreciating man which has for two hundred or more years been the custom of much scientific writing cannot continue under this new impact. Nor can the new temper be kept out of philosophical and religious reflection any more than from scientific thought. All this is incompatible with despotisms of every kind. The triumph of authoritarianism can now be seen as betokening the death not only of religion and philosophy but of science as well. The issue is at last clearly joined.

Such is the strangle-hold of ancient absolutisms that to offer the person as the cure for present ills seems absurd, yet here is surely the most promising solution. History should have convinced us long ago. For instance, we have in the past vainly imagined that the future of religion could be assured by compelling men to the lip service of an institution, a creed, a literature, or a form of words. Men have professed allegiance to all these and then have proceeded to break the spirit of every truth to which they have subscribed. The most sacred and devout formulas, the most eternal truths and principles have been appealed to in the pursuit of the most selfish, avaricious and diabolical schemes that are known to mankind. Nothing can preserve these principles but personal character itself. Where the person has a will and a desire to goodness, success seems to blossom out of strangely illogical credos. Where personal character has been re-formed there is no argument against religion but only the convincing power of a great dynamic. However pure may be the professions and principles of any institution it is in reality dependent on actual achievement of character by the persons who compose it.

In much the same way is science convincing when its pronouncements proceed from disinterested, skillful, honest observers, who have no hypothetical axes to grind and who fearlessly report what they see and discover. It is perhaps a strange thing that so little attention has as yet been paid to the necessity for moral and spiritual integrity in the scientist. In reality an integrity is called for which is no less than religious in its scope and sense of responsibility, and the field of science has never been wanting in its martyrs to the cause of truth. Morally irresponsible persons cannot approach the world of scientific knowledge without distorting and misinterpreting what they find there. In the last analysis even science depends for its credibility on the personal character of the scientist.

If the person, his integrity and character are bound up with the success of science and religion, it is no less true that democracy is dependent upon the person. Democracy has achieved its highest measure of success only where the greatest pains have been taken for the development of the person. The granting of suffrage itself can only presuppose the existence of voters who believe in the spirit of democracy and that they are intelligent enough to recognize the common good. The voter is by implication something of a statesman. Far more than this, he is presumed to be self-controlled and moral, using that suffrage not for selfish benefits but for the common welfare. There has been no difficulty with democracy where the average person has been thus enlightened and self-restrained. Where these conditions do not generally obtain democracy becomes impossible. It can only follow the alternative of relapsing into the violence of mob rule on the one hand or of autocracy on the other. In general, men have the choice of ruling themselves through self-control or of being ruled by others. In any case the success of democracy rests with the intellectual, moral and spiritual status of the person.

III. THE COMPLEMENTARY CHARACTER OF OPPOSING CONCEPTS

To set before us the extreme danger to democracy of absolutisms is not to be blind to the service which hypotheses and dogmas must render in providing ideals as a backbone or skeleton to furnish the forms of organization. Democracy is a point between chaos on the one hand and tyranny on the other, and it exists in varying degrees. The peculiar gift of human personality is the power to formulate ideals of action and to work toward them. Organized and purposive life calls for ideals. Nor can the human personality be satisfied with an aim short of perfect achievement. The achievement of absolute perfection is by human beings impossible but not inconceivable. The dream of perfection is a human creation calling for inspiration no less than divine. But it must grow with man's own intellectual and spiritual understanding. If there is growth or progress, the ideal of yesterday must give way to a larger one today. The attempt to fix a conceived ideal or absolute into an infallibility which will command all the future is therefore futile. However well expressed may be our credo, ideal, or hypothesis, it can be no higher than the best interpretations of those who seek to understand it. It suffers the fortunes of the age which holds it. Our strictest absolutes are relational in spite of all our devotion. This does not mean that they are to be discarded any more than as formerly they were blindly worshiped. It means that we must grow to their larger meanings. They are necessary to any ordered life.

The danger in absolutes from which democracy suffers is the peril that some form of organization, some method or watchcry, some governmental credo will be allowed to crush out the just rights and liberty of individuals. Quite true it is that society has a right and duty to protect its citizens from the violence of its antisocial members. This can be justly done even to commanding the life and resources of the individual for a common good, but it cannot be done justly except for the preservation of a common freedom for persons. Such powers cannot be rightfully exercised for a dream or formulary of state, an institution, or an absolute of any kind without regard to persons. Whatever its name, such exercise of powers becomes a tyranny. The thought to be kept in mind at this point is the supreme value of the person as such. The person can realize his value only in a system of freedom. The aim of democracy is to hold such a balance between chaos and tyranny, between anarchy and despotism as will grant the individual the highest freedom consistent with the common good. This precarious position between two mighty forces arrayed against it from opposite poles is what has made democracy seem at times so hesitant and futile. Obviously the person, his education, and enlightenment, must be the supreme guardian of democracy as he is also its chief goal and end.

IV. THE ANSWER TO TOTALITARIANISM

Although totalitarianism is a word of recent coinage and, in our day sadly hackneyed, it seems most expressive of that type of absolutism which most influences our own time. The chief characteristic of totalitarianism of various kinds is its denial of the supreme value of the person. Not only does it overlook the rights of the common man but it would force him to conform without regard to freedom, morals, personal self-expression, or achievement, to its own pattern of society, its own social, political or religious concepts, its own organization or to a single despotic will. In totalitarianism the form is everything, the person nothing, except as the tool of an ideology. Totalitarianism becomes thus the chief foe of democracy. The reason for this lies in the relation of persons to democratic practice. A true democracy attaches the highest importance to the development and self-expression of the person because it looks upon such development as essential to its own success. Democracy is a venture, a living growth which gives greater promise for the future. Totalitarianism, on the other hand, is certain that its hypothesis is the only correct one which can brook neither change, growth, nor variation. It is not subject to individual interpretation or opinion and its success lies in its being imposed on all alike. The very nature of totalitarianism as of absolutisms of every kind, is, that while they offer an immediate advantage as best fitted to meet a definite situation, being hostile to growth or change, they cannot satisfy for long the demands of the human spirit. With all their show of power and force they are therefore unfitted to meet the changing exigencies of society and whatever form they take or however complete, their success can be only ephemeral. This is the long verdict of history which tyrants never seem able to learn. The power of growth and of life is bound to undo them. Democracy is, in contrast, able, because resting on personal development and character, to meet the demands of life and change. It seeks living values not forms. Seemingly weak in a given situation, it holds the future in its hands because it alone can command ultimate respect and obedience. To win then, it needs only to be true to its fundamental principle, the supreme value of the person.

Never in human history has mankind been faced with greater exigencies than those which are to be met by this generation. A crowded world, becoming more crowded through growing populations, conquest of disease, conquest of space through transportation, and universal dissemination of information presents problems for the solution of which there are no precedents.

One thing should be clear if a world thus crowded is to continue in peace and respectability, some type of organization must be found that makes life possible for all. The easiest solution and the one calling for the least intellectual effort is the assumption of the totalitarian state. Here it is hoped to spare the individual citizen the labors of democracy or the distractions of governmental policy by placing all power in the hands of a dictator or at the most in that of a political cabal. Not only is the effort made to relieve the citizens of a given state from the perils and problems of self-government, but arguing from the thesis that there are ruling races, the totalitarians would restrict rule to their own kind. Any scheme which assumes the superior right of any one ruler, race or class to govern all the others is totalitarian in principle, regardless of excuses offered. Democracies can never long exist half-slave and half-free. Restriction of suffrage for any other reason than that of intellectual incompetence or criminality is a betrayal of democracy.

Evidence is increasingly at hand that absolutisms which outrage the finer qualities of the human spirit cannot be the final answer to the problem. The reason for this is that they do not meet the needs of men on the higher levels. Men can be satisfied only for a time with being well fed and well housed at the price of intellectual and moral slavery. Authoritarianism is an anachronism in a scientific age like this, for the very breath of science is freedom. If despotism failed in simpler times it is no less stricken with death at the present moment. The present conflict must be considered the death struggle of ideas that have been made obsolete by the general enlightenment.

The strength of modern absolutist movements lies in a capacity to confine the thinking and planning to one man or to a small group. This makes possible immediate organization and quick action. It is the most effectively instant form of human co-operation. To meet the peril, democracy must present an equally potent co-operation and organization, but how can democracy with an unwieldy variety of opinions which must be consulted, do this? The notion of regimentation is repugnant to any practice of democracy we have known. It must be admitted that this is the stark and unwelcome fact of the present hour. Against such a peril democracy has one resource; it can regiment itself. The present dilemma of survival then is whether we shall regiment ourselves as free citizens of a democracy or whether we shall be regimented by some totalitarian power, domestic or foreign. There would seem to be no escape from one of these alternatives.

Self-regimentation is not easy. It is slow of movement. Its power is a long-range power but its eventual strength lies in its conservation of freedom. It can be brought into being only by deep convictions, convictions with the pervading strength of religious beliefs. It is thwarted and hindered by every avaricious, self-seeking or crackpot citizen, but it is ultimately convincing as it appeals to those higher motives which human beings can respect. Self-regimentation means self-control, self-restraint and in a final analysis such self-control—the amalgam of all democracy—is dependent on the achievement of personality by persons.

SECTION IV
THE SURVIVAL OF THE WEST

CHAPTER XXII

THE DESTINY OF THE WEST

. . . .

SPENGLER ATTRIBUTES THE program of Western civilization largely to the "sense of destiny" that has characterized it, but, adopting the ancient Oriental concept of history as moving by cycles—that philosophy of history so characteristically set forth by Schelling, who saw it as the Iliad of the soul away from God, followed by an Odyssey of return to God—he believes we have reached the end of the cycle and that the decline of the West is assured. Whatever may be the appropriateness of its application to Western history, the scheme itself will be recognized as distinctly Oriental, the ancient theory of emanation and return, and as essentially alien to the arithmetical concepts of Western thought. It is this alien quality in Hegelian philosophy which, perhaps more than any other, has made it disturbing to the modern mind. Our intense individualism is all in the opposite direction. We do not think of ourselves as emanations, and even our extremest mysticism is not a longing to be lost beyond recall in the being of God. The genius of the West has looked toward a permanent mending of human conditions, social, political, educational, and religious advance. The Western man has not conceived of himself as an animal at an unending treadmill of progress and retreat. He believes he is advancing toward the perfect society. He looks upon his gains as permanent. This is, perhaps the chief distinguishing feature of the Occidental from the Oriental outlook. It is the source of Western impatience and unrest as distinguished from Oriental passivity and calm. It is not strange that to the Eastern man this seems the besetting sin of the West. To him progress is something so entirely foreign, so presumptuous, so futile, that it seems quite crude, quite lacking in insight and dignity, entirely unphilosophical. He is quite likely to feel outraged by what appears mere Western bustle, aggressiveness, thirst for power, and dependence on the new.

There is much of cogency in the Oriental distrust of Western manners and philosophy. The West no doubt needs the refining impact of Orientalism, but the present need is for mutual understanding, that each may profit by the best which the other has to give. This ideal of permanent gains for human society is perhaps the noblest thing that can be said for Western culture and should be considered quite apart from the question of how incompletely it has been achieved. So long as the ideal lingers there is hope. Should that ideal vanish from its dreams, the decline of the West would be swift and certain.

Herein lies the redeeming principle in the Western "sense of destiny" which Spengler has overlooked and which completely changes the essential interpretation. Without this element of social advance concept of destiny becomes mere selfish aggression, the manifestation of the power of the strong over the weak. Too often the hidden idealism has played into the hands of selfishly designing parties who have used it for oppression. Sometimes these elements have been so strong as to seem to include whole nations. But the ideal has survived, winning its major conflicts now against governmental autocracy, now in the interests of universal education, now in the advance of democracy, and equality of opportunity, now upsetting threatening systems of caste, now freeing men from the pretensions of religious tyranny, now abolishing slavery and every sort of peonage. These inner conflicts which Western civilization has waged within its own body in the interests of its ideal must be considered if we are to look upon it with understanding. It has been attended by weaknesses that would have been fatal had there not remained the suppressed, but never extinguished, gleam of great humanitarian ideals. As always, however, the camp followers of her progress have been on hand to loot and oppress, to exploit and enslave. Frequently they have shared the plunder so widely that the moral virus of their corruption has spread to multitudes, but grafters have never been looked upon save with contempt by the most significant members of Western society. Western culture has expressed her hopes in a score of utopias, and had it not been for this redeeming dream, the iniquities of her children would long since have accomplished her destruction.

In the light of these facts it may be valuable to make reappraisal of the Western "sense of destiny," and to press the inquiry as to whether she has a destiny or will survive.

I. THE GOAL OF THE WEST

Facing the Golden Gate at the bay of San Francisco stands the statue of an American Indian on horseback, entitled "The End of the Trail." Both horse and horseman present the dejected appearance of extreme weariness and hopelessness. They have reached the end of trails and journeyings. There is a physical sense in which the statue symbolizes the present condition of Western civilization. From before the days when Trojan refugees streamed into southern Italy and its adjacent islands, Western culture has been the story of one long migration. It is only a superficial interpretation to say they were searching primarily for wealth or power or conquest. They were not nomadic, erecting transient dwellings of insecurity. Wherever they have gone, after the first days of pioneer adaptation are over, they have built of stone. They loved their homes and the institutions of an ordered society. Even when they fled from their enemies they did not hesitate to build themselves permanent habitations, as when, within the sheltering lagoons of the Adriatic, safe at last from pursuit, they raised the fair palaces of Venice.

Even the Westerner's colonizations have been so universally conspicuous as an effort to found a home for himself and his children that colonizations of mere conquest and exploitation are negligible in his history. He has ever hoped in the new home to secure a footing for the blessings of a larger freedom and a better social order. Everywhere with him has traveled this sense of destiny, the founding of a new civilization.

But his advance into the unpeopled and unsubdued parts of the earth has blinded him to existing weaknesses. His perfect society, though unrealized, seemed possible across the ranges or the plains or beyond the seas. He had neither time nor patience to fight at home the beasts of entrenched wrong and special privilege. It was easier to escape and to face the wild beasts of the wilderness or the solitudes of the desert, or the bitter wastes of the Poles. In the new land to which he was going there were to be better conditions, temporal, political, and religious. He and his children would there be as free from the tyranny of custom as from political and religious autocracy. These moods kept him moving, ever moving, into the West. There was something of that very look into the sunset which called for the completion of his yet imperfect day. This progress could continue in these terms, however, only so long as unsubdued wilderness lay before him.

He has now obviously come to the end of that trail. The question is: Will he lose his ideal when it no longer appears achievable across the mountains or in the environment of new surroundings? Will the pioneering spirit enter into a reappraisal of institutions already established? Will his "sense of destiny" take on a new import into which he can throw his old enthusiasms? Will he sublimate the old urge for new surroundings to the higher level of a new and better civilization? Will he turn to the achievement within the present order of the dreams that have sent him trekking around the world? In that former movement he had frequently to forsake all that was dear to him— stable society, personal security—for a life that was filled with peril, accompanied by hunger and hardship, and whose end was hid from all but his own ideal vision. One cannot but believe that the hardihood and heroism that have led him through long centuries will not desert him in his hour of greatest need. Were one gifted with the spirit of prophecy we would predict that with the same energy and with equal ideals he would proceed to set his own house in order. Just now he has reached the end of the lower trail. Will he go forward to the higher? The hour of his decision is here: it is critical, and it is full of import for the civilized world.

II. The Test of Destiny

The present crisis will provide the proof or disproof of the correctness of the Western sense of destiny. The physical progress of the West has become the source of its critical problems. Its scientific discoveries have brought all nations and races into its own dooryard. Its financial and business organization have driven it into relations with all people. If the Westerner begins to feel crowded, it is his own fault. His religion has emphasized to all men the essentials of a world-wide brotherhood which embarrasses any claims to political, social, or religious superiority. The virtue of his own ideals has emptied of all glory the force of military supremacy. Scientific achievement, in which he has long prided himself, falls under the same judgment. He sees his numberless and unlimited factories adding not to the richness of society but to the exploitation of the weak, the degradation of artisanship, no less in his own land than among alien races. The competition of his own machines, in the hands of peoples of low economic standards now threatens him with starvation at home. The tragedy is that this counter-attack has been led by men of his own race who were ready to betray him and all others for their personal gain. It is another case of camp followers who are quite content to cause defeat so long as loot is to be had. At the same time the activities of these hangers-on have laid him open to world-wide suspicion and made him the object of universal hatred. He faces bitter enemies without and treacherous foes within.

From such a situation there is no way but up. It is up or perdition. But it is also the opportunity and the culmination of the centuries, the fulfillment of many generations of hopes, dreams, and migrations. It is now for the first time possible to provide for a narrowed and expectant world the way to a higher civilization. The ultimate victory in the present conflict will go not to the most forceful arms, nor to the will to power. The victory will go to that order of civilization which shows itself best fitted for the arts of peace, which is able out of the present chaos to set up a government that shall protect the weak, that shall cultivate initiative and give to all its citizens the opportunity for their best self-development. The ultimate leader of the world will be the nation which, accomplishing these things, can also live in peace and friendship in a crowded world, which can win universal confidence for the disinterestedness of its intentions. Such a nation must have as fine a sense of justice and of tolerance for aliens as it has for its own.

One can imagine easily a Gargantuan laughter at propositions which at present seem so preposterous, for some will look upon them as a vain and foolish idealism, but society in general must rise to such an idealism or Western culture will succumb to effacing wars and barbarism.

In such an hour arise numerous false prophets whose blunted foresight and lack of insight would urge us to overlook the task of educating, moralizing, and improving the conditions of the people. In addition to arms for defense we must have also seriousness, power of thought, social disinterestedness, and, in its highest sense, religion. Such problems as these have never been settled by arms alone. The uncounted hordes of Persian soldiers could not conquer the Greek love of freedom. The Romans in turn subdued the Greeks, only to find themselves conquered by the superior philosophy of Stoicism. Ostrogoth and Visigoth overthrew Rome's prestige, only to be overcome by Roman institutions of law and letters. It is a commonplace of human experience that he who conquers by force of arms often becomes the vanquished of history, in some subtle way being conquered by the very ideas and ideals he set out to overthrow. This is the judgment of time from which there is no appeal. The reason, we suspect, lies here—that the poorest judgments of reason are better than the best judgments of force, and the identification of any ideal with military force alone is sufficient to secure its ultimate defeat. Men are eventually conquered by superior institutions. The present struggle is one between institutions, between civilizations, and only the best can ultimately survive. Here must lie the proof or disproof of the value of Western "sense of destiny."

III. What is "Western Culture"?

It may be that to this point we have been so occupied with the external aspects of Western culture, such as "sense of destiny," freedom of speech, press, and opinion, of universal education and equality before the law, that we have not sufficiently considered the inner essence of Western culture of which these are only the implements. Let us ask again what we really mean by the term. What is the underlying spirit or motivating principle which has given the man of the West a sense of destiny to be fulfilled? What did he hope to bring to the world, or to achieve by his recurring treks across desert and mountain and sea? What were just laws, universal education and free speech to accomplish?

The intention he had in mind is as apparent in his failures, in his consciousness of frustration, as in his successes. At the moment we are very conscious of the shortcomings of Western society. We have already recounted the failure of the West to capture the ideals at which it has worked and the attendant sense of frustration. Even-handed justice has been turned aside in many ways. Attempts at an education which should satisfactorily enlighten all the people have been disappointing. Inroads have been made on the rights of free speech and free press. Democratic and representative measures of government have been perverted by the demagogic, the selfish, and the strong. The great scientific advances and discoveries which have been fostered by the freedom of democracy now threaten to engulf the more precious achievements of the spirit. These are some of the dark shadows that becloud us at noonday. Perhaps if we seek the sources of our discomfiture we shall discover that they are part and parcel of our ideals themselves, due to the greatness of our dreams. No such uncertainties seem to attend the totalitarian concepts of society. Their complete and cyclic view of history seems to create a notable smugness and self-satisfaction. They turn man's thought away from himself and fix it on an established ideology which promises a perfect, if theoretic, solution of all problems, at the same time releasing him from the obligations of individual thought, action, or responsibility. He has no sense of personal frustration at the ills of society. They are presumed to be due only to the failure to adopt the favored scheme. Their solutions are as easy as dialectic.

The contrasting Western concept is on the other hand wrapped up with the achievement of personal freedom. Events are seen to flow, not from ideologies but from individual actions and decisions. Every migration the Westerner has made has been in the hope of escaping some deadly conformity and regimentation with which an older order has attempted repeatedly to enslave him. The same spirit moved the Puritan who fled to Massachusetts, the Roman Catholic who took refuge in Maryland, and the Quaker who sought the forest solitudes of Pennsylvania. They fled from the securities of a conformed world that they might be free. If somewhat narrowly, they sought to impose their own decisions upon those who followed or attended them it was from the fear of losing those very liberties they came so far to seek.

It seems clear that the reality and substance of Western culture cannot be held to lie in external achievement, nor in material prosperity, not even in its institutions as such, since the Westerner is not like his totalitarian brother a mere worshiper of ideologies. Western objective is a spirit of freedom based on the right of every person to the completest self-expression and fulfillment possible without the invasion of similar rights in

others. There are obvious weaknesses in such a system. The sea
of liberty is as dangerous and uncharted as in the days of our
fathers, for it holds as uppermost the welfare of persons as
persons. Doing so it is like the organism of the plant which must
continually readapt its living processes to changing environments
of climate, necessity, and growth. The free development of the
person is the end toward which all these other things, just laws,
free education, free speech, and representative government are
but the means and safeguards. It is only when these means are
considered as ends in themselves that the foundations of Western
society are endangered, for more important than any theory or
institution is the freedom of the individual. Here must be sought
the essential reality of the genius of Western civilization.

iv. What is Likely to Survive?

We seem now to be standing in one of those interludes of
history which are momentous in the decisions between contrasting concepts. Western civilization is threatened by discordant
and competing theories within its own body. Our world has come
too largely to prize its accomplishments rather than the vitalizing
spirit that made those achievements possible. We now face the
hazard of overthrow by violence of the gains so hardly won. To
many observers it must seem quite incredible that Western
democracy should not necessarily pass with the external institutions it has founded. We are forced to ask what there is sufficiently stable, substantial, or enduring to survive the attacks of
totalitarian ideology on the one hand, and the very necessity on
the other of a regimentation strong enough to repel it. It is not
to be wondered at that men look with dismay upon the type of
organization demanded if we are to defeat the forces of tyranny.
This incompatibility is the source of much present confusion and
despair. Very little consolation is to be gained indeed if we consider primarily the preservation unchanged of the institutions we
have already erected and which are so dear to every one of us.
The face of these structures has changed appallingly (if change
is necessarily appalling) within a short lifetime. Is there that in
Western culture which can survive threatened changes in our
social foundations?

The only comforting reply we can get to such a question must
come along the line already suggested, and it seems to us like a

strong anchor of hope in our troubled age. The important thing is to cling to and foster that spirit of personal freedom which has survived the tyrannies and changes of the past. Whatever regimentation must be entered into to meet the peril of the hour must be sponsored from within rather than from without. A strong and free people must pull itself together, forgetting selfish interests, in order to preserve the spirit of personal freedom. But the preservation of this spirit as a fact is the main thing. If we can keep the spirit of freedom, we can again in happier times rebuild all that we have lost, and infinitely more and better. There is no devastation either of resources or of institutions which free men may not rebuild. Our founding fathers in every trek westward were forced to begin without other resources than their own devotion to freedom and their native strength. Their very necessities became the source of new strength and inventiveness.

The persistence of this spirit of freedom in Western life which has enabled it to overcome untoward circumstance is exactly the element which is lacking in totalitarian philosophies. They replace confidence in the essential capacity of the person with trust in a shibboleth and system. They are dependent on a form of expression. They offer no chance for individual freedom in action or judgment. Every man is presented with a complete system which he must not criticize but to which he must submit. Initiative becomes a danger or a crime. Such a system dies at the top because its intelligence must spring from limited counsels, and foreshortened information. There is no opportunity for growth, development, or change to meet varying conditions since these are looked upon as hostile or revolutionary. "Purges" of its enemies deprive it of exactly its most valuable counselors. In contrast with all this the spirit of freedom looks upon liberty in each man as superior to and necessary to all other values. Democratic methods are made the sources of its power. Moreover the demand for freedom is natural to every man. It grows more insistent in the midst of oppression, survives every persecution, possesses a common appeal which cannot forever be suppressed. For these reasons it may be safely assumed that the spirit of freedom will survive in spite of every oppression, and that it will eventually rebuild "the old waste places."

v. The Conflict of Philosophies

We are witnessing at the present a conflict between incompatible philosophies of society. At the possible expense of repetition let us get the differences clearly in mind.

The underlying principle of totalitarianism, however diverse its outward aims, is identical with that of all sorts of authoritarianism or absolutism. We are presented with a supposedly perfect system, springing from the ingenious brain of a Marx, or let down from heaven, but in any case forever above criticism demanding submission. The good embodied in such systems need not be denied. They provide platforms of belief and worship which serve as valuable rallying points for people too weary or too incapable for independent judgments. But like geometrical figures they cannot be changed without destroying their original character. There is no place for individual genius or invention. The processes of such a society are stereotyped. The individual must conform to the system imposed upon him. Departure from the accepted philosophy is treason. There is no sanctity of the person which is recognized as inviolate. Men become pawns in the service of a great and infallible idea.

The only effective opposition to such systems can come through recognition of the intrinsic worth and value of the free person. The spirit of freedom is a living urge as insistent as life itself against the molded forms that would captivate and confine it. The very essence of Western culture is to prize that invention and discovery which any given personality may reveal and to reward such a person as a benefactor of society. This fact is vividly illustrated in the case of scientific inquiry. The very moment any scientist is bound to discover facts in keeping with any preconceived notion, that moment science would be at an end. It is so with the spirit of democracy. There is safety for it only in freedom. Its future prosperity, its very existence is dependent upon the promotion and encouragement of new and fruitful ideas. Because each person is a potential contributor to the common knowledge and welfare, his right to full expression becomes the strictly guarded treasure of the state. This is the essence of Western culture most frequently overlooked, and the one most often endangered by the lethargy of society. Such danger to the structure of democracy arises when we forget the spirit of free-

dom in the interest of maintaining the *means* to freedom. For it
is possible to so worship the established forms of democracy as
to pass over into totalitarian ideology. Hence comes the abuse
of law, of free speech and press. They do not include the right
to be used for the suppression and oppression of other persons.
They do not constitute freedom to indulge in false and damaging
statements or even in misleading propaganda. There can be no
freedom to invade the full rights of other persons except for
the common welfare. Whenever the institution becomes more
important in the eyes of men than the right of the least and
weakest of persons, we have resorted to a totalitarian philosophy
even though it be in the sacred name of democracy.

The present conflict then is one between that concept of society
which considers the person and his freedom of less importance
than some concept or organization of the state, and a belief that
the free person is the supreme aim and achievement of the social
order. Never before in human history have these contrasting
philosophies presented so clean-cut and so world-wide a conflict.

CHAPTER XXIII

CREATIVE IMAGINATION IN FUTURE CULTURE

N O ONE COULD justly claim that Western culture is at the
present time lacking in creative imagination. The difficulty lies not in its amount, but rather the point at which it is
directed. This must be held as the source of the present incongruities in our economic, social, and religious life. Our effort
has been bent so exclusively on production that overproduction
and economic want, bursting granaries and starvation, colossal
fortunes and dire poverty, are the strange bedfellows that share
our household. Organization, which should be the handmaid of
the social order, has along lines of mechanical production never
been equaled in the history of mankind, but social organization
lags far behind, still in the swaddling clothes of infancy. One
dares to assume in spite of popular opinion that no period has
ever witnessed a wider financial or missionary interest in religion
than at the present time and yet the external prosperity, diversi-
fied programs, enlarged churches and multiplied resources bring
a consciousness of frustration on the part of those within organized religion.

This unfortunate jumble of circumstances, opinions, and lack
of convictions is not to be laid so much to the evil wills of men
as to the fact that the creative imagination of our age has been
trained too narrowly to a pervading commercialism which has
not only quenched the springs of the broader economics which
the times demand, but has likewise blunted the social imagination, perverted the ideals of education and has dimmed the ardor
of religious conviction.

Generation after generation of a race cannot be trained to
the single belief that achievement of wealth, commercial prosperity, and physical comfort are the outstanding marks of success,
without bringing into being a civilization distinguished by commercial genius, but dwarfed socially, politically, and spiritually.

Overemphasis on material things cannot fail to draw in its

train consequences far outside its natural realm. Commercialize a man's heart by making the monetary the chief interest and you transform his outlook upon society, education, political life, and religion. In fact, we have been spectators of such a movement which has left no nook or cranny of our life untouched but has molded even our attempts at art and literature. The chief artistic creativeness we can actually point to is along the line of the commercial—our temples of business, our means of transport, and communication, the increase of physical comforts. To recognize this is not to be unmindful of the artistic and social merit of these creations, but to call attention to the narrowness of the field and to expose the causes of our creative poverty in the broader domains of culture.

Our great achievement in lines of invention, mechanics, commercial enterprise, and business organization has resulted from an almost exclusive attention to these things, an absorption so complete that it has marked our age as deficient in political wisdom, social organization, creative art, and religion. The overemphasis of the material aspects of civilization has dwarfed the life of the spirit, dulled the creative genius of art, and left us without true standards of judgment in that which is most worth while.

In the sources of present weakness must also be sought the means of strength, and it may well be worth our while to study the relation of a broadened and surviving Western civilization to the cultivation of the creative imagination.

I. THE CREATIVE IMAGINATION IN DISTINCTIVE CULTURES

In estimating the different racial and national cultures it is quite the custom to follow a naturalistic interpretation and to assume that the differences are first of all geographical, and after that economic, and finally, physiological. From these three as causes, mental and spiritual characteristics are held to have their rise, whereas, on the contrary, they are at least the modifiers and at most the creators of the external features of any civilization. This can be admitted without denying the natural influences acting to change human choices and outlooks. If we can sometime achieve a history of civilization which will take into account these more creative forces rather than the less important ones, much of value will be added to our understanding.

Even a little consideration will indicate that climate, food supply, and physiological differences, if there are such, cannot be held as the main factors in determining a culture. Equatorial climate cannot account alike for the mental superiority of the East Indian and the inferiority of the African. Neither can the difference depend on a racial basis, for the African has under the proper conditions shown himself not intellectually inferior.

If we cite economic demands, as is often done, the question at once arises as to the source of the sense of economic need. Our own Nordic ancestors were long enough wandering nomadic tribes content with very simple satisfactions. We would be so now but for the rise of a creative imagination that led us no longer to be happy with nomadic life. If association with higher civilizations like that of Rome is named as the cause, we have still to remember that the new wants came as the result of acquaintance with hitherto-undreamed ideals. It might have been quite possible for those contacts to have been without result but for the creative imagination of the people influenced. One of the earliest American Indian tribes to be entertained by the Great White Father at Washington is said to have climbed out of the luxurious quarters in the hotel to sleep in the open air on the roof. Even those aborigines who have enjoyed the doubtful blessing of a state-administered college education do in many instances go back to the forms, habits, and cuisine of the tepee, once they have graduated. All of which indicates that contiguity with a so-called higher civilization is quite insufficient for results unless there is a stirring of the imagination which gives the individual a desire to enjoy and to be like that which he sees. This is a mental and spiritual and not a physical process. A man's economic demands will move no faster than his capacity to visualize his wants. The showman must precede the salesman.

Neither can tools be said to make a civilization, for there must first be a man to make the tools. The tools are themselves the result of creative imagination and until it operates there is no sense of need, nor capacity to use the new tool.

Language is sometimes cited as the main prop of distinctive civilizations and there is no doubt that, once formed, it exercises a powerful influence to expedite or to slow up thought, literature, and communication. But to say that language makes a people is to put the cart before the horse, for it is the people who first make the language. The language springs from inventive and pictorial creativeness. Inept and ponderous verbal forms do undoubtedly slow up or even make well-nigh impossible great literary expression, nevertheless these forms were not a natural but an imaginative growth. Their ineptness and lack of facility must be laid to a lack of imagination in those who originated them. Liberation from inferior forms of expression can come only through the inventive genius of the more visual-minded of such a language group.

Racial retardation is frequently laid at the door of tradition. We need, however, to ask after the sources of tradition and we find here as in the case of language certain symbols evolved by the genius of a people to conserve certain customs held to be beneficial to the race, tribe, or clan. These traditions are nevertheless man-made, possessing mental and spiritual content, and are in the highest sense the work of the creative imagination.

Obviously, then, if we are to get at the essence of a civilization, we must inquire not only about the climatic and geographical conditions, the sources of economic need, tools, language, and tradition. None of these alone can be held efficient causes of any historic culture. It is not only his world but man's reaction to his world which builds the whole fabric of his common wants and his common achievements.

II. THE SOURCES OF GENIUS

In discussing the sources of genius we have much popular misapprehension to deal with. To the unthinking, genius is the result of birth or accident or magic. Nothing could be farther from the truth. Genius is the flower and fruitage of a long discipline which has deposited what may be called technique in the subconscious mind. No artist can become creative while he is conscious of brush, paint, or canvas; no musician can find original expression of musical concepts who is hampered by the consciousness of the relation of his hands to the keyboard. Until technique becomes quite thoroughly unconscious it stands in the way of creative achievement. Technique does ordinarily have to be laid down by very slavish and very attentive habit. Every creator is aware of the necessity of detachment for his task. So long as the effort is a conscious one he remains an artisan but does not rise to the artist.

The Prince of Lu asked Ch'ing, who had finished a bit of furniture that seemed of supernatural execution, "What mystery is there in your art?" [1]

"No mystery, Your Highness," replied Ch'ing. "And yet there is something.

"When I am about to make such a stand, I guard against any diminution of my vital power. I first reduce my mind to absolute quiescence. Three days in this condition, and I become oblivious of any reward to be gained. Five days and I become oblivious of any fame to be acquired. Seven days and I become unconscious of my four limbs and my physical frame. Then with no thought of the court present to my mind, my skill becomes concentrated, and all disturbing elements from without are gone. I enter some mountain forest. I search for a suitable tree. It contains the form required, which is afterwards elaborated. I see the stand in my mind's eye and then set to work. Otherwise there is nothing. I bring my own natural capacity into relation with that of the wood. What was suspected to be of supernatural execution in my work was due solely to this."

Sometimes it takes the specialization of generations to develop this technique. Sometimes the technique becomes nation-wide, as in the case of American business. When a family thinks, lives, eats, and sleeps in the thought of some particular activity, to the idea of which it has been reared from childhood, we have families of musicians or merchants, or of distinguished clergy and literati, as illustrated by the Beecher family.

The inventive genius of our age takes its rise from such a concentration of thought and purpose until it seems as if man were capable of doing anything which he strongly wills, desires, and to which he gives himself completely. Such is the definite background of our present scientific achievement. It is the appearance of genius on the basis of a technique laid down through several successive generations.

Such being the case, we can produce the kind of a world we will, provided there can be a sufficiently definite, compelling, and widespread interest to create it. It is thinkable that we might have a world with a genius for art, for music, for poetry, or religion. What has been done sporadically by the attention of

[1] H. A. Giles: *Chuang Tzu, Mystic, Moralist and Social Reformer,* 2d ed., Shanghai: Kelly & Walsh, 1926.

individuals is certainly possible on a larger scale whenever humanity in large groups is ready for it and willing to pay the price. About such a result there is nothing of magic or haphazard, as it follows the regular laws of all achievement.

If our age can become so obsessed with commercial success, industrial organization, scientific invention, that it is able to constitute a new physical world and in fifty years bring about differences in men's wants, needs, outlooks, and ambitions, may we not hope that devotion to the more spiritual ideals of deeper values may bring results more vital and more useful than any yet achieved? What we need to remember is that the sources of such achievement lie within the gift of the creative imagination.

III. Leadership and Visual-Mindedness

If the foregoing be true, one of the most essential qualities of leadership must be visual-mindedness. By this is not meant the shallow kind of "go-and-get-it" variety. To sight must be added insight, and insight is the gift which fools despise. The shallow mind believes only in sight—what is obvious, what it can seize, what seems momentarily desirable, without inquiry into long-range values, ultimate consequences, or moral and spiritual fruitage. This is exactly the kind of leadership which curses the world of our day. It boasts of callousness, is proud of its incredulity and has no capacity to understand those underlying factors in any situation which are at the moment not obvious but which will ultimately control. These factors are the philosophical, the sentimental, the artistic, the religious, the emotional, such as "the world's cold thumb and finger fail to plumb."

It is this deeper visual-mindedness amounting to insight which is necessary to true leadership. Those old, old words are eternally true, "without vision the people perish." For without insight the sources of artistic genius, religion, and all those things which give lasting satisfaction to a people dry up.

Chestov has somewhere written: "People with little imagination live by the past and the new life they create hardly differs from the old." Here lies the secret of all backward races, the clue to the unprogressive peoples. The Chinese were a civilized people with highly developed arts, superior culture, and a genius for inventiveness that made them possessors, thousands of years in advance, of many luxuries of the present age. All this took place while our ancestors were for some millennia still destined to the life of nomads, wandering about in sheepskins and goatskins and without written language or art. However, at this moment in their history arose one of those movements which change the face of civilization. In this case it may have been a recrudescence from their patriarchal past of the philosophy of filial piety, or it may have arisen through the repressive measures of such conquerors as the Mongols.

Amazement is often expressed that a culture so full of promise should have been checked so suddenly in full career. One need not be unmindful of the surpassing genius of Chinese art in those fields into which it has been turned, to realize that this arrest of development took place because of the conquest of a philosophical idea or a governmental tyranny which attacked the creative imagination at its root, and like the trees of a Japanese miniature landscape compelled a civilization to be not less cultured but more narrowed in its scope.

Thus it will be easily seen that the development of the creative imagination is not necessarily an evolution forward. It may quite as easily take a backward direction. There is in the nature of things no Providence or law which apart from the will of man will insure progress in the arts of civilization.

IV. A WORLD DREAM TO CAPTURE THE IMAGINATION

Christopher Dawson in his work *The Modern Dilemma* suggests that an international world order is dependent on such a world culture as does not yet exist.[2] This truly states the dilemma that faces modern civilization which cannot endure on the present narrow nationalistic and circumscribed basis. It must become cosmopolitan or perish. This situation is due to the narrowing lines of commerce and trade, swift communication and travel. The lone inhabitant of a desert isle may indulge to the point of madness in idiosyncrasies which could not be tolerated in a center of population. Insanitation in China threatens the health of Los Angeles, false ideals in New York exert a contaminating influence in India. Economic distress in Germany imperils the financial structure of the world. This condition becomes more aggravated every day with every increased facility of steamer, radio, or airplane. In this steadily tightening and narrowing world

[2] Sheed & Ward, Inc., New York, 1933, p. 18.

we are attempting to carry on as if none of these modern factors were in existence. That is the tragic meaning of the effort to galvanize the ancient nationalisms into the semblance of life. Such is the import of new tariff barriers, the slogans to "buy British" or American or French. Such expedients even at the best could be but a stopgap against the restless and overwhelming tides that threaten to engulf us. So far we have done no better in dealing with the problem than to dream of wars and to indulge in war, but such a course can only mean inevitable destruction for a large part of the human race. The only effective way, quixotic as it may seem to the politician of our time, is to meet the problem by mutual and international understanding. Yet the means of that common understanding appear everywhere to have broken down. And why? Because too widespread is the imagination of national, racial, or class privileges to be had at the expense of others. Avarice, that foe of peace and democracy seems to have a seat at every council table or peace conclave. And behind avarice stalks unfaith, a suspicion of secret treaties and understandings which themselves amount to nothing in a world where promises are made only to deceive. There could scarcely be more complete evidence that the present trouble with the world is fundamentally a spiritual insolvency. And now there can be no peace short of destruction or the re-establishment of good faith.

Narrow nationalism, idiosyncrasies of manner, of custom, of language and literature, false propagandism, appeal to racial or national prejudice, bear the ring of a false heroic, and aggravate the problem bringing no solution for anyone. Increase of benefits, enlargements of understanding, progress in civilized wants, these are needed for that larger world of which we dream. The conditions are such, however, that it cannot be achieved by any one nation alone nor by any block of nations, if any considerable portion of the world is left out. The time has come when, if we are to continue, we must achieve a world civilization. And for this, some concept is necessary, some dream so vast as to conquer the imagination of many peoples. Such a dream might have been very near fulfillment at the close of World War I, had the great peace conference been free from political chicanery and open fraud. Still, world disarmament, a great gesture of peace, a bona fide act of surrender to the larger exigencies of the time, might bring a renewal of faith in the better way.

Let no one call this an appeal to magic, where natural forces have failed, for itself is a natural force. If we have not the greatness of mind and heart to achieve it, perhaps our children or grandchildren may. Such a dream, which will partake of the nature of creative genius, can be prepared for by practicing the technique of the coming civilization in our own time. The words of Herbert Wildon Carr in his posthumous papers apply here with power:

> In all the great movements which mark the advance of the human spirit, the force is to be traced not to reason but to the creative imagination . . . It is this universal, omnipotent power of imagination which philosophy should make its first study.[3]

If we cannot ourselves bring in the dream on a large scale, we can practice the international habit of thinking and speaking, individually. We can teach our children so to speak and think; we can frown upon and vote out the cheap politician who lives by provincial appeals. In other words, we can begin to practice the technique of a world understanding that will eventuate in the expression of genius in world organization.

[3] In *The Personalist,* Winter, 1935, Vol. 16, pp. 52, 53.

CHAPTER XXIV

THE SIGNIFICANCE OF RELIGION

. . . .

SOME DAY AN historian of civilization may arise with the scientific spirit but sufficiently free from prejudice to recognize the commanding significance of religion in the achievement of culture. That time is not the present, which finds it easy to neglect religion as unimportant.

One reason for this antireligious attitude is the shallow assumption first made by certain students in anthropology that the source of all religion is fear. Having behind it the assurance of men who called themselves scientists, the dictum has received popular acceptance. One recent writer in particular has rung the false note by closing each chapter of his book on religion with the phrase, "It was fear, it was fear."

Fear as a psychological factor can lead to many inhibitions. It can render cruel, it can induce persecution, it can make people bloodthirsty. It has the power to raise hatred and to arouse war. It can produce cowering subjection, inhibit good impulses, and stifle the creative imagination. All these things fear can do, but it may be suggested, popular notions to the contrary notwithstanding, fear never caused any man to be religious. It never laid the basis for any religion though it may have for various fetishisms and taboos.

Religion is a reverence for a universe and a power within it which is vaster than ourselves. It springs from a desire to seek a mental, moral, and spiritual unity with that of which we feel ourselves already a part. There is awe (not fear), there is reverence, there is worship of that which we feel represents a nobler and better part of us. There is a feeling that to be on right terms with it will make us the recipients of greater powers, and because it outspans our earthly life it can be trusted for that which is after death.

This is certainly the common heart of all the great religions the world has ever known, and to leave this out of consideration

239

in favor of some baleful practice of uncivilized tribes is as unfair as it would be to judge the authority of modern physics by reference to the superstitions of alchemy and astrology.

However, this unfortunate and false estimate of religion has done vast harm and is delaying the progress of human culture; for religion needs to be considered with tolerance, its salient features separated from the incidental and traditional, and its place in human advance truly evaluated.

Fear in any case is detrimental to advance of any kind, quite as detrimental to religion as to anything else. That it should have been considered the handmaid of religion is of a piece with Spengler's contention that war is the secret of progress in culture.

1. Paganism Versus Religion

If we trace the history of the word "pagan" we find that it was the term of derision cast by the Christian cosmopolite upon the countryman who worshiped on the local hilltop to propitiate the local gods who had within their keeping the fertility of adjacent fields and other benefits. Their chief significance was their limitation to a locality. Paganism was and is a denial of the cosmopolitan, cosmic, and spiritual nature of religion. Its benefits are for the few, it denies the universal and unprejudiced character of God. It seeks special and undeserved advantages for individuals, communities, tribes, nations and races. Its rituals are designed to appease and cajole into participation those higher powers that could confer success in battle with neighboring tribes or assist in the chase or in the field.

The confusion of paganism with religion is the mistake of modern opponents of religion. The characteristic feature of paganism is the effort toward personal privilege and benefits without regard to others. Its chief means of propagation and sustentation is fear. Fear of the active anger of the gods or of God, fear of the forces of nature or the smiting hand of disease. It opposes because it fears innovation and it has not the living power of readjustment to new ideas.

Paganism is always opposed to the spirit of prophecy because it is at enmity with the God of the prophets. The prophetic task in Israel was to break up the pagan concepts of religion that too widely prevailed, lingering on in "high places" and about natural objects and creeping into the services of the Temple as well. The prophets taught the cosmic character of God, that he was a respecter of righteousness rather than of persons and peoples. The older type of paganism has now pretty generally been done away with around the world. Where it still lingers its knell is sounded by the progress of science and the growth of intelligence. To meet it forms no great part of the present task of contemporary religions.

There is, however, a new paganism, far more widespread and subtle, the overcoming of which is the immediate task of all religions and particularly of Christianity. This paganism prevails widely in modern life, invades and is the reproach of Christendom as of all the world. The phenomena it presents are new, appearing in new forms, but the principles of ancient and modern paganism are identical. Both deny the cosmic and universal nature and love of God.[1]

To some modern pagans, who would be the last to recognize their paganism, God is a respecter of persons, to be individually appeased, to bring benefits to a limited few at the expense of other individuals, classes, or nationalities. God is thought of not as the God of the whole earth nor of all men, but one who will yield unfair and prejudiced advantages to his cultists. One is appalled at the present progress of this paganism which characterizes the advance of nationalisms over a great part of the earth and lingers too long in Christian concepts in the minds of those to whom prayer is a begging for undeserved individual favors, and religion a charter of special privilege.

Another form of the new paganism consists in the denial of a universal God and turns to self-worship, the accomplishment of salvation by scientific and natural means alone. It scorns as superstition the cosmic and deeper forces of life, mystically discerned, and misses or denies altogether the sources of inspiration. The old paganism, though parochial and selfish, had some respect for powers above and within itself; the new paganism discredits all values of the transcendent order or of the inner spirit. This type of paganism registers in modern life in many

[1] The term paganism is used here in contrast with religion. Paganism characterized by the search for material benefits is at enmity with that devotion to goodness, truth and brotherly love which is the religious element in any system. In this sense there is paganism which is false religion wherever it appears and there is true religion, the salient elements of which are present in all religious systems.

ways, but it is evidenced in the widespread breakdown of the
moral sanctions; in the flair for vulgarity; in the emphasis placed
on sexuality; in its scorn of those delicacies of life and honor
that characterize the gentleman and gentlewoman; in the spirit
of falsehood which mocks at the most solemn promises in business, in matrimony, in international treaties. Last and perhaps
greatest of all, this paganism rears its ugly head in the spirit of
a selfish nationalism that seeks its own gain at the expense of
others and foolishly imagines that one can prosper without the
prosperity of all. It may truly be said that this Machiavellianism
is no new thing in the world. It is also true that we now live in
a smaller world than has ever before been known. The growth
in communication, the interlocking interests, economic, social,
political, and religious, have brought the old problem to an acute
issue in our day, and given it a new and more sinister meaning.

Such is the new paganism [2] that faces us today. The old
paganism entertained a lingering respect for religion and moral
values, though unworthy. The new paganism confronts us with
the prospect of the world-wide prevalence of antimorality, the
cult of a supreme selfishness. No hour in the history of mankind has been more critical since the days of Augustine.

Wherever it appears, paganism is incompatible with all religion and most of all with Christianity. Since the heart of paganism is the exaltation of material benefits it is always at war with
the spiritual concept of value and reality. It is forever substituting
goods for good in its estimate of life. This can be easily shown
to have been the *bête noir* of other religions than Christianity.
What is not so easy to realize is, that within organized Christianity has lurked an ever-present Simon Magus willing through
all centuries of Christian history to trade in spiritual values. In
fact, the achievement of material and selfish benefits either here
or hereafter has been too often the idolatrous appeal which has
been made to men to become Christian. Men have been urged to
become good not for the reward that goodness holds in itself
but for the sake of material prosperity or escape from future
very material suffering. Many religious devotees have not sensed
the materialistic character of such appeals. Such measures are

---

[2] The term "paganism" is here retained for what would be more strictly
called "heathenism" in order to emphasize the essential spirit of self-seeking
in all forms of irreligion.

however essentially pagan, in that they do not ground themselves in the supreme value of goodness, the virtue of the clean heart and the right spirit regardless of earthly bliss or woe. It is this pagan element persisting in Christian institutionalism which is now on trial before the world and which accounts for whatever powerlessness now manifests itself within such organizations.

Wherever it exists this spirit of paganism is incompatible with Christianity even though, like Simon Magus, it would or does operate under the Christian name. Men are to be constrained by the love of Christ, which means by the love of goodness, truth, righteousness, mercy and self-sacrifice, which virtues carry their own enriching and self-sufficient rewards. Putting ahead of these rewards, others, such as escape from bodily pain here or hereafter, and the trading of a strenuous Puritanism on earth for an eternal feasting in heaven, is an evidence of apostasy. It overlooks completely the reality of the spiritual values.

The resort to such inducements will always be found to be the result of an unfaith in God and in man, an unbelief in the power and existence of the spirit.

It may very well be that modern religion has come upon the present era that it may purge itself of paganism and demonstrate its spiritual and living character.

The world is growing tired of all sorts of paganism, though at the moment it seems to be wholly devoted to the false gods of mammon, of material fame and success, of militarism and of nationalism. The very wildness of the present pursuit gives abundant indication of desperation at the unsatisfying rewards enjoyed by its devotees. Their imprecations, gyrations, violence are as emblematic of the transitoriness of their satisfaction as were the antics of the priests before the altar of Elijah. Their gods are not hearing their prayers.

The times are ripe for the manifestation of the true God. There is hope for a religion sufficiently living to dare to stand forth and stress the spiritual values as the only enduring ones: to write "love" upon the erstwhile banners of war, to replace worn-out shibboleths which have lost meaning to the multitudes, with words of common speech which shall convict men of sin, of righteousness, and of the inherent judgment which attends all wrongdoing—that living hell of torment which pursues the unrighteous soul, which can never altogether silence its own inner protests.

There is an evangel of the eternal spiritual verities which is as cogent in this age as it ever was and far more demonstrable to an era of science than to any other. The opportunity for a new emphasis on spiritual reality is present already in the collapse of materialism in scientific hypothesis. We need to read through the violence of our times to see that it is after all the expression of souls that are disgusted with their own materialistic repletion. They plunge into the wilder distractions, hasten the tempo in order to forget those inner dissatisfactions which only spiritual values can remedy. At no time has there been such opportunity for a true religion which will commit itself to its own authentic methods and character. The age needs to be shown that religion means deliverance to captives, and sight to the blind and peace to the inner spirit. It is this interpretation which, more than any others, has given wings to the speech of the modern missionary. It is the best evidence of a living religion, for the time has come for religion to demonstrate its living character. There is only choice between the two. Religion must now be true to its essential mission and teaching or it must be classed as only another type of paganism.

II. Religion and the Creative Imagination

Perhaps the very best evidence that can be adduced to show that fear is not the source of true religion is the fact that religion has inspired the world's best and most enduring art. The reason for this is that it rids the human spirit of the constrictive influences of fear and makes it conscious of a new freedom in which it finds devoted and loving self-expression. It is exactly in this release from fear inhibitions that religion takes its place as the greatest inspirer of the creative imagination. Creative freedom does not, as some assume, call for a plunge into all sorts of excesses and transgressions against the conventions of society. True liberation can never be found in that which eventually enslaves the individual in evil habits, and base thoughts. Man's highest self-expression, the true deliverance, can be only a spiritual and a mental one, and for this only religion is adequate. In art, or literature, or social organization human nature can realize its own greatness and its latent potentialities only through deep religious experience, devotion to spiritual principles. One writer has recently gone so far as to declare that "our religious insight is the source and guide of our scientific insight."

It is very easy to check up this truth by the facts of history. Every great era in artistic expression has sprung from religious revival. Egyptian or Greek, Gothic or Renaissance, great art has been attended by great faith, a period of spiritual liberation.

The same factor may be traced in individual lives, in which the first ambitions for a college education, a burning desire for nobler self-expression, have grown in innumerable instances directly out of individual religious experience. After all, when we have lashed Christianity as the enemy of intellectual progress, it is only fair to remember that every one of the great universities owes its existence either directly or indirectly (sometimes through emulation) to religious organizations. Even the narrowest of Christian sects have their educational institutions, and however dogmatically these may begin they inevitably broaden into intellectual freedom. That this is so is due to the privileged relation which religion bears to creativeness.

This being the case, and the place of the creative imagination bulking so large in any sort of human advance, it is well-nigh useless to look for the appearance of great genius in social and political reorganization apart from the religious motive. The dream of a community of nations, a brotherhood of man, cannot arise out of the fens of greed and commercial self-seeking. There is need for a higher mandate, the urge of a finer feeling, before men will willingly surrender the fruits of avarice and oppression. What form such a movement may take who can say? It may arise quite outside of institutionalized religion. It may bear no relation to any creedal form, but to be strong enough to move the souls of wide masses of men, and to be potent enough to succeed, it will of necessity take on a religious character.

III. RELIGION AND WORLD UNITY

One reason for this part that religion must play in the coming world order lies in the fact that it is the most natural vehicle for the expression of the higher emotions. Religious devotion is a universal instrument of mutual understanding, with power to unite in a common cause men of various gifts and of every grade of intelligence and to direct them toward a high goal of achievement. Undirected by religion, emotional excesses, instead of finding embodiment in institutions valuable to the whole of society, become the easy tools of selfish interest and special propagandists. There is much truth in the claim of revolutionaries that their chief enemy is religious conservatism. If they would look a little deeper they would also see, as in the case of Christianity, that religion is the chief ally and inspirer of a juster social order. But as such it must be the foe of every selfish special interest both high and low, both revolutionary and conservative. It cannot look with equanimity on the exchange of one tyranny for another. This deeper fact will probably never dawn upon the seeker after power who dresses his special interests in the guise either of patriotism or of freedom. No movement for the reordering of society will be strong enough to accomplish its purpose without widespread convictions so deep as to be compelling and none can be so deep without also partaking of the nature of religion. By religion there is no reference to set forms but rather to the feeling of a divine sanction, an appropriateness to the character of God, or of nature, or of the universe, and also to the highest spiritual achievements and needs of the human soul.

When ideas achieve this deeper range, and only then, does society find itself acting as one man toward a common end and that a constructive one.

Unbalanced and selfish emotion can destroy and tear down but is unable to build because its basis is self-seeking, which drives men farther apart. Many a disciplined army has been destroyed as soon as the looting began. Unless the result is to be repeated any social movement must take on the force of religious conviction even if it declares itself to be hostile to all religion.

Religion, then, in offering a common vehicle for the higher emotions, provides for wide understandings and general communication of ideals to be had nowhere else. Its emotional power unites high and low, learned and ignorant. Its intuitional character is the source of its power. It speaks with compelling mandate directly to the souls of men. It is the universal language which all can understand. Out of such an experience sprang the far-flung lines of the Apostolic Church because Parthians and Medes, and dwellers in Elam, Jews, and proselytes, for a brief moment outstripped the necessities of language in a common understanding.

The international world order which must arise, if civilization is not to perish, can come forth only as the world becomes widely moved by a spirit of good will. There will be many to declare that unselfishness is an impossible dream, but there are already sufficient examples of it in the world to give such cynicism the lie. Men do not always act in accord with selfish interests. Often in the higher ranges of action they have shown a capacity to forget every physical self-advantage in the enthusiasm for a cause, for the person of an admired hero, for the welfare of a loved object. The release of creative powers by devotion to unselfish ends is amply illustrated in history and literature.

These facts contradict the allegation of Spengler, who declared that this higher self-forgetfulness can spring only from war. In fact, war of itself has no power to produce the spirit of self-sacrifice; for of itself alone, war, like any kind of hate, is a disintegrating influence. It is only because war has been able here and there to attach to itself the religious impulse of sacrifice for others or the triumph of a great and righteous principle that it could put on the semblance of more admirable virtues. Religion alone can rightly bring to pass an era of good will, for good will is of the very essence of religion.

One cannot have followed these thoughts thus far without a feeling of the apparent fatuity of any hope that humanity will arise to a common insight so self-forgetting as to result in a new world order. The voice of the cynic is heard on every hand. The age-long strife between individuals, nations and races is glibly cited as the indubitable proof that struggle is divinely ordained and must always be. To people who are satisfied with our present uncivilized state such an argument will appear convincing. They will overlook or deny the fact that there is in the present inequity some seeming advantage to themselves. Perhaps men will sometime acquire sufficient insight to understand that not one inequity can exist anywhere without peril to the established order everywhere; in fact, that no enduring order can be established while such inequity is condoned. It must be admitted that the task of a righteous world order must from every material standpoint seem impossible.

There is but one situation from which there is any hope, and that situation lies within the realm of the religious impulses. Only religion of the highest type has the courage to attempt the impossible and to discover through the network of difficulties the thread which unravels all. Contrary to popular opinion, religion flourishes most under adverse conditions. That is what religion is for. Its main function is to turn man's extremity into God's opportunity. When human ways and means break down, religion opens the unsuspected treasury of endurance, of faith, of vision, and of insight. Patronized by the state, petted by popular support, widening the borders of her phylacteries, the church makes a pitiable spectacle indeed. It is only under the stress of difficulty that she rises to her highest spiritual capacities. There is need that material props and dependencies shall be removed before she can stand forth in spiritual power. Adverse conditions are the forces which unlock the larger human capacities and lead men to perform the heroic and Godlike.

In any situation involving the depths of human interests to the extent of re-ordering a civilization, the backbone of success must be sought in religion. For the sacrifice demanded will be forthcoming only to its appeal. Once again must warning be given that no institution of religion, no creed, no rite must be taken as the definition of religion here. It is rather a living experience of God, a love for humanity, a devotion to righteousness so sincere that it will pay any price to bring in the true world order and in doing so will find its proper worship.

IV. A New Approach to World Problems

If religion offers the open door to the cosmic fulfillment of the spiritual aspirations of all men there is need to seek the basis for a new religious unity. The foremost and undebatable approach to world unity is the life of love. Alas! that the life of love has made so little appeal to religious people. Yet it is more apparent in religion than anywhere else. The life of love must become the object of striving among all faiths before there can be religious unity. This love is something man cannot achieve for himself; it is the gift of God to such as seek it. This is the evangel which is already running out through the whole earth, known and read of all men, in hospital and educational institution, in devoted individuals who count not their lives dear unto themselves, who everywhere reincarnate the spirit of true religion. No method can ever supersede this. It is the all-conquering dynamic and wherever it is wanting, all efforts and pretensions become but as sounding brass or clanging cymbal. But there is always danger that this cosmic appeal will be obscured under the partisan wrappings in which it comes. Sometimes our very zeal for an institution or credo has concealed the religious message and made it a partisan and hateful thing. This always occurs when we are more zealous for our ecclesiastical party than for right-eousness.

We need to ask ourselves perhaps if it is not possible to dull the sharpness of this inconsistency by seeking the intellectual sources of world unity, not as a substitute for faith but as a schoolmaster to more general understanding.

An intellectual approach to the problem of world religious unity might be found without the raising of partisan questions and yet form a basis for deeper mutual understandings. What if we were to begin with better intellectual understandings and end in religious convictions? While such a method has often been proposed it has not yet seriously been tried. As far back as 1707 the Jesuit missionary, the Bishop of Rosalie, appealed to the philosopher Malebranche to write a Christian philosophy for the use of the missionaries. The reason he assigned was that China would never be converted except with the aid of a Christian philosophy. Malebranche's effort was characteristic of the out-look of his age. Instead of identifying the correspondence of Christian concepts with those of the Chinese, he labored to show the unworthiness of the Chinese idea of God. Thus in a partisan spirit he threw away an opportunity for understanding.

The Oriental world with its long intellectual development is particularly susceptible to philosophy. Under the form of philosophy the profoundest problems of religion can be dis-cussed without offense to religious belief. This is because of its character of give and take. All religious beliefs have a common ground in the belief in God, in a supreme good. The whole force of educational and scientific enlightenment is moving to-ward the assumptions of a reasonable theism. A recent visit to the Orient demonstrated the eagerness everywhere to listen to a modern form of theism. Men of various faiths have confessed that it deepened their religious faith, their rational assurance of God. That it cleared them of misconceptions and false emphases

Apparently here is the discovery of common ground, yet the complete implications of this type of theism would seem to be ultimately and satisfactorily met only by the Christian system.

Emphasis was laid, it is true, upon points of agreement rather than of disagreement. This may seem apostasy to some because it depends not upon a revolutionary violence but upon the power of an inner assurance. It may be that this will be as it always has been, more fruitful for the common understanding of religion than more spectacular methods. At any rate, the man is not convinced until his mind is convinced and this method opens more doors to larger groups of intellectuals than have as yet ever been opened. If one is met with the contention that after all "not many wise are called" we need to ask the immediate question whether the power of the spirit of God is limited to the ignorant. Such would be a weakening admission for any faith which claims efficacy for all men. At least these intellectuals of the Orient, whatever we may say of them, wield a mighty influence in the very places in which our own faith at present wins slight recognition.

It may seem strange to carry to philosophy the appeal for religious tolerance and understanding. Yet history indicates that at the great periods of Christian success it laid the ground for effective advance. Paul could not be said to be a philosophical zealot yet he did not despise philosophy, using it as the open door by which to win the Stoics, that best and highest group in the world of his time. The Greek fathers of the Christian Church wrought their triumphs by not despising the aid of Platonism. Thomas Aquinas laid the basis for the Medieval Church in a revived Aristotelianism. The movements of the Protestant Reformation were philosophically grounded by Luther and Calvin. It is not without significance that John Wesley was a Fellow in Philosophy at Lincoln College, Oxford.

The best *persuadant* to Christianity lies in the indwelling spirit, the living experience of God manifested by a life of love and self-sacrifice. This breaks down prejudice, succeeds where other means fail. It is the true propaganda which cannot be gainsaid nor denied. Let this fact be noted in view of what is to follow.

But though religion is of the spirit, it partakes also of the intellect since it has to do with the whole man. The satisfaction of the intellect may be a prior step to the satisfaction of the spirit. In this light alone can the existence of philosophy finally be justified. If religion is properly to meet the sweeping tides of change it is not enough that it should present only a mystical side. It must also appeal to the intellect. To this end it must call in again the service of philosophy as it has in the great periods of its past.

It is not sufficient merely to present the same arguments that appeared cogent to Greek and Roman society. The movements of thought are different under new aspects of knowledge and discovery. There is no more sense in approaching the intellectual world of today with the philosophical weapons of the first century than to oppose to a modern army the famous Macedonian phalanx which laid the ancient world at the feet of Alexander. New mental outlooks must be approached on their own ground. Least of all can we afford to distrust truth and righteousness from any quarter. The power of early Christianity lay in its capacity to clear itself from the limiting concepts of Judaism and meet the Greek world on its own terms. In this respect Paul was the great plowman who broke up the stubborn glebe. He offered a working mental agenda for that day and time without rebating one whit the essential teaching of a true faith.

We must be prepared to meet the objections of men of other and contrasting faiths, and of men of no faith. Our purview of the situation must include provision for meeting the general problems of religion—problems that face all religions. We must ask such questions as these: Have the religions any common desiderata? Are they seeking after the good life? To what extent may they cooperate in mutual understanding for common ends? How may the problem of exclusiveness be met by the recognition of a common God and Father of all men? Do the religions seek to unite the individual with some power not himself that makes for righteousness? Do they believe the universe or God to be friendly to goodness? Do they trust the higher powers to aid man's own development? Is there forgiveness for man's sin, a power for overcoming temptation and a way to inner peace? How can all this be brought into accord with the general reason and the best scientific knowledge? What are the terms on which individuals may rise to the highest self-expression and the largest social usefulness? What are the social obligations of the religious man? What injury may be done to one faith through recognition of the valid goods and truths in others? Is there a common basis of theism on which all men of religious mind can build? Are goodness, love, compassion, charity, uprightness, sincerity, self-sacrifice, devotion to ideals, the heart of true religion, the evidence of the divine Spirit, of the indwelling of the God and Father of all?

If these are taken as the marks of God's presence in man it is possible to arrive at religious understanding and cooperation despite theological differences, for here we deal with the actual evidences of religion. Once these principles are recognized all else follows. Divinity is evidenced by indubitable testimony, the existence of perfect moral character, the life of perfect love in any religion.

At this point, philosophy may be of exceptional service, just as it has been in the past ages of religious history. It possesses to a great degree a non-partisan character. It can easily become the meeting-place and the medium for the comparison and equitable appraisal of contrasting and even of contradictory ideas. It offers a field of amicable discussion far from the heats of sectarian or partisan religious claims. It may be made the common ground from which all forces of good-will, of love, and of truth may proceed together. It offers a standing ground where hands may be united against all that would substitute hate for love, violence for peace, or that would foster misunderstanding, suspicion and that which morally degrades. Men may not at present be able to come together to discuss the relative virtues and values of their religion, for religion calls for complete and exclusive faith on the part of its devotees, sincerity being its first law. But men may come together to discuss the basic philosophy of all religion because religion springs from recognized common needs everywhere present. This ground for mutual discussion and understanding is provided by philosophy.

Here at last is an approach to religious understanding which is at present almost totally neglected and in which both Christianity and Judaism are by the terms of their own faith under obligation to lead the way. No religious man whose faith is sufficient but will welcome the test and comparison in the confident belief that whatever is true, whatever is of good report, will survive.

Perhaps it will be affirmed that the Buddhist, the Brahmin, the Confucian, the Shintoist, the Moslem, will approach philosophy in a like confidence. So much the better. The more we believe in the cosmic value of our own faith, the more willing should we be to submit it to the common tests of reason. Let the test abide by the great moralities, the great experience of God, the great service of humanity, the evidence of love. It is safe to say that no religion *in its present practice* could altogether win out—none that would not need in humble contrition to beg forgiveness from all the rest for the existence within it of practices unworthy of its avowed principles. But out of such contrition, mutual respect, and love there would no doubt spring a new illumination of the Spirit, a new and widespread manifestation of the presence of God, a new realization of brotherhood, a new theophany, a new homophany, a new Pentecost that would lead to the creation of a new world.

Some may indeed question whether Christianity is yet ready to lead in the great renunciation which is her only way to supreme service and fulfillment. Such renunciation implies the bringing of institutions, formularies, modes, manners, characteristics of thought, philosophy, and theology, made dear and venerable by age, to cast them into the crucible of time. This will not seem impossible except to men of little faith. But this fact and this necessity lie buried in her fundamental and all-conquering principle, the doctrine of the cross.

v. Personality the Universal Goal of Religion

It is very obvious that the simple statement of this proposition will call forth question and protest. Can it properly be defended in face of the probable doubt of a great proportion of the world, at last of such as make Nirvana and the unconsciousness of Taoism the culmination of religious effort? Without pretending in any sense to be the master of these religious concepts, it may be that there is not the distance between religious concepts that a casual usage of language seems to imply. It may be that in attempting to flee what might be called a crass and embrangling individualism these diverse faiths seek the same goal that is attempted by a true personalism. The object of their religious effort is perhaps to lose the individuality in a higher unity, believing that only as they cast off the garments of individuality can they enter into that communion in which there is no discord, which is God. It cannot be claimed that this is in any way an adequate definition of the meaning of Tao or of Nirvana but this would undoubtedly be included.

Now the Personalist as well feels that individuality must be lost in a higher unity, the love of God, the love of our fellowmen, the good of all mankind before one can fully realize his own truest selfhood. The true personality, the highest realization, and the completest expression of himself comes only to him who forgets self, selfish interest, individual advancement in the greatness of a divine experience. This philosophy is on its religious side summed up in words with which the devout of all religions will find themselves in hearty agreement. "Except a corn of wheat fall into the ground and die, it abideth alone; but if it die it bringeth forth much fruit. He that seeketh to save his life shall lose it, and he that loseth his life shall keep it into life eternal." These words addressed to the Greeks, are the key to any enduring philosophy of life, but far more than that, they are the clue to common understanding between all the great religions. Christianity has as a whole not taken them seriously and has deeply failed in practice; but throughout her history she has never ceased to provide some witnesses to their truth, as some pure souls have here and there entered upon them and found in them the true way of life.

After all, any Nirvana or Tao we seek is one into which a definite person comes to orientate himself, and the object of his search one cannot believe is so much utter extinction as extinction of that in him which is strictly individual and contrary to the universal harmony; it is ultimately a nobler self-realization which he seeks. With this in mind there is a great universal goal of all religion which is the achievement of this higher personality.

Still another question is sure to arise, which is whether this personality of which we speak is compatible with a complete self-sacrifice. Here again the question is partly answered by the foregoing discussion. Understanding depends on the distinction between individuality and personality. It is at the core a distinction which the entrance of Greek culture has prevented Western Christendom from achieving. The Greeks were individualists, and in putting their stamp on Western thought and particularly in the great Creeds they created a confusion at this point. Christianity has never yet become fully Christian and never will until it accepts to the fullest this Oriental view-point which to the Greeks seemed foolishness. Here lay the essential conflict between Greek and Christian culture, between what some have aggravated into the problem of Paul versus Jesus. However, they have no right to this interpretation, for Paul, in spite of his Greek sympathies, was at heart Oriental, and expressed personally this doctrine of the mystic experience.

Still the question remains, is this altruism which is considered necessary to a renewed world-order compatible with the possession of personality? To me it seems not only compatible but necessary. We have seen how any creative art calls for the completest mastery of technique. It is only as the artist loses the sense of his hands, of his instrument, of measured time, that he can become creatively self-expressive. Self-consciousness is the bane of all artistic action even as it is in the simplest forms of social intercourse. Here stark individuality is recognized as a flaw, a blight. So with the painter, while he loses his individuality by becoming unconscious of himself, his brushes, his colors, his hands, his canvas, it is only by losing this other-consciousness that he finds that self-expression which we call genius. The submission of individuality eventuates in the realization of a sublimer painter, a nobler self, until all are amazed at the work. A real artist must perforce become a person.

The friend of the social order who is chiefly conscious of personal benefits to be realized, of commercial self-advantage, of fame, or of reputation, can never be the leader of a world order, the liberator of a people. Genius of such order does not grow on the individualistic bush. When the true leader comes it will not be with the sound of the trumpet, but he will be such that in his love for the common weal he will find his own self-realization. The freedom to which he will lead will be not of the body only but of the mind and spirit as well. The end which he seeks and the devotion he must show will be in the truest sense religious, and it will be achieved not through individualism but through personalism.

CHAPTER XXV

THE NARROWING WORLD AND THE COSMOPOLITAN MIND

ON THE FATEFUL morning of her execution as a spy, Edith Cavell is reported to have written, "Patriotism is not enough; I must have no hatred or bitterness toward anyone." Our difficulty in attempting solution of world problems in the past has been that we have tried to make a cosmopolitan garment out of the shreds and patches of nationalisms, race feeling, provincialisms and parochialisms. Such is the main reason that our efforts to reach world understanding have failed. Each nation sends to the peace conferences parochially minded men who go to "protect" the national interests, which means to profit by the gullibility of the peacefully inclined, or to intimidate the weak. If there could once be an international conference made up of cosmopolitan men bent on peace instead of on "protection," an agenda of understanding could be arrived at. So far these conferences have themselves been wars, wars of diplomacy, with the greatest honor to the most skillful trickster who was able to trade nothing for something. The result has been a tide of ill will increasing with every conference that has been called. Each wants peace only to his own advantage. Of course it is a travesty to call such gatherings peace conferences. They are attempts to gain by diplomacy what could not otherwise be had except by war. One hesitates to name the sources of this hypocrisy but it does not lie with the great masses of the people whom the diplomats are supposed to represent.

I. THE PROBLEM, MORE THAN RACIAL OR NATIONAL

It must be admitted that the introduction of the larger view along with a genuine desire for peace seems to be eternally delayed. The roll of history yields only negative examples. The cynic has history on his side. "Things having been must ever be," is his last word of wisdom. But certainly most cynics believe in evolution, and if they do it is incompatible with their cynicism.

The question must be frankly faced, however, whether there can be any more powerful and more universal appeal than that of greed and self-interest. If there is not, then the sooner humanity perishes the better, for even the ant and the bee have power to teach our sluggard souls the necessity of surrender for the common good. To assume that man cannot be reached eventually by the higher appeal is to assume that his intellect and judgment are inferior to the unthinking intuitions of the insects. Such an assumption is negated by the haste of our ease-loving youth to enlist for hardship and death. One must admit that moments of despondency settle down when one is almost ready to fall into the mood of the cynic, but it may be that man is the participant in a larger purpose, a nobler end than the instinct of the bee, which with all its marvelous intricacy, rises no higher than food and propagation. As long as the goal of mankind subsists or attempts to subsist on this level, there can be only the old antagonisms; as between hives and swarms so between tribes and nations. It is quite apparent that these are not the bases on which it is possible to establish a new world order. Can race consciousness ever be eliminated?

To answer in the affirmative poses what seems at first an impossible problem except for this: outside of occasional personal repugnance it is difficult to hate the people we know. Great hatreds spring frequently from ignorance, unfamiliarity, lack of acquaintance. Contempt is often the child of ignorance. Men of other races at a distance may darken my horizon, fill me with all sorts of fear, arouse in my mind the most cruel intentions, but not so with the man who sits at my table and shows me he is quite as much of a gentleman as I consider myself to be. The educational results of contact have been observable in all history. Peter the Hermit could arouse the nobles of Europe to the hatred of Saracens at a distance. The cry of "Infidel" has a certain potency for the pious. But the nobles who returned from the Crusades had made the discovery that these "infidels" they had gone out to slaughter were foemen worthy of their steel. Many of them were much better trained in the art of being gentlemen, and on occasion both chivalrous and generous. The "Infidel" of Peter the Hermit turned out on investigation to be a rather lovable and in many cases superior gentleman. It is notable in war that the hatreds spring up not so much among the combatants as with the people at home.

This being the tale of history, education is seen to bear a large part in breaking down that feeling of seclusion which makes possible strong national hatreds and suspicion, and for this the world is better organized than ever before in history. Means of communication are now so swift and easy, that the far-separated tribes of men can scarcely avoid a growing knowledge of each other. The most benighted spots of the earth are yielding before such enlightenment. Maybe the tragedy of common disaster, the threat of total engulfment in horror will crystallize the wide world of civilization into a common understanding, to bring about a community of feeling that will unite us all.

II. THE APPEAL TO EMOTION

Since the appeal to sectionalism lies deep in the emotion of fear, of self-preservation, of provincial pride, it is clear that even education cannot of itself alone dispel the emotional sources of parochialism. Such emotions cannot be eradicated but must be raised to a higher level. The emotional ground of civilization has been suggestively pointed out by the late Professor Dennison in a work the title of which is *Emotion as the Basis of Civilization*.[1] In the scientific organization of society we have too much overlooked this important factor. We are all of us far more the creatures of emotion than we are willing to admit. The late Glenn Frank[2] pointed out how, due to a Puritanic respect for austerity, our scientific men have been patronizing toward that which smacks of emotion. They do not consider quite sane the man who puts artistry and emotion into his work, thus preferring "the burrowing mole to the singing lark." But the present day of confusion, perplexity, and misunderstanding calls for insight, and insight is never cold-blooded, pedantic, and academic. Insight is intuitive, artistic, and interpretive, and we must have interpretation even more than investigation, or rather, on equal terms with investigation. As has already been shown, there is a close relation between the emotions and the creative imagination

[1] Charles Scribner's, Sons, New York.
[2] *Thunder and Dawn*, The Macmillan Company, New York, 1932, pp. 147-148.

and genius for leadership; for social organization can never be wholly rationalized, it must partake of the mystical, the artistic, and the religious.

Any attempt to ground a culture upon training or education alone must fail, since an enduring culture must satisfy the whole need of the man, emotional as well as rational. There must be food for his soul as well as for his mind. Yet many have dreamed and are dreaming that a permanent ordering of society can be built merely upon the basis of economic needs.

Economic needs are various and uncertain but, worst of all, their satisfaction gives no ultimate peace. More than one man has dreamed that plenty meant peace, only to find the harrowing disillusionment that in it he had grasped but dust and ashes. In spite of all wishes to the contrary, there is a spark that disturbs our clod. The world is full of experiments of a social order with religion ruled out or remanded to a pagan worship of the material; but reforms of that kind are reforms against nature and cannot endure. The ultimate result of such a course must be a great reaction toward some sort of religion, worthy or unworthy.

But the final reason why a cosmopolitan world order must be built upon great emotion is because in the emotional plane alone can men of varying interests, intelligences, habits, colors, creeds, occupations, come together and act together. Any appeal to pure intellect will but break them up into sects, and parties. There is no end to differences of opinion even among philosophers and scientists. Men act together for common ends only under great emotion.

III. THE SUPREME EMOTION

The emotions might be said to be primal and intuitional since they grow out of physical, mental, and spiritual functioning possible to all men. Because of this universality the emotional appeal is then the one that can be made with the surest results. What we need to discover is the nature of the supreme emotion. Doubtless there will be differences of opinion here and some may disagree, but it would seem that of all the emotions that of self-sacrifice is the highest as perhaps that of self-preservation is the most common. There are of course those who argue that the latter is also always the stronger emotion. Reflection will show, however, that this is a mistaken notion even in the lower ranges of life. The beast of the field will evidence complete indifference to individual peril for the sake of its young. In the higher ranges of intelligence where there is greater opportunity for the imagination, the principle of self-sacrifice becomes increasingly commanding. Here the interests for which the individual will recklessly give himself multiply. Not only for the immediate welfare of offspring attacked, but in the dream of a distant and sometimes fanciful future for one's descendents, multitudes of people give themselves in uncomplaining sacrifice. Even more, such sense or emotion of sacrifice becomes to most fathers and mothers a consuming joy. Giving ourselves for those we love is not the rare and unaccustomed experience we are sometimes asked to think but is the practice and the highest happiness of most people.

In presenting self-sacrifice as the supreme emotion we are not, then, going far from common practice to some academic proposition. We are rather coming close home to universal emotional fact. It is safe to say that this emotion is not only the universal source of joy but also that those who have never experienced it have never known an hour of real happiness. Man's spiritual nature dogs his most materialistic intentions and grants its deepest satisfactions not to the selfish person but to the self-forgetting one. Selfish gains have always a way of palling on the appetite, the more so in proportion to their completeness, and only the joy of self-sacrifice smacks of the permanent and the eternal.

Herein lies that power of appeal which brings renewal to religion, but in it lies also the possibility of social renewal and the reorganization of civilization. For man, with imagination and intellectual grasp, can give himself not only to his own immediate posterity but can spend himself with an equal freedom on any good and noble cause or, if an ignoble one can be so dressed up as to appear worthy, he will without reluctance die for that. Dying for causes is one of man's commonest occupations. If the cynic would once look about him with insight and understanding of the deeper meaning latent in the activity of most people, this would become for him the most obvious of facts.

The ennui and boredom that afflicts individuals arises in specific instances from the failure to discover a cause worth dying for. This is the stern and never-ceasing demand of the spiritual within us which cannot find satisfaction until we have given all.

We seek this gratification sometimes in ways that are illegitimate, sometimes by physical excess, sometimes by fanatical religious flagellation; but there the principle stands, the commonest of the motives which dominate men. Even our selfishness is covered over with the average excuse both to ourselves and others that our purpose is to secure the good of others.

One cannot pretend it an easy task to turn this human spirit of good will into channels that will make for the well-being of society as a whole. At present we are prone to think it sufficient to exercise it toward our families, our communities, our lodge members, our churches, our denominations, our countrymen, our race. It is difficult to realize the wider appeal. But this is largely through our incapacity to visualize people and needs with which we have never been in touch. The narrowing of our world changes all this and brings home to us with a new force the truth that these whom we most intimately love and care for are continually imperiled unless our love shall also embrace those others, whose poverty, ignorance, misery, bondage and disease constitute a permanent menace.

Any event, then, that with startling clearness can bring these realities effectively to the understanding of men, any leader with power to stir the minds of people widely to action, might find the whole course of history prepared for him.

IV. THE UNIVERSAL LANGUAGE

One cannot have wandered widely about the world nor have reflected deeply thereupon without having discovered that there is a universally understood language, which is love. It formed the basis of comprehension between Livingstone and the African natives who knew no word of the English tongue. His interest in them, his care for their welfare, his self-forgetfulness toward them, are honored still and memorialized among the tribes with whom he worked. His practice and his life among them made the understanding complete. Here, then, is a language which requires no long tutelage, no extensive harangue to bring men to a common cause, to unite them in a common devotion. Good will is the universally understood speech which needs no interpreter. It seems rather simple, to be sure, to apply such an expedient as unfeigned good will to the ills and misunderstandings of society, but there is little doubt that its wide practice could heal the bickerings and bitternesses that now render the world an armed camp of conflicting interests. Every individual practice of good will adds to the total of peace whether it occurs between individuals or between nations. There is need only that it should be expanded to include all.

Violence is tempered by acts of good will. Love is the universal solvent, the language which beats diplomacy for being understood, which silences and, eventually, overcomes thoughts of hostility and reprisal. The working of this principle is evident in the common relationships of life. The man who acts the boor is the one who most commonly meets insult and opposition. The gentleman finds himself surrounded for the most part by gentlemen. The hateful and unkind live in a hateful world. The appeal to love is not to an empty idealism. Mutual courtesy, respect, and love, yield the largest and surest dividends. Because a materialistic world does not trust this eternal truth, it is now rushing violently down the steep places into the sea of a common ruin. Hate threatens to overwhelm us where only love can find the way.

CHAPTER XXVI

THE NEGLECTED FACTOR OF PROGRESS

AN ANCIENT HABIT among the unthinking has been the depreciation of philosophy. Nearly always this disparagement has been due to an absence of acquaintance with philosophic thought. Contempt is easy toward that which we do not know or cannot understand. Yet philosophy is nothing more than an intellectual look about us. It views the facts, considers the various theories about them, examines the relation between given facts and given theories, includes the imponderables which frequently determine human happiness and destiny, and faces the possibilities. Such a program would seem to call for applause rather than detestation. Philosophy arises with advance out of barbarism into the higher forms of civilization and its gifts, as Alfred North Whitehead reminds us are insight and foresight.[1] Barbaric and simple orders of society can get along with a hit-and-miss method, but the finer civilization cannot arise except by planning and forethought, a consideration of all those influences which affect society. Such insight and foresight are the special task of philosophy. Whitehead is correct in declaring impossible the existence of democratic society unless education bears in general a philosophic outlook.

The direction of history is determined by the reactions of society to the course of events and those reactions depend upon the moral, intellectual, and spiritual watchwords that dominate the average mind. Such watchwords summarize the philosophy of the time. If the common mind is impregnated with faith in worthy ideals, with a right comprehension of the things that are worth while, any age may arise to new opportunity and advance to a great destiny. Lacking courage, weak in intellectual grasp, dominated by materialism, it may fail entirely of the occasion and bind the future to shallows and to miseries. Western society now stands at the culmination of an old order, that of individual-

---

[1] *Adventures of Ideas*, The Macmillan Company, New York, pp. 125-126.

ism, in which the ruling philosophy has been one of unrestrained competition, of private possession, of complete noninter-
ference with the individual. The ruin of competitors has been
considered a natural necessity, and death and disaster mercifully
removed the failures from the field for the benefit of those who
survived. This philosophy received the official sanction of science
through the doctrine of the survival of the fittest, the warm
support of the avaricious, and the timorous consent of such
religionists as felt the shame of being called unscientific. But the
outcome of naturalism, materialism, utilitarianism, and the ruling
ideas of the nineteenth century have led us into the Serbonian
Bog of the twentieth. The natural suggestion is salvation by
dictatorship. Many do not yet see that such a cure may be worse
than the disease, is in fact the climax of the disease.

Why not, someone is sure to suggest, try to get along without
philosophy in the future? But alas, he who proudly boasts he has
no philosophy is likely to be the most dogmatic philosopher of
all. Proud of his ignorance, he blunders forth with well enough
defined dogmas and catchwords of the hour, but without any
purpose of examining or comparing his theories with those of
others or even with the facts. He substitutes sight, the appearance
of the moment, for foresight and insight. His lack of philosophical training renders him uncritical.

Whether it wills to or not, any age of conflict and change
grasps at whatever philosophy it finds occupying the field of
attention and this philosophy is likely to determine the future.
In the light of these facts there is no other study of greater importance to any people than the study of philosophy. There is no
other task which begins to equal that of the clarification of ideas.
We cannot safely launch into the future on the trial-and-error
policy which belongs distinctively to unreflective animal minds.
We can reconstruct a world civilization that will endure, only
upon the basis of wise philosophical principles. We have tried to
discover what those principles are which brought our civilization
to the present point of excellence. Let us try to determine the
sources of failure to the extent that we have failed. But let us
not throw out the baby with the bath. If twenty-five hundred
years of Western culture have taught anything, let us learn the
lessons they bring. They themselves may suggest the alternatives
for world renewal.

We have already seen how in the youthful day of our civilization the glosses of Porphyry's *Commentary on Aristotle* left open the burning question of freedom. Boëthius would not decide whether individuals or universals were the ultimately real and so left open the door for discussion. If the former were true, democracy was given philosophic standing; if the latter, then authority and autocracy were in the saddle. To this idea of freedom both Augustine and Boëthius clung amid the falling rafters of the ancient culture, but out of their loyalty sprang the democracy of the new culture that was already on the way. The constructive power of their ideas changed the face of Europe.

One can but wonder why, with the powerful forces of individualism which did so much in the way of impetus to the development of democracy, the triumph of democracy is yet incomplete. More than an inkling of the answer may be found in the survivals in modern civilization of concepts which are diametrically opposed to those of democracy. These concepts still linger in philosophy, in social organization and theory, in statecraft, in religion, and even in science itself. The last value to be evaluated in civilization is the supreme end of civilization, the person. The chief bane of our civilization so far, with all the advances which individualism could bring, has been its impersonalism. The shadow of this impersonalism which has had in it so much power of defeat is typified by the wavering and uncertain attitude of Boëthius in his failure to declare positively for personalism as against its opposite. Boëthius lived in a world impregnated with the ideas of Neoplatonism. He felt the binding hand of authority. Although himself a thoroughgoing personalist he dared not tread boldly where Porphyry had refused to render decision. Thus the one voice that could have spoken effectively to the educational ideals of more than a thousand years was rendered largely nugatory.

I. INDIVIDUAL AND PERSON AS TERMS OF CONTRAST

Since the neglected element in progress is here assumed to be the person, it becomes necessary to define meanings. The two words individual and person are often confused and frequently treated as synonyms. Anything is an individual which is not susceptible to logical division or to actual division without loss of character or which cannot be separated into parts without loss of identity. While the dictionaries sanction the use of the term as applied to persons, the etymology of the word indicates that this is a strained and unnatural usage.

Individualism is apparent in whatever sets the individual out in contrast with his fellows. The word contrast is used advisedly here, for individualism is divisive, selfish and antisocial. One can easily be individualistic in the cut of his hair, the style of his clothes, the color of his necktie, the unconventionality of his speech, the shocking nature of the ideas he expresses, the offensiveness of his tastes, his nonconformity, his abnormality. Most individualists consider such manifestations exhibitions of personality, but usually they are not. They are most often exhibitions of individuality. They are frequently the evidences of belated adolescence, of early inhibitions and complexes, such as the inferiority complex, or of a pathological egoism.

Much of the product of individualism masquerades under the guise of enlightenment and freedom but is in neither category. The individualist is neither enlightened nor free. Enlightenment is prevented by his failure to entertain all sides of a proposition since his egoism presents only the side of his selfish interests. He is never free because he is the slave of the unworthy interests.

The personalist on the other hand knows that the highest self-expression he can achieve must lie along the line of an unselfish devotion to the best. This holds in the world of business, of toil, of art and of religion. Only that man who fears not the face of any man, who challenges the rewards and advantages of any position is in the truest import free. He has power to take up his life and lay it down again in the sense that he can apply the power of that life to any point that will count for the most. He is under no obligation to man or party, and lusts not after any reward of the world. Such a man is in the strategic position of freedom. He answers to God and his own soul. Such is the stuff of which real artists, statesmen, creators and saints are made. Only such are open to the inspirations of creative freedom. Such only possess full power of self-expression and become in the highest sense persons. The gift of self-expression has too often been taken in a narrow sense. Until the artist can eliminate his special idiosyncrasies of thought and technique he cannot achieve true artistry. If his thought is primarily of sensation or rewards, these ulterior motives prevent him from the highest achievement. It is only as he risks the common emoluments, perhaps even life itself, that his personality becomes uniquely creative and expressive. So long as he holds back anything for motives of gain or fame or personal advantage he fails of full expression. To do less than this is to be dominated by ideas and impulses that are hostile to his art and contradictory to his personality. He fights a losing battle for self-expression because of inner conflicts. He cannot free himself from these inner conflicts except by being true to his best self. This principle holds true in the whole realm of human values. Most of us labor against odds which we lay to environment, accident and circumstance but which actually we ourselves impose. To have an inner conflict with conscience over the pursuit of ideals we know to be false to our art or our business is to render ourselves slaves to that which is the enemy of art and hostile to true self-expression. If to be true to our higher personality is to be called a "slave morality," well and good. We then know ourselves to be slaves only to the highest master. If we choose the lesser way we yield to a "slave immorality" which destroys and degrades our creative and artistic power and ourselves with it. While this truth is commonly expressed in terms of religion, it is as binding and as universally applicable to human life as the law of gravitation to the movements of the heavenly bodies. None of us can successfully challenge or change it. It holds just the same whether we believe in religion or do not. Religion is the simple recognition of, and obedience to, this common fact of human psychology. Denial of it would be in the same class with refusal to believe in the law of gravitation. The dictum "he that seeketh to save his life shall lose it, but he that loseth his life shall find it" is the complete expression of personalism and is as real and as irreversible as the laws of nature. There are no exceptions.

Should anyone at this juncture, point out that such a service of one's highest ideals is a species of slavery, and as such it is commonly considered, it must be admitted as true. One has the choice of slaveries; to be increasingly the slave of evil and selfish desire which burns out the very heart and soul of the higher cultural life, or to become the slave of that Power whose service alone is perfect freedom. The true personalist comes to the highest self-expression but reaches it through self-forgetfulness in the service of God and the common good. Hence this type of living is the only one that can bring peace for the world and the salvation of society, and this it does because it has an eye to the supreme value of all culture, civilization, or human existence, the person.

II. THE BANE OF INDIVIDUALISM

Individualism as thus outlined may be seen as constantly at war against the highest interests of persons and therefore of society. The good is frequently the most effective enemy of the best. There are various influences at work in society which have brought about this state of things. The most important of these has been the hold-over from Greek-Hellenic-Alexandrian culture of an undue subservience to absolutes. We have been unable to free ourselves from an authoritarianism which is not verified by the nature and inner sensibilities of the person. Absolutes however attractive, authoritarianisms however good, are to be judged by their personal values, their response to the needs and interests of the person. If this seems an abrogation of all values, let us pause to reflect that the person himself is not only a part of nature, but the most rational and highest part, and even his interpretation of the highest and most sacred revelation cannot be greater than his own best, and all revelations require interpretation.

There was a time in Western society when the individualism of Greek science and arithmetic might have yielded something better than abstractions, integers that might mean much or nothing. That was the moment when Socrates would amend Sophistic skepticism with a reinterpretation of the Protagorean dictum, "Man is the measure of the universe" by pointing to man himself as the source and custodian of truth. Then it was that Plato perverted the Socratic *daemonium* or inner conscience into an abstract Idea, and the harm had been done. Aristotle with his individualism meant to do better but could not break the heavy weight of authority and through the dark night of Greco-Roman collapse only Plato was widely known. When Aristotle returned to the Western world, authoritarianism was everywhere in the saddle. Science and the inductive method had always to pay lip service to authoritarianism in order to be tolerated. Galileo's despairing cry under torture, "but it does move," spoken of the movement of the earth, is the specific and vivid reminder not only of the power of absolutism but of its disregard of the person. Science was led to put up as a bulwark and defense against such influences a few absolutes of its own, since it seemed necessary to fight absolutes with absolutes.

The outcome of all this was a science that looked in the direction of democracy but was still committed to the contempt of the person, and often by reaction, to a contempt of personal values. The absolutes it set up were its own hypotheses, concepts or conceptual constructs, infallible laws. In its own way and field it reflected the absolutes of church and state and had frequently to justify its importance by open warfare on common opinions and authorities, in which destruction of the good was involved with the bad. At the moment of success with the forces of authority retreating from the field, science has discovered the fallible nature of her own absolutes. She learns at last the human nature of knowledge, and that her best absolutes like the theologies she has so often resisted, grow out of the interpretations of experience by persons. We have no longer a world of ideas independent of persons as with the Platonists, nor one of basic matter or absolute phenomena abstracted from meaning as with the older science but a world of persons, of personal understandings and interpretations which if they are not dependent upon the opinions of individuals must at least respond to the reflections of human interpreters. For the first time in the movements of Western society do we have a rationale for a correct evaluation of the person such as is essential to a true democracy.

The curious perversion of what should have led to personalism into the impersonal standpoint may be clearly seen in the development of Western thought. The heart of Aristotelian philosophy lies in the double idea of *purpose* or teleology and *entelechy* or organism. Purpose and entelechy require the presence of personality to invest them with meaning, and this was overlooked. Reality was to science discoverable only in a functioning organism. Its truth lay in its activity. The best test of its reality was to be found in how it fulfilled the purpose for which it was intended. One was to judge of what lay behind it from the way in which it functioned. The fact was an individually functioning unit. The method of scientific knowledge was a study of these functions by experiment and the classification of individuals according to their observed functions in a given case. The individual was then not to be known by studying the class to which he belonged but rather the class was to be understood by the growing group of individuals that could be rightly said to comprise it. Classification was only a convenient arrangement of knowledge acquired by investigation of individual realities.

In a day given to autocracies of every kind, political autocracies in which the Emperor was the state and the people existed for it, when individual opinion must uncompromisingly bend the neck to dead and canonized sages, when religion itself was guaranteed by authority from above and must be received without question or criticism, this individualism of Aristotle was viewed with alarm as the dynamic of revolution, which indeed it was. It had come into Europe from suspicious hands, for hitherto Europe had known only the *Organon* or *Logic* of Aristotle. Now the complete Aristotelian system was the gift of "infidels," the Moslems and Moslem-Jewish scholars, who were heirs of the ancient manuscripts. The new learning they brought was not only revolutionary, it was captivating. The former interdict of the church against Aristotle was no longer of avail, and the subversive nature of his teaching to institutions of authority was even more apparent with the influx of new writings. Moslem teachers, at first gaining foothold only at Padua, had later been installed at Paris itself, seat of theological orthodoxy.

Then it was that the insight of Albertus Magnus and the literary facility of Thomas Aquinas saved the day for orthodoxy. Aquinas had the genius adequate to rendering Aristotle acceptable after specific proscription by the church, and authority from above won out, as against authority from within.

The mandate went forth that the individual must be judged not by what he was, but by the source from which he sprang, the institution to which he had vowed allegiance, the body of superior opinion to which he clung, and by these was he to be saved. Thus was Aristotle perverted into a Platonist of sorts and in the interest of authority. Out of this perversion arose the conflict between science and orthodoxy. It is the source of that ancient fear among those of "sound doctrine" that some truth in God's world of nature may be discovered that will upset some truth in God's world of moral values, as if the

standing of the Ten Commandments were not in nature itself
and could be bolstered into authority only by attendant magic.

The result of this misinterpretation has retarded institutional
religion by removing nature from the realm of the divine into
the special kingdom of the diabolical. It has engendered distrust of our best instincts and thrown discredit upon intelligence
itself. It elevates into high importance the creed the man pro-
fesses and emphasizes too little what the man is. It would
seem astonishing that science, nurtured on the Aristotelian
principle of induction, finding itself at continual variance with
authority, making its advances only through ever-renewed conflicts with orthodoxy, should itself become bound by a perverted Aristotelianism, but such is the case. Nevertheless,
science has been bent on the study of the individual more and
more segregated, by smaller and smaller units, which is to be
Aristotelian but without any eye for the more important Aristotelian principles of purpose and entelechy or organismic unity.
To science the unit has been less a functioning organism than
a meaningless corpuscle, an Epicurean atom, which in final
analysis was unintelligent, senseless, inert matter.

With Aristotle the stress is not on the unit but on the organism. That is the reason for the great gulf fixed, whether
one likes it or not, between chemistry and physics, and between
both these sciences and biology. The emphasis of modern science (till within twenty-five years) has been on parts, *not* on
working relations within an *organism*.[2] Hence our search for
the ultimate unit of matter has landed us in the embranglement
of an arithmetical abstraction which often even the mathema-
ticians cannot intelligently interpret.

A similar perversion of Aristotle is observable in the realm
of political theory where the stress is laid on the individual,
with no questions asked as to how he may function or as to what
his functions are. Thus democracy has become identified with
universal suffrage or free competition, which is the source of
the present discredit into which it has fallen. It may be seen
as the acceptance of the Aristotelian principle of individualism
without the qualifying notion of purpose which can be exercised only by persons.

[2] For extended discussion of this one-sided attitude of science see Alexis
Carrel: *Man the Unknown*; Harper & Brothers, New York, 1935.

III. The Person in Evolutionary Theory

Attention has been called to a certain discrepancy in modern thought in the most surprising of places, the method of modern science. It has been quite easy to note and deplore that discrepancy in religious thinking, less easy perhaps for most of us, lovers of democracy, to believe there was a fatal rift in the lute of our political theory, but that our scientific method might be faulty seemed the most incongruous and least believable of all.

If now the latter suspicion has reached formulation, it has clear and convincing illustration in the past and present status of the theory of evolution. The theory of the evolutionary origin of things is not the original product of the nineteenth-century thought. It existed in Western thought as long ago as the early Greeks, was artistically set forth in immortal literary form by the Roman poet-philosopher Lucretius, and even earlier by certain Chinese sages, from whom the Greeks may have derived it. At any rate, it is not to be considered a newcomer in the realm of thought.

Nearly always the evolutionary theory of origins has been broached in the interest of scientific method. It has been set forward in the hope of scientific knowledge and as such has frequently served as the servant of mechanism, materialism, naturalism, or whatever *ism* of the moment found itself in opposition to mysticism and religion. The curious fact about the whole matter is that without the mystical element which it pretends to discard, the theory of evolution has no legs to walk on. One can note this fact with a sense of humor for the diatribes of interested parties of religion or of science against each other; actually they were closer together in fundamental principles than they imagined. This is obvious even though the evolutionary principle seems a sound one. Most of the world's famous controversies would never have reached expression if there had been in either party a saving sense of humor. The alliance of evolutionary theory with materialism has always been a bastard one that arose from absence of reflection. Far from being a theory that dispenses with an intelligent and purposeful creator of all things, the theory of evolution cannot be logically maintained without assuming such a Creative Intelli-

gence above or within the process. A rising order of life fitted
for ever-widening complexity of function, with man at the top
of the scale, differentiated from all the rest by the possession
of a mind, cannot be logically accounted for by any combination
of senseless and wandering atoms in chance juxtaposition. If
intelligence arises, to say that it has no source in a Primal
Intelligence is to say that something can be created out of nothing. *Creation ex nihilo* has been the chief charge of materialism,
against religion, its principal object of scorn. But materialism,
mechanism, and naturalism are quite as credulous in such belief
as the theologian. The old superstition, if such it be, has simply
passed over from the theologian and become the basic principle
of much naturalistic science, concealed it is true, under a form
of words. The theologians by their doctrine assert that mind is
itself creative and can bring to pass what did not before exist.
The materialist denies any causal connection, and if he is logical must at the same moment deny the possibility of science.
If the theologian, in posing that the world of matter and of
mind proceeds from a Creative Intelligence, can be charged
with creating something from nothing, then the naturalist may
with even greater cogency be accused of producing something
from less than nothing, by assuming that matter can be the source
of mind.

If evolutionary theory is to be logically maintained, it must
be through the assumption that within nature or above nature,
or supreme through nature, is a creative mind and purpose that
foresees the outcome of the growing complexities of the cosmic
order and is working toward ends that are desirable and that
represent progress. Far from being hostile to religion, a consistent evolutionism demands a belief in the existence of God
though not necessarily of the theologian's God. At most the
theory of evolution can be seen as a striking hypothesis that is,
in spite of itself, rooted and grounded in the belief in a Creative
Power not ourselves that works for progress.

But the supreme lesson of the evolutionary theory is scarcely
ever alluded to, and the presence of this factor puts it more
closely in line with a truer Aristotelianism. The struggle for
survival has been falsely assumed as the heart of the evolutionary principle, its working basis, which it is not. Many years
ago Henry Drummond set forth the more basic fact in the

striking phrase, *the struggle for the survival of others*.[3] This
is the principle which makes evolution possible. The individual
even in the animal world is less concerned over his own survival than with that of his offspring. Here is the telltale of the
whole system. This is the light that shines in the dark world
fierce with claw and talon. The great fact in evolution is not
struggle for survival but rather for the survival of others. It is
a story of fine co-operation, such as that wherein the bee toils
for the flower to further its propagation and the flower in turn
yields its dying sweets for the benefit of the bee. By such co-
operation in millions of instances the whole process of nature
goes on. In other words, the world of reality is a world of
organisms which work together to make the, as yet uncom-
pleted, larger organism of the still-evolving universe.

IV. THE CREATIVE PRINCIPLE OF EVOLUTION

It was a most unfortunate concomitance of events, that brought
together French Positivism, the Darwinian theory, and theological fundamentalism. The result was a misunderstanding of
Darwin's meaning and intentions. The hostility of the religious
arose out of this misunderstanding and by reason of the fact
that the theologians of the time possessed no philosophy adequate to the new ideas. Darwin was embittered and Positivism,
eager to discount religion, seized the opportunity in the interests
of naturalism and materialism. Had the church been friendly it
might with much more logic have appropriated the theory in the
interests of theism, as the proof of the existence of purpose in
creation, and the evidence of a supreme Creative Intelligence, but
the times were not prepared. The outcome of the unfortunate
controversy was to give a false turn to the doctrine of evolution.
Falling quite completely into the hands of the materialists, the
dominant development was in the direction of an evolution by
external causes, which is a contradiction in terms.

The term "evolution" in its very etymology indicates a movement from within outward, yet the constant effort has been made
to explain and substantiate evolution by reference to external
forces. The great stress was laid on environment, chance, and
accident which are quite inadequate at any point, to account for
creativity, progress, or development. The attempt was made to

[3] *Natural Law in the Spiritual World.* J. Pott & Co., N. Y. 190.

construct a world of novelty out of one where, by initial definition, novelty was impossible and all things proceeded by mechanical necessity. The principle of "the survival of the fittest" was
treated as something apart from the indwelling "will" to survive
on the part of the persisting organisms. The whole argument was
made to hang on the exterior accidents of food, segregation, or
climate. In some cases strength of muscle and jaw, the possession
of fighting qualities, were taken to account for survival, as in the
saber-toothed tiger who didn't survive; and when the case required it, the survival was accounted for by the absence of fighting qua'ities, as in the sheep. In other words, whatever survived
was fit, and whatever was fit survived. In a similar way "natural
selection" instead of being assumed a matter of choices from
within organisms mutually attracted, or moving from within the
heart of nature herself acting as an organism, has been generally conceived as the forced result of survival.

None of these methods of external force has the least significance in the face of what a consistent theory of evolution
demands. They lack the vitalizing element of novelty for they
deal only with realities that are already here and whatever power
they may have to reproduce themselves they have none to create
anything unlike themselves or dissimilar to what has previously
appeared. Change of quality is an internal process not to be
accounted for by external force. If our universe were made up of
bricks, we might pile them in many fantastic combinations, but
we would never get other qualities than those already possessed
by the brick. Such a world would be as devoid of the touch of
living creativity as the block house of the infant, and more,
for the blocks would in this case be forced to pile themselves.

Our views of the progress and evolution of society have been
hampered by the same mechanical and materialistic concepts.
Malthus was the classical example of this. He treated society as
if it were a problem in mathematics and time has made him
ridiculous. Society is a living organism, moved more by the free
forces of emotion and spirituality than by external circumstance,
and it is this fact that provides all the hope we can logically
indulge that the future of society will not be as the past. Yet
the daily social experience would teach us this were we not so
dogmatically set on our materialism. Here, again, we falsely
assume that society is primarily dependent for its *progress* upon

means of subsistence, economic wealth, commerce, trade and communication. We dream in these days, of the renewal of society by some forceful inhibition of free speech, some dictatorial regime, the private arming of those portions of society whose ideas correspond with ours, not seeing that such would mean the death of civilization, the end of progress. Or, on the other hand, we vainly imagine that the equal distribution of wealth, or advantage, or education, will mean the renewal of society. All these expedients suffer from a similar defect. They look only to mechanical, external forces which have no vitalizing power. Power of police does not mean the regeneration of society. Even if we could build jails sufficient and could incarcerate the political majority, that would not indicate social redemption and a growing society. The great strength of society is now being spent on the securing of reforms by force and force is the father of its own destruction.

The fact remains that all creativity of every kind is from within. It seems strange that the world has so long remained blind to the constructive and creative internal forces that are the sources of all progress made to date. The marvel is that minds, priding themselves on their scientific detachment, could have remained blind to the facts of history, except, indeed, that fanciful history of an unknown past which they could construct in keeping with their own scientific dogma. Perhaps, however, we should be charitable, for men have been obsessed by ways of looking at things and the most blinding of all influences is dogma, either theological or scientific.

It was Socrates that first, in the Greek world, discovered the confirmatory evidence of the inner light as the guide to truth and the unerring reflection of the moving forces of the universe. Plato, in magnificent dream, disclosed the creative power of ideas and saw them as the fundamental realities. There was power, as well as truth and beauty, in the concept and for this we have the testimony of history. But Plato's ideas were disembodied ideas. He had his finger on the very forces of life and creativity and then failed through abstraction. Ideas are creative but apart from bodies, organisms, or individual wills they are nonsubsistent and powerless. Someone must have the idea and someone must act on the idea. Someone must likewise be free to act, choosing one rather than another course, if anything new is to come into existence. The one necessary attendant of all creativity is freedom, and the perfect and supreme creativity must be attended by perfect freedom which is also supreme Personality.

Nor is some measure of freedom so rare as might be supposed. While it comes to largest exercise in reflective consciousness, there's not the simplest organism that grows which does not in some degree give evidence of choice. Even the unthinking atom itself has shown unpredictabilities of action that have made in science "the most certain of all principles the Principle of Uncertainty."

Much neglected in argument has been what might be called the moratorium in evolution, the apparent absence of evolutionary processes from life as we know it. The nightmare of the mechanistic evolutionist has been his inability to produce the evidence that is to show specific cases in which the struggle for survival or natural selection has actually produced a new species. In the absence of facts, he has resorted to analogies about as scientific as Kipling's *Just So Stories* to account for how the giraffe got his neck or the elephant his trunk. These scientific fairy tales have quieted the public mind and held in abeyance certain uncomfortable questions. When pressed, we have been forced to admit that there are no specific instances, but either we have appealed to the fallacy of the abstract by saying it could happen in millions of years, or resorted to dogmatism by saying some day we shall discover "the missing link." The question is a far more serious one than at first appears. If evolution is the dominating process that has made the world and us what we are, why does it now seem to have ceased to operate in a living world?

We hold no brief to protect the theory of evolution from its own mental shortcomings, but we think there may be a reasonable answer to this question. Possibly with the appearance in man of reflective consciousness, the world has entered on a new phase or epoch of evolution. Other aeons or stages of evolution have been distinctly marked. Perhaps what amoeba and cell, and bird and beast, have been blindly groping for in the following out of an inner consciousness, has now come in man to the stage of reflective self-consciousness. Plainly, in any unprejudiced view of evolution, man should view himself as a part of the process.

Obviously he has reflective powers which are not the gift of the lower organisms. The production of such a being must have been present in the purpose of evolution. If so it is not too much to say that any further evolution must depend on what is already evolved, will not take place without the aid of man himself. Some day we may have the good sense to discover that the appearance of mind, of moral and spiritual self-consciousness was quite as important in the history of evolution as the change from a fin to a foot or to a wing.

What if evolution has made as much progress as is possible without the presence within the subject of evolution of reflective self-consciousness? Should this be proved to be the case, we can see that the halt in evolutionary progress may be but one of those aeons of transmission like that from sea to land life, in which these higher embryonic powers may find themselves. Instead of a moratorium in evolution, it may be true that evolution is now in process of bringing in some new and higher phase.

Such an answer cannot be returned upon the old basis of an evolution forced by external circumstance, but only on the condition that it is an internal movement, an inner expression of life itself. This view of evolution has several advantages of which we may name at least three. First, it uses the term in a meaning consistent with the word, in that it places the force of evolution, the creative element within the organism itself, where it obviously must be to work. In doing this, it likewise establishes a place for freedom in the structure of creation, thus ceasing to offend one of the most universal of human instincts. Second, it vacates the demand for an automatic progress, which gives us the present apparent moratorium in evolutionary process and has the further disadvantage of dulling the moral consciousness. Evolution ceases to be automatic (if ever it was automatic) with the appearance within the organism of reflective consciousness. Future progress in evolution is now dependent upon the exercise of brains and moral qualities, the choice to live by spiritual values. We may reflectively refuse to co-operate but we cannot escape moral responsibility. Third, since future evolution is dependent upon the reflective, mental, emotional, and spiritual powers granted to man, it is able to overcome the physical limitations that hitherto have bound it. The future of the evolution of culture is discovered to be without known limit.

The present need in the wide realm of human thought and endeavor would then seem to be to turn from a vain questioning as to what things might be apart from their functions and purposes and to begin to define them in terms of their activities. In religion we may very well leave off evaluating men in terms of their beliefs and begin to ask after what they are from the basis of what they do. The test would be a difficult one for most of us who continually flatter ourselves with the virtues of our beliefs in extenuation for our frailties. The method would, however, be wholesome for religion and might lead to a revival in that neglected realm. Something exactly similar might be said of science if now it will turn away from the unprofitable question of what matter is and begin to inquire into what it may do, or may be creatively induced to do.

Wherever the purposive principle has been applied nature has shown what to our shortened vision must seem little less than miraculous responses. We have trusted her, put her into harness, and she has eased us of half our burdens, carried us overseas or on the wings of the wind, reported our small talk to the ends of the earth, and revealed the face of a friend in front of a far-off microphone. The miracles of modern science have the mythology of all the ancients done to a neat brown because they forever excel the imagination of the ignorant and unskilled. If we had further need of emphasis on the fact that nature is an organism, part related to living part, surely the responses of nature to our attempts to use her in airplane, radio, and television should be sufficient. And if in all this nature there is a benevolent Creative Mind, it should be no longer possible to doubt that not one sparrow falls to the ground unnoticed.

V. THE PRAGMATIC AUTHORITY OF LIFE

If the so-called failure of democracy has been due to the over-stressing of the ideal of individualism without due regard to the other basic principle of personality, the individual acting in harmony with and for the whole system of relations; if the failure of religion has again followed a like line on the one hand, betraying the principle of personality in the interests of authority, or on the other losing itself in an unlicensed indifference to the order of which it is a part; if the efforts of science have been negated by a too-determined devotion to particulars without proper consideration given to the facts of the functioning organism; if social economy in exalting the individual has overlooked the good of society at large, then the way out may be by the route of this overlooked element of the person, of an organismic world evolving in response to an inner urge, a cosmic self-consciousness.

The prime effects of such new appraisal of our world are several. Turning science away from the deadening dogma that units are more important than functions, that analysis is a surer method of knowledge than synthesis, will lead to a renewal of scientific interest and bring new confidence in its results, but, what is of greater importance, it will give a new emphasis to values. The old science has pretended to be indifferent to values. It has boasted this indifference at times as the charter of its intellectual freedom. But such indifference could hold only for a disjointed world in which everything would be out of relation with everything else. In a world of such complex relation as ours values present us with the most important facts. Doctrines of relativity are fairly ablaze with this import.

Moreover, the old science in its pursuit of units has had a tendency to belittle man. In a mock humility it proclaimed man insignificant as compared with the extent of the universe, whereas on the contrary man is the most significant of all things. To the unthinking, planets and suns, the vastness of distant places, can have no meaning nor significance. Man, it is true, is hemmed about within the garden plot of his mental mastery of space. Shut in within the morning and evening of his human day, he lays all time and all circumstance under mental tribute. Any philosophy or science which attempts to diminish or ignore the fact of man, however far it may throw a line into the universe, is guilty of the simplicity of one whale-fishing Simon, whose only ocean was in his mother's pail.

Here we have hit upon a fact which the age and which all ages have too much overlooked—the significance of the person. For the man who swings his telescope into the wide vastness of interstellar spaces brings back only the interpretations that are the mirrors of his own soul, his own intellectual grasp. An astronomy which ignores the man who made and uses the telescope may be considered of minor importance. There is no fact it can gather which is in any sense so important as man, no fact it can grasp which is unrelated to man's own existence. Self-respect will bring a finer regard for and appreciation of nature; for we shall see her as a part of ourselves and ourselves in a new light as a part of her. Out of this will arise a new co-operation and influx of power.

In the same way, no system of political and social economy can be good, nor can it be thoroughly democratic so long as its gaze is turned away from the rightful needs, the highest development of the last and feeblest member of society. Nor must it be content to throw him the stone of political platitude about freedom when it should provide him with bread for his body, food for his intellect, and liberation for his soul.

Neither in the renewal of Western culture toward which we look can religion forget its duty to persons. There is a vivid sense in which no one of us can save his own soul unless he saves the souls of other men with his own. There is no authority from above nor from beneath that can pull an iota of weight in the balance against the authority of one human life. The true democracy can never come but with the realization that we are members one of another and that we can realize ourselves and reach religion, happiness, creative genius, economic order, only in giving ourselves without reservation for the good of all. If ever there shall come a day of true outstanding creative genius, of true democracy, of religion, pure and undefiled, of a world saved from disorder, and a golden age come into being, it will be the day which witnesses the advance from individualism with its self-seeking to personalism with its self-giving. Nor can such a movement be gainsaid, however much it may be scoffed at, because it bears within it the unimpeachable and pragmatic authority of life itself. If such a view could capture the imagination of man, the whole universe would rise up to back it as surely as the faithful air sustained the accordant hopes of the Wright brothers.

VI. THE CREATIVE PRINCIPLE AND THE FUTURE OF THE WEST

Let us attempt to summarize briefly our findings to see what light they may throw upon the future of Western culture. We have had revealed to us several facts.

The appearance of reflective self-consciousness as the product of evolution must be held to mark a distinctly new stage in cosmic progress. The economy of nature has always been to employ each advance in progress to produce the next. We should then bend the energies of our minds and souls to a co-operation with nature to bring a new era of progress. In the character of facts now known to exist, the progress called for is not so much physical but primarily intellectual and spiritual. Since an extreme individualism has led us into a mathematical, quantitative view of nature and life which is inadequate for present problems, science must apply itself to an organismic, even a personalistic, view of facts. Einstein has disclosed the relativity of all human interpretations of nature but that is only the threshold to yet greater truths of a relational world. No one thing in it can be properly understood apart from its multifarious relations which make it what it is. No part of the living body nor of the living world, can be known by itself alone. Values created by relations are the supreme realities.

A new emphasis upon a reasonable theory of evolution in logical keeping with the idea itself will disclose that the secret of progress, the solution of the various problems raised in this book, must be found in the internal forces of life. Modern anatomy reveals the human body as made up of many nerve centers, each with very definite functions under normal conditions of health. Under the shock of accident or disease, however, all strive through some inner urge to make up the deficiencies of diseased or missing organs in the interest of the whole organism. Under certain conditions they assume additional functions to meet the demands of the body as a whole.[4] The body social is an analogous case. Here, too, we have a relational system. Modern invention has intensified the relationship until society at large, the whole world, must begin to co-operate if the social organism is not to destroy itself. But we need frequently to remind ourselves that the sources of progress and of health are from within. We must realize that law and order spring primarily from within the hearts of good citizens and not from external mandate or decree. Such law and order are impossible of maintenance without the active assistance and cultivation of moral persons. Where morals and religion prevail, law-

---

[4] See Alexis Carrel: *Man the Unknown*, Harper & Brothers, New York, 1935, chap. vi, pp. 191 ff.

breakers are reduced to a minimum. Where they are neglected no law can be drastic enough to compel obedience.

Education must be seen as resting on a like internal principle. So far our educational system has depended on a quantitative regimentation of genius and stupidity in the same classes and grades, exposed to the same tedious curriculum and dedicated to the theory that the consumption of courses, books, or "units," was the equivalent of education. At its very roots, however, education is personal and inspirational or it is nothing. One teacher with a sympathetic interest sufficient to discover and inspire the individual genius of his different pupils is worth more than all the books ever written on scientific pedagogy. Modern educational pedantry can be quite as deadening as that of the past. Education can take place only where there is a love of study and such love can frequently be induced by the right appeal. The problem of education is not predominantly one of organization, technique or apparatus but of an inner spirit.

The decline of influence of philosophy can be met only by a new appreciation of personality as containing the heart of all true insight and understanding. A philosophy which seeks to include in its purview everything in the universe except man himself cannot have a vital message for an hour of universal cultural crisis.

Religion also must take account of this inner secret of progress and of life. Such internal forces are the very heart and soul of religious faith, the one consideration without which it cannot exist. And yet, religion has too often fallen from its high estate of reverence for the inner light to the mechanical beating of ecclesiastical tom-toms, the frigidity of theological or liturgical conformity. It is in sore need of a revelation of the enshrined and potential God within the human spirit itself, which is the meaning and the message of the Incarnation.

But what of the future? Western civilization in its "sense of destiny" has conceived itself as moving along the straight line of progress to a distant goal. This concept has been of unutterable value in all the advances it has made. But it has reached its first goal of physical achievement or nearly so. However, its dream has never been wholly identified with mere physical wellbeing. There has always been a moral and spiritual residuum. This must now be trusted to turn the tide upward to a new all-embracing world progress. Such advance cannot be upon the old plane of national selfishness and self-aggrandizement; it will be an advance for all, and it will include new moral and spiritual understanding among all men. There are many reactionary forces at work in international politics and in class misunderstanding which it must be allowed, seem to give the lie to so earnest a hope. But Western society has through its history dug itself out of much deeper pits in the past. Recall the situation at the downfall of the Roman Empire and again during the Hundred Years' War. From the death of learning and order of the former it built itself up to its brightest achievements in education and law, and from the misery and poverty of the latter, came the period of greatest production and most luxurious comfort. There is reason to believe that from the moral and spiritual debacle of the present time there will be reaction to a civilization whose crowning achievements will be witnessed in the internal status of man himself. There is hope for the higher destiny of the West, so long as any considerable portion of society does not give up hope. Though unseen and unobserved of men, the internal and creative forces of Western life are already at work, for as of old, "the Kingdom of God cometh not with observation," it is within.

Epilogue

CHAPTER XXVII

A QUANTUM VIEW OF HISTORY

. . . .

IT MAY SEEM to some an odd notion to apply the Quantum Theory to history. To all such it will probably appear that in atomic action quanta find their sole justification. The principle is revolutionary, even in physics, to suggest the application of a physical principle to a whole cosmic, as well as social, order. However, if there are any complaints from the house of the scientists, we have as a ready answer that it was they who first insisted on the application of scientific principles to all phases of human experience, and if they find the battle going against them through a more rigorous employment of their own principles, they of all have the least right to complain.

The theory of the continuity of force in physics has for many generations been one of the surest of basic assumptions. Predictability has been the proud boast of science over both philosophy and religion. These latter disciplines seemed so insusceptible to any mathematical, measurable, ponderable demonstration that it has been common for many scientists to declare them therefore negligible, since they do not yield to quantitative demonstration or proof. For this reason the world of practical knowledge was philosophically unprepared to receive the shocking and revolutionary discovery of Max Planck that forces are not continuous but discontinuous; that they move in waves like the beat of the surf on the shore; that the action of individual atoms is unpredictable; that the so-called iron-bound laws of nature hold only in a general way and not in particular cases; that what we really observe are statistical averages upon which we have to depend. Even in the physical world there is a demand for organization. Always an organism of some kind seems necessary to explain activity on any scale, anywhere. The downfall of the ancient tyranny of purposeless mechanism can be safely predicted.

Since the Quantum Theory is coming to wide acceptance among physicists, it may not be amiss to inquire if its application is to be confined to a single phase of nature, the activity of the atom. In biology we have long been lost in the barren and fruitless search for the so-called "missing link." This has been nothing more nor less than a doddering trust in the hypothesis that force is continuous and always in a single direction, that of a mechanistic evolution. The theory has always raised more questions than it answered, and the poverty of 'results should have led to abandonment long ago. Emergent evolution, as it is now called, is an effort to let ourselves down easily from a position which even the materialistic evolutionists were beginning to discover to be no longer tenable. It is easier now to understand that evolution may be an illustration of the quantum principle—it may proceed by jumps, "mutations," or "sports," and there may be no need for a "missing link." Thus the "missing link" is seen as merely the hobgoblin of ancient conjecture.

Our view of the formation of the earth itself is taking on new aspects. We have thought that in the interests of theories of nature the making of the earth could be viewed only as the part of a universal process. It seemed illogical to regard it as in any sense a unique occurrence. We felt that there must be countless other earths, with atmosphere and vegetable life and stores of metal, oil, and multitudinous supplies for animal subsistence. Not to think so was unscientific and displayed an ignorant provincialism quite unworthy and narrow. However, it now seems possible that the earth may have been formed by a unique cataclysm, a collision of asteroids, such as may never have taken place before nor since. There seems a sense in which the Quantum Theory could apply to the forming of the earth. In the face of ascertainable facts the claim that the universe is doubtless crowded with other worlds like our own is wholly gratuitous and calls for verification from the claimant.

The Quantum Theory seems even more applicable in the field of history; for here we find that there have been certain periods of history which in achievement and results have appeared the possessors of powers unknown to any other age. Such eras have occurred which have set particular human achievements forward to a state little short of perfection and which have become the standard and the despair of later generations. Such an epoch arose in the concept of moral law in the days of Hammurabi and later of the Jewish prophets. Such an age was the high-water mark of

Greek philosohy and sculpture. Such a period was that of Rome, when the genius for empire and world peace reached its climax. Such a time saw the invention and development of Gothic architecture, appearing, it might almost be said, like a sudden inspiration out of the nowhere into the here, and subsiding like an exhausted flame after a brief flowering of a hundred years. Such an era may be that of modern science and business organization, typified by the vast steel-and-concrete structures which mark our cities while they constitute the marvel of our age. There are evidences that our genius for organization may have exhausted itself, and that in the future the changes of society may be so great that these vacant and unprofitable structures may grow as rusty as are the empty cathedrals of an earlier day. Whether we are entering upon the light of a new Renaissance, or plunging into the shadows of a new Dark Age, who can tell?—but there can be no doubt of the momentous character of the days that have called us into being and placed in our hands the future of the human race.

In each of the previous periods humanity seemed to have spent itself, and to have become incapable of carrying further the high emprise. Is history about to repeat itself, as with Spengler, or are there elements in the situation now that have never been present in the epochal crises of the past? Here seems to lie the narrow pathway of a larger hope, and the only hope, maybe, for future progress. The following are perhaps the vital questions which must be answered.

Does our world differ from the ancient and passing civilizations in the general dissemination of culture? New phases of civilization, new developments of already achieved civilization, are never secure so long as they remain in the hands of the few. It was doubtless the parochialism of Grecian education that made possible the quenching of her intellectual torch. She made no effort to bring the lowest members of society up to the standards of the highest. Much the same might be contended as true in every other instance. The priceless secrets of civilization were kept in the hands of a small dominant class, the priesthood, some esoteric cultural fellowship, some political freemasonry. And then, because the untutored classes were so prolific, any sweeping social change, epidemic, political disorganization, pressure from barbaric hordes, any of a hundred different types of events, has been sufficient to turn a classical civilization to nothingness, or at least to a memory and a regret. There is an element of hope in the wider dissemination of ideas that characterizes our age.

A further source of cultural collapse was inherent in the provincialism of ancient achievements. They were confined to small areas, to small extensions of time, to national boundaries that could be swept away by war, or other disaster, and even by civil disintegration. Rapid transportation, the radio, organized educational facilities, widespread literacy, knowledge of printing, vast collections of books in many places—these are facilities making for the preservation of culture which no other period has known in equal degree. There have never before been in the hands of men such world-wide capacities for the dissemination of ideas—such powers of universal appeal—such possibility of arriving at quick and extensive world understanding.

One other question must be held as vital to our situation. Perhaps the most significant fact about our age since World War I, and certainly more recently, has been the sense of insecurity. This mood is in one way paralyzing, fruitful of inhibitions of the worst sort. This is the psychological effect of fear. It easily accounts for the surprising reversion to nationalistic sentiment and narrowed concepts of world responsibility so powerful at the moment. But this same uncertainty may be the forerunner of a better day. Especially if man can be brought to a new spiritual achievement. Uncertainty can be accepted with fear, or it may be accepted with confidence as a challenge to the higher powers of man. To meet the present dilemma calls for faith in spiritual values. Perhaps the most illuminating question of all will be whether our age has within it the spiritual resources to turn the horror of war into a victory for a new and better civilization. These are the questions that we now face.

I. Dependence of World Culture upon Ideas

Every epoch-marking culture has resulted from the rise of controlling ideas that have conspired in one direction. Men have been deeply moved by similar thoughts, and out of that simultaneity in time, place, and background they have been able to advance a given outlook to its highest possible perfection. But such achievement does not spring except from convictions so deep that they seize upon both the emotions and the imagination. It may be the inspired dream of universal moral law, promising to remake a world, as in Babylonia and Judea; or the appreciation of beauty as proportion, where beauty is seen to represent cosmic law and order, as in Greece. It may arise from burning religious convictions coupled with the dream of a new freedom for the human spirit, as in the rearing of the Gothic cathedrals. With us now the integrating idea may arise out of the prospect of universal ruin.

The question arising is, then, whether or not our age is capable of ideas of sufficient moment. That it has been widely moved is evidenced by the epoch of clever invention, of high-powered organization, of exhaustive command of the physical powers of nature. But we may have come to the end of what these powers can do for us. Our success as organizers has all but ended our civilization, even as Frankenstein was destroyed by the monster he had created. The only forward step which lies in that direction seems to many to be the mechanically complete organization of an oppressive Communism or totalitarianism. In such organization the individual must fall prey to the institution. There could be neither individual initiative nor freedom; the whole concept is implacably hostile to the ideas that have been so laboriously engendered in Western culture for twenty-five centuries. We may even now be witnessing the final conflict between the program of a free society and a complete paternalism. But philanthropy with the necessary autocrat at the head is not only repugnant to Western notions, the idea has so clearly failed in history that we already know its outcome. The new idea that can save modern culture from collapse cannot, therefore, come along the line of organization unless it contain some other and transforming idea. What shall this be? The easy way will be to assume that the problem is one of more organization—the application of business organization on a world-wide scale, somewhat as the Medievalists presumed that the cathedrals and creeds had made their theological ideals forever secure, and that at the very moment when the revolting minds of the Reformation were about to make them insecure. The creative idea must include something more than organization. In general it must bear a promise of universal benefit; it must be easily understood by and communicable to the greater portion of world citizens; it must be sufficiently cosmopolitan—that is, human—to appeal to all classes, faiths, conditions of men; and it must be so freighted both with conviction and emotion as to move the greater part of mankind with an impulse akin to or partaking of religion. These qualifications cannot be fulfilled by any promise of regimentation, however great or of whatever kind, unless the benefits to be realized shall reach past all the divisions of warring nationalities, races, sects, and religions. It must reach up into the moral and partake of the spiritual. For this great end nothing would seem to suffice short of a theophany. But the pressing need is that the thought of mankind should run ahead, far ahead, of its actual achievement. Once an idea has become so visualized, so vivid, and so widespread in the minds of men that it touches the imagination, the swift transition to a new order of civilization is possible almost overnight. It needs but the disturbing jar of a world heroism, a transcendent deed, the common recognition of a threatened social cataclysm, to cause crystallization in the whole mass of society.

II. The New Capacity for the Dissemination of Ideas

To this end our own age is in possession of powers that have never before been known in the history of mankind. The invention of space-destroying machinery such as the steamship, the airplane, the telephone, the wireless, and the radio—these are rapidly bringing about a homogeneity in ideas such as has before been utterly impossible. Heretofore it has been an insuperable task for widely divided races to possess ideas in common; now they are so close together in trade, in health, in political fortunes, in community of interest and ideas, that they must be moved by a common concern or else all must perish. The new capacity for sharing ideas has removed the last security from any autocratic or tyrannical or conservative nationalism. We cannot successfully hold to the parochial mind when the world has become one vast whispering gallery. To endeavor by various repressions to keep out the influx of new, contradictory and revolutionary ideas is a task as unpromising as the attempt to sweep back a Bay of Fundy tide with a housewife's broom. Of course there is the danger arising from perilous ideas. Humanity may be stampeded into running amuck. Some noble conservators in our midst are sure there is salvation only in their own ideas, and would undertake the benevolent task of censorship, but the fates are out of the box and nothing but the destruction of the machinery of locomotion, of dispatch of information, can now shut us back into the old small-town ways and provincialisms. Whether we like it or not, whether it is safe or not, the world at large is going to settle the problems of the world at large, and our greatest contribution cannot be by way of repression or of suppressing information, but by way of enlightenment. If, therefore, you have a constructive idea, cast it forth and watch its ripples reach to the ends of the earth. If the world is captured by radical principles, it will be because the conservative party has offered nothing but criticism, has presented no constructive concepts for the betterment of society. For the race cannot stay at any point already achieved. Its new problems compel it with the insistency of a boy who outgrows his clothes. If you do not wish for the radicalism of extreme styles and wild sartorial adventure, get busy with the tailor in the interest of something better. It will be of no use to upbraid the boy because he demands a new suit. The only safe society is growing and progressive, and the day is already here when wise ideas can run around the earth like wildfire. If we are alert to our day and generation, we shall bear in mind the value of transmission of true concepts to the eager world. If the cyclic theory were true we should already be prepared with the solution. We are however faced with problems never before appearing in history.

III. Spiritual Renaissance and a New World

Social and political insights lie buried for centuries waiting for opportunity to spring into action. Then their day and their occasion appears. This may be the great hope of the present age. In his work on history[1] Benedetto Croce has shown how salient concepts have lain fallow and dormant for centuries, waiting for the intellectual and spiritual sympathy of an age capable of appreciating them. Thus it was that Aristotle was lost on his own times and had to wait fifteen centuries for that new understanding that sprang up with the Middle Ages. Our need lies in a widespread renewal which shall bring back into general focus long neglected and motivating truths of the human spirit. These

[1] Croce: *On History*, Harcourt, Brace and Company, New York, 1921, pp. 24, 25.

truths need not be new truths in the sense that they have never before been conceived. They cannot be truths which have to do with tests of orthodoxy, nor truths of merely academic nature; for they must be so living, so practical, so universal, that to be set forth in the right spirit shall bring them universal recognition. It was something of this kind which must have been in the mind of the great spiritual leader of Nazareth when he announced that the advent of the new social and spiritual order should appear "as the lightning cometh out of the east and shineth even unto the west." It may look fatuous to dream of such a possibility in a day which seems so completely resigned to the ways and the sins of the flesh, a day so characterized by the breakdown of idealisms, so overwhelmed by greed and avarice, so trustful in the power of falsehood and violence. But the quantum view of history gives hope that we may be near the turning point toward better things. The old assurances of material success are gone. There is no longer a sublime confidence that business organization can solve every problem, from social want to spiritual ideals. We have been profoundly shocked to discover what that kind of organization could do when it was not backed by integrity. We have discovered that integrity was not itself inherent in the size of corporate effort. It is found to be something that may be wanting from the countinghouse and may be absent under an exterior of faultless dress, engaging manners, and social prominence. Our financial house has been wrecked because the old moral traditions that involved integrity and honor had seemed out of date. Nor shall we fare better at the hands of a greedy and unprincipled proletariat which would sink all to a common level.

What we distinctly need is not better business organization nor even a more popular social regimentation. What we need is a genuine repentance for our sins of greed, avarice, dishonesty, credulous gambling, unsocial and unearned profits, our reckless abandon to the wiles of illegitimate pleasure, our smug self-content while toiling children weave our clothes and our profits out of the warp and woof of blood and starvation and our sweatshops groan with the murmurs of a new slavery and our homes are warmed at the price of lifelong and poorly requited darkness for the miners. Neither can peace be won by indulging hymns of hate and arraying class against class. There are none of us who have not sinned against the just claims of persons. I and you and other respectable people have dwelt in the unthinking security of an unchristian system, lisping prayers to the Father of the orphan and the oppressed. We go on even now to compound our insincerity by reducing our taxes at the expense of countless women and children whose natural guardians are without power to resist the narcotic effects of alcohol, or those mentally doped hordes who can be depended on to impoverish their families under the lure of the lottery and the professional gambler.

Better social organization is a sore need, but unless it is founded on the spiritual and moral readjustment of society it is as empty of virtue as the sounding brass or tinkling cymbal. We need a wind in the world which shall sweep away our whole refuge of lies. Once around the wide, wide world, there is a real regeneration, a genuine search for the submerged spiritual bases of the social order, we shall see eye to eye with other men, and war and slavery, crooked business, grafting politics, enervating nationalism, fraud and oppression will be abolished.

But we need not so much a new organization as a new soul.

IV. THE DESTINY OF THE WEST

In the corridor of human history there seems never to have been a gift more rare than that of prophecy. Men who can expertly read the proclamation of cloud and sun with respect to the weather fail utterly in applying their knowledge to the actions and reactions of human society. The main reason for this is the freedom of human response to circumstance and the influence thereon of the imponderables. Under such circumstances we shall scarcely be expected to usurp the role of prophet. Nevertheless, having essayed the problem of the destiny of the West, we must not leave the task without asking the direct question whether the West has a destiny, or whether the lugubrious promise of her final decline which Spengler makes may not be the true answer. Naturally, individual prepossession and latent philosophy will enter into any attempted solution of the problem. No one can quite rid himself of the personal equation, and the more conspicuously one may claim an utterly detached attitude the more surely is he blind to his own prejudices.

In the estimate of human progress there is one factor which is frequently misinterpreted because society is looked upon as a static achievement rather than as a living organism. For purposes of study and comparison it is well to take a given social order as the astronomer takes a "frame of reference" for the study of comparative facts. One should, however, at the same time recognize the relativity of his judgments. The highest standards of human culture as conceived by the Egyptians, with their tenets of all but universal slavery, would not seem adequate as a norm of judgment today. Even the best social and political maxims of the age of Louis the Great would impress the modern age as quite inadequate. We cannot, then, be sure that any present-day definition of the meaning of civilization can form the norm for tomorrow. Indeed, if we have a mind to history, there is nothing quite so certain as the certainty of changed ideals.

If we hold to the static theory of society, we shall be alarmed and disturbed by every threat of change; for if the good of society is always to maintain the *status quo*, then society is always in danger and the decline of its civilization is certain.

There is, however, another point of view. Change may be looked upon as the evidence of growth. The changes that come to the child, though they render him awkward and at times impossible to his elders, are not looked upon as catastrophic. They are seen as part of a process both physical and mental by which he works his way out to maturity and usefulness. In a living social order, uniformity of opinion, quiescence in present achievement, are signs of death, while, on the other hand, dissatisfaction, political and social experiment, up-flaring of untempered theories, accompanying unrest, may be signs of life rather than of decline. What under the first concept would be taken as token of the expiring gasp of the present social order, and so of all order, would under the other interpretation be taken as the outward evidence of growing pains. Such a view is entirely in keeping with the words of the world's greatest social prophet, who declared: "When ye shall hear of wars and rumors of wars, be ye not troubled . . . these are the beginnings of the birth-pangs." [2]

Seen from this standpoint, Western society shows many signs not of disintegration but of growth. In a living society the only fatality arises from quiescence in things as they are. In the biological structure the bursting of the shell is necessary to the unfolding of the new life from within. The task of Western society is to assist the process of change, directing it into the widest channels, seeking the broadest co-operation, and moving hopefully toward ideals for the largest benefit of all men. That

[2] Mark 13:8. Marginal rendering.

we cannot predict the final result is not an argument against the movement; for the consummation will appear only to the late participants as the struggle toward a renewed society is itself a part of the achievement and brings new goals and objectives into view. Here we have something essentially different from the biological history of a plant or of a tree, which rises no higher than physical achievement. In the mental and spiritual organism of human society lies the possibility of never-ending and unlimited progress.

The West, instead of reaching the nadir of accomplishment, shows by its spiritual discontent with material achievements the greatest promise of advance to new mental and spiritual goals.

That such is no empty dream is indicated by the fact that the West is for the first time in human history in possession of material subsistence for all mankind. For the first time it is possible to encourage the creative capacities of individuals. There will for a long time remain those with such intellectual and emotional equipment as will be satisfied to continue as hewers of wood and drawers of water. But with the possession of machinery, and under the wider impulse of creative effort, hopeless drudgery may give way and man generally be liberated to the wider achievements of mind and spirit.

But the possession of material resources adequate for the whole world, though a great part of the problem, is not the greatest.

For the first time in the history of modern science we are being freed from materialistic dogmas which were hostile to a true appraisal of humanity. The doctrine of relativity, the new theories of the atom, the changed outlook in physics have released us from the deadening load of a single point of view.

For the first time in civilization we are glimpsing a new social outlook which is able to discern the fact that any underprivileged portion of society anywhere is a menace to the welfare of all, that the prosperity of the whole is involved in the prosperity of the most ignorant and neglected.

For the first time it is being borne in upon the world of politics that transportation and communication have made the world too small to be endlessly divided into narrow nationalisms and provincialisms. Present events are but the reactions of narrow minds that refuse to admit the larger truth that is becoming plain. There is no way out even to material prosperity for any one of them through exclusive boundaries of trade and interest.

The nations will be compelled to come to mutual understanding in the simple process of self-preservation.

Concomitant with the revolution in scientific theory, there is coming in philosophy a new understanding of the importance and place of the person in any adequate view of reality and the cosmic order. Mind, purposive thought, understanding, and creative will must come to be acknowledged as themselves portions of reality. They can no longer be treated as negligible and extraneous to the universe. They will be seen as the most important clue to the solution of the secrets of nature when the present mania of materialism shall have passed away. Out of this new appreciation are sure to flow discoveries and practical applications arising from a new knowledge of the person in his relations with nature. There are undoubtedly unlocked powers, undiscovered resources, arising out of man's connection with the objective world which present an all but virgin field of investigation.

For the first time we have the presence of a widespread conviction in the realm of religion that any goodness, purity, or love anywhere in the world is a manifestation of the Divine Spirit without respect to the special religious system under which it appears. Such recognition bespeaks a coming tolerance which will enable men of good will everywhere to join forces for the furtherance of world peace, of international amity, of a new impetus to the life of the spirit.

These are some of the possessions of the present which make for the rise of a new civilization. No age nor period that can really claim them can be truly said to be in decline.

All these are considerations which may be justly taken into account in any consideration involving the survival of Western culture. To some they will seem feeble and utterly inadequate because all of them may be reckoned among the imponderables. But it is the imponderables that dictate the future. Should Western culture succeed in rising to the new opportunity that faces her, should she take a step forward, it must now be toward a more spiritual interpretation of life and society. Material progress has reached its bound and end until there is broader and deeper pioneering in the spirit. The genius of her past, the tenseness of her disillusionments and dissatisfactions with material things, point to a nobler and ultimate survival.

INDEX

Absolute, the 22, 75, 154, 168, 191
Absolutes, in philosophy, 175-176
   in religion, 176-178
   paradox of, 179-180
   scientific, 191, 192
   theological, 192
Absolutism, 21, 22, 59, 172, 176, 185,
   188, 190-193, 213, 228, 269
Adams, Henry, 73
Albertus Magnus, 60, 63, 270
Alchemists, 66
Alcuin of York, 64
Alexander, 251
Anaxagoras, 23, 24, 33, 49, 56, 85,
   185
Anaximander, 183
Anthropology, 5, 6, 139, 239
Anthropomorphism, 139, 141-142
Aquinas, Thomas, 60, 63, 250, 270
Archimedes, 6
Aristophanes, 179
Aristotelianism, 60, 62, 65, 66, 68,
   100, 129, 250, 269, 271, 273
Aristotle, 24, 26, 60, 62, 63, 65, 77,
   79, 103, 268, 270, 271, 293
Astrology, 66, 77, 79, 240
Astronomy, 142, 280
Atom, 13, 78, 161, 195, 197, 200,
   273, 277, 287, 297
   Daltonian, 172, 175, 178, 196
   Democritan, 191
   Epicurean, 271
Atomism, 33, 79
   attraction of, 22
Augustine, 60, 62, 86, 87, 89, 210,
   242, 265
   conversion of, 86-87
Autocracy, 58, 63, 106
Authoritarianism, 103, 185, 188, 189,
   193, 206, 211, 215, 228, 268
Aztecs, 9

Babylonian captivity, 25
Bacon, Francis, 77, 81, 183
Bacon, Roger, 66, 68, 81
Beecher, 234
Behaviorism, 104, 151
Berkeley, Bishop, 160

Boccacio, 63, 67
Boëthius, 6, 62, 63, 130
Bohr, 196
Bragg, Sir William, 196
Branch, 196
Bray, 196
Bruno, Giordano, 149, 185
Brutus, Marcus, 190
Buckham, John Wright, 171

Caesar, Julius, 184
Caesarius, 64
Calvin, 250
Capella, Martianus, 63
Capitalism, 112
Carlyle, 38
Carolingian Empire, 57
Carr, Herbert Wildon, 238
Cassiodorus, 63
Cavell, Edith, 256
Charlemagne, 64, 67
Charles the Bold, 64
Children's Crusade, 58
Chivalry, 72
   rise of, 58
Christianity, 27, 30, 42ff., 53, 56, 60,
   72, 75, 86, 103, 131, 241ff.
   dangerous position of, 130
   effect of, on Graeco-Roman thought,
   24
   influenced by sense of destiny, 26
   greatest foe of, 45
   influence of Stoicism on, 42
   misinterpretations, 28-29
   power of early, 251
   rise of, 45
City of God, The, 60, 87
Civilization, aims of, 10-11
Cleanthes, 43
Commentary on Aristotle, 265
Commercialism, 115, 230-231, 235,
   276, 294
Communism, 9, 63, 112, 187, 189, 291
Confessions, The, 62, 87
Constantine, 45
"Contraplete," 171
Croce, Benedetto, 293
Crusades, 58, 72, 135, 257

Index